# *Managing the Four Stages of TQM*

Also available from ASQC Quality Press

*The Change Agents' Handbook: A Survival Guide
for Quality Improvement Champions*
David W. Hutton

*Excellence Is a Habit: How to Avoid Quality Burnout*
Lon Roberts

*A World of Quality: The Timeless Passport*
Xerox Quality Solutions

*Reengineering the Organization: A Step-by-Step Approach
to Corporate Revitalization*
Jeffrey N. Lowenthal

The ASQC Total Quality Management Series

*TQM: Leadership for the Quality Transformation*
Richard S. Johnson

*TQM: Management Processes for Quality Operations*
Richard S. Johnson

*TQM: The Mechanics of Quality Processes*
Richard S. Johnson and Lawrence E. Kazense

*TQM: Quality Training Practices*
Richard S. Johnson

To request a complimentary catalog of publications, call 800-248-1946.

# Managing the Four Stages of TQM

*How to Achieve World-Class Performance*

Charles N. Weaver

ASQC Quality Press
Milwaukee, Wisconsin

*Managing the Four Stages of TQM:*
*How to Achieve World-Class Performance*
Charles N. Weaver

**Library of Congress Cataloging-in-Publication Data**

Weaver, Charles N.
    Managing the four stages of TQM: how to achieve world-class
performance / Charles N. Weaver.
        p.   cm.
    Includes bibliographical references and index.
    ISBN 0-87389-311-5
    1. Total quality management.   I. Title.
HD62.15.W4    1994
658.5'62—dc20

94-30676
CIP

10 9 8 7 6 5 4 3 2 1

ISBN 0-87389-311-5

Acquisitions Editor: Susan Westergard
Project Editor: Kelley Cardinal
Production Editor: Annette Wall
Marketing Administrator: Mark Olson
Set in Palatino by Precision Graphic Services, Inc.
Cover design by Paul Tobias.
Printed and bound by BookCrafters, Inc.

ASQC Mission: To facilitate continuous improvement and increase customer satisfaction by identifying, communicating, and promoting the use of quality principles, concepts, and technologies; and thereby be recognized throughout the world as the leading authority on, and champion for, quality.

For a free copy of the ASQC Quality Press Publications Catalog, including ASQC membership information, call 800-248-1946.

Printed in the United States of America

 Printed on acid-free recycled paper

 ASQC
Quality Press
611 East Wisconsin Avenue
Milwaukee, Wisconsin 53202

# Contents

# Preface

Most managers understand that total quality management (TQM) requires organizations to undergo a substantial transformation, or change of state, so that they don't operate as they did before. Many understand that after being transformed to TQM, organizations have a different style of management, focus more on improving processes, produce higher quality products and services at lower cost, satisfy their customers, are more innovative, and capture a larger and larger share of the market. Yet, many managers do not understand exactly how organizations change from what they were before TQM to what they are after TQM. They fail to understand that there is a sequence of four distinct stages through which organizations undergo this change. They know TQM is a journey, but most are unfamiliar with the stops along the way.

Not understanding the four stages of TQM puts managers in an awkward situation. If they don't understand where their organizations are in the sequence of stages, they won't be as successful as they could be in leading their organizations into the next stage. This lack of understanding is not limited to managers. Many consultants are unaware of the stages of TQM and, as a consequence, are less helpful than they could be in advising their clients about TQM. This book describes the four stages through which organizations are transformed to TQM, from point of origin to destination.

The TQM transformation begins for most organizations in the *traditional stage*. Consider briefly what organizations in this stage are like. For the most part, traditional organizations are backed by owners who expect to get a reasonable return on their investments. To get this return, they hire professional managers who organize enterprises into pyramids of authority or wedding cake organizational structures. Within this structure, managers administer activities according to what is taught in business schools: the principles of management based on the concepts of scarcity, competition, and behaviorism. Organizing and managing in this way is the source of the crises and problems that give owners and managers gray hair and ulcers; that make employees feel unfulfilled, depressed, and often humiliated; that disappoint and anger customers; that frustrate suppliers; that prevent organizations from being truly efficient and effective; and that have put many organizations with good prospects in the ditch. In the worst traditional organizations, employees are expected to make their bosses happy, and everyone's attitude toward customers is "Here's how we do it here. Hope you like it like that!"

When chief executive officers (CEOs) of traditional organizations wake up to the fact that their survival depends on satisfying customers rather than disappointing and angering them, they begin to move into the second stage of TQM, *customer awareness.* In this stage, customers are called *guests* or *clients,* customer complaint departments are added, and employees, called *associates* or *partners,* are trained to provide customer service that CEOs can boast of as "legendary," "leading edge," or "whatever it takes." The customer awareness stage often goes on forever, but it brings about many needed improvements and has forestalled bankruptcy for countless companies. It reduces customer delays, insults, and abuses, but these improvements are almost always made by exhorting, overworking, and exploiting employees who asked only for an opportunity to do a good job in the first place.

Eventually, many CEOs realize there is more to satisfying customers than creating customer complaint departments and exhorting employees to smile. They realize that treating customers well comes from a multitude of factors in addition to the contributions of employees. Having well-trained employees is important, of course, but other factors, such as high-quality materials, appropriate tools and machines, well-thought-out methods, and pleasant working conditions, also are required. Many CEOs eventually see that these factors collectively exist as processes that must be identified, actively managed, and continually improved in a spirit of system optimization. They realize that much of the important work in their organizations is conducted in processes that extend horizontally across functional areas or departments. They realize that the work that gets done in these horizontal processes is at least as important as the work that gets done vertically, within functional areas.

Improving cross-functional processes begins for most organizations with the creation of a transitional organizational structure composed, at the level of senior management, of a quality council. Among its other responsibilities, this council provides guidance and resources for a large-scale effort to improve cross-functional processes. This council identifies the most important such processes and charters the second part of the transitional organizational structure, teams, to begin the work of continually improving these processes. Not only do teams improve processes, but, if an improvement effort is to be fully successful, they must be the vehicle by which the work of improving processes is transitioned to existing departments so that continual improvement becomes accepted throughout the organization as a way of life. In other words, teams must be a force for changing an organization's culture. These activities comprise the third stage of TQM, the *process improvement stage.*

The fourth stage of TQM is the most difficult to enter, and the thought of it never occurs to most CEOs. Most of them are either stuck hopelessly in the traditional stage or are utterly overwhelmed by what is required to move out of the traditional or customer awareness stages. In fact, many courageous CEOs devote their entire careers to trying to get their organizations out of one of the early stages.

To enter the fourth stage of TQM, CEOs must become aware that merely satisfying customers and improving processes will not expand or even maintain their market share. Satisfying customers and improving processes are critical in today's competitive marketplace, but these activities are simply insufficient. For instance, improving customer satisfaction and improving the manufacturing processes for stagecoaches, buggy whips, single-action revolvers, single-shot rifles, fountain pens, typewriters, carbon paper, tabulators, punch cards, and accounting machines did not maintain and expand their market share. These splendid products and thousands like them were the result of streamlined, cost-efficient processes and enjoyed the highest customer satisfaction and market dominance. Yet, today, they have virtually disappeared from the marketplace.

If an organization expects to expand its markets and truly prosper, something beyond satisfying customers and improving processes is required. That something is innovation. Innovation is providing products and services customers are incapable of asking for or even thinking possible. For instance, did any farmer in 1874 pulling a wagon with a team of horses call out for a pickup truck? In 1879, did the 1800 British soldiers using single-shot Martini–Henry rifles against 30,000 Zulu warriors call out for machine guns, mortars, and hand grenades? Did clerks using turkey feathers, fountain pens, or typewriters call out for word processors? Did any accountant running punch cards through a table sorter for accounts receivable call out for a mainframe computer and interactive terminals? Innovation requires knowledge of how a customer's processes work and of how these processes are influenced by forces in the customer's social, technological, economic, and governmental environment. It is only through understanding and forecasting the impact of these forces on customer processes that suppliers can see into the future and innovate products and services. This is the fourth stage of TQM, the *innovation stage.*

For many CEOs, TQM leads to an awareness that they must reengineer their organizations from a strict hierarchy of functional areas to place more emphasis on the horizontal nature of many important cross-functional processes. In this way, many organizations are transformed gradually from being organized and managed mainly around vertical functional areas to being organized and managed mainly around core processes.

There are many important differences between the four stages of TQM, and, if you know what to look for, it is easy to see where an organization is in the journey through these stages. The easiest way is to understand that CEOs of organizations in these different stages think about very different things. For instance, what CEOs of traditional organizations think about is different from what CEOs in customer awareness organizations think about. The same can be said of CEOs of organizations in all four stages. There is some overlap between the stages, but the differences are quite pronounced and easy to see. What CEOs think about and don't think about in the different stages of TQM is explained in this book.

As this book will explain, the 14 points and profound knowledge provided by the late W. Edwards Deming are a brilliant road map for making the transformation away from the traditional stage of organizational development. But, as I struggle to make this transformation for my clients, an interesting thing happens. I realize that Deming left much work for us to do. I find myself faced continually with the need to build new knowledge about how this transformation works beyond what Deming said about it. At first, I was hesitant to think about improving on Deming's teachings. It seemed presumptuous. But I remembered Deming's point about constant and forever improvement, and I doubt that he would exclude his own teachings from this advice.

This book reports the current state of the new knowledge I have developed with my clients about the TQM transformation. For instance, there is a chapter about tasking, an indispensable part of the successful transformation of any organization. Tasking is a tool for optimizing a system. Yet, to my knowledge, nothing has ever appeared in the literature about this subject. Deming stressed the need to optimize organizations as systems, but he did not explain in his books, or at any of his six seminars I attended, how tasking can be used to bring optimization about. Tasking is new knowledge; I knew nothing about it two years ago. It came from helping people with active minds who were transforming their organizations within Deming's framework. The same is true of other new knowledge contained in this book, such as the iron law of the hierarchy, laws of organizational development, the rule of when to compete, the three improvement strategies, the principles of innovation, the enhanced nominal group technique (ENGT), finger voting, and the expanded, more precise role of CEOs in the TQM transformation.

What's presented here is *not* the one best way to make the TQM transformation. It's a snapshot of the current state of a body of knowledge that's rapidly expanding and improving. I'm certain that in a year my clients and I will see much of this knowledge in a different way, in an improved way.

But my clients and I don't have a monopoly on developing this new knowledge. My experience is that if you'll begin to think within Deming's framework as I present it here, you, too, can learn to build new knowledge for yourself and for your organization. The overriding aim of this book is to show you the way through the four stages of TQM. And, after I've taken you as far as I know the way, you'll be able to build the new knowledge necessary to continue your journey.

# Acknowledgments

From the late 1970s to the early 1990s, I was affiliated with the Armstrong Laboratory of the United States Air Force. As a contributor to this laboratory's research and development program in organizational performance measurement and enhancement, I came in contact with the principal figures in the TQM movement, including Deming and Joseph M. Juran, through their books, videotapes, and seminars. I learned much from these contacts. I was selected in the late 1980s by Anthony Gallegos, director of Installations Assistance Office—West, and Robert A. Stone, deputy assistant secretary of defense—Installations, to make two-day TQM awareness presentations and provide team leader and facilitator training at military installations. Over a three-year period, I made these presentations to more than 20,000 military personnel at bases and posts across the United States and in Hawaii, Panama, Puerto Rico, the United Kingdom, the Netherlands, and Germany. Seeking to make these presentations meaningful to others was another way I learned about TQM. As I developed and made these presentations, I thought about which approaches to TQM made the most sense to me and to my audiences.

As military installation commanders attended my TQM training, many sought my assistance in implementing TQM in their organizations. A surprising number needed my help to recover from false starts in TQM caused by the bad advice of consulting firms.

Commanders who sought my assistance were applying TQM in organizations on military bases and posts. In many ways, military bases and posts are like cities. They are home to all kinds of organizations doing almost every kind of work you could name, including housing, barber shops, hospitals and clinics, food service, grocery stores, accounting and finance, civil engineering, headquarters, research and development, construction, law enforcement, legal offices, printing, personnel, power plants, maintenance, and recreational facilities. Each base and post has all these different kinds of organizations because in wartime they must be able to achieve their missions in the possible absence of support from the civilian community.

About this same time, I began working as a TQM consultant to organizations in the private sector. These experiences were also in many different kinds of organizations. There were many similarities and differences between public and private sector organizations, but I had the opportunity in a wide variety of organizations to learn much about what works and doesn't work with TQM.

Many people made it possible for me to learn about TQM, and I would like to acknowledge them. In my first book, *TQM: A Step-by-Step Guide to Implementation* (ASQC Quality Press, 1991), I expressed my thanks to the many military personnel who helped me learn. After that book was published, other people in the Department of Defense made it possible for me to learn about TQM: Major General Ernest J. Harrell; W. E. Daughtery, U.S. Army Engineer Division, North Pacific Division, U.S. Army Corps of Engineers; and James Smith, master statistician at San Antonio Air Logistic Center at Kelly Air Force Base, Texas. Incidentally, nothing in this book is intended or should be inferred to represent the policy of the Department of Defense or any of its components.

I also had educational experiences working with Mary R. Hamilton, U.S. General Accounting Office, Washington, D.C. and Toby Summers, Coca-Cola Bottling Company of the Southwest. I am indebted for opportunities to learn provided by people at five organizations with which I enjoy a long-term relationship as their TQM consultant. I could fill pages with the names of their employees who made valuable remarks during training sessions, at team meetings, in hallways, and over diet sodas. But, I am especially indebted to some of them. At Southwest Texas Methodist Hospital in San Antonio, they are John E. Hornbeak, James C. Scoggin Jr., Dr. E. Ann Hillestad, Steve H. Bancroft, Newt Courtney, Geoffrey W. Crabtree, Donna Smith, and Gregory A. Seiler. At Methodist Hospital, it was especially educational for me to serve as the facilitator to Newt Courtney and his patient accounts department improvement team (PA DIT). This team is a model of what a DIT should be. At Sid Peterson Memorial Hospital in Kerrville, Texas, I am indebted to the following for educational experiences: F. W. Hall Jr., Dianne Parrish, Terry Napper, Jean Williamson, Bob Walther, Martha Carlson, Stephanie George, Edwina Miner, and Charles B. Goodale. At Sid Peterson Memorial Hospital, I learned much serving as the facilitator to Dianne Parrish and Jean Williamson, leaders of the laboratory process improvement team (lab PIT). Dianne and Jean helped me think through many of the tough issues presented in this book. They are examples of what Deming had in mind when he said we need people with active minds. At the Electric Utility Department of the City of Austin, Texas, I learned much from my association with John Moore, Laura Doll, Milton Lee, Joe Maleski, Dr. Clarence Bibby, Lenny Molbert, Shelby Barnett, and the other members of the quality council. At the City of Kerrville, Texas, I learned from Glenn D. Brown, Kirk

McCarley, Dane Tune, and Jim Harvey. And, I am particularly indebted to Louis O. Garcia, Children's Regional Health Care System, for the many diverse learning opportunities he shared with me.

Associates who helped me learn include Dr. Karl J. Krumm, a consulting organizational psychologist in Austin and San Antonio; Donald Scooler, a TQM management consultant and trainer in Charleston, South Carolina; Debbie Prost, a marketing consultant with Prost Marketing, Inc., San Antonio; and Dr. Michael D. Matthews, a consulting organizational psychologist in Springfield, Missouri.

I appreciate the editorial assistance of Dr. Michele L. Trankina, San Antonio.

# Chapter 1

# The Traditional Stage: The Foundation

Many organizations in the Western world are managed in essentially the same way. This style of management is not new. It evolved from a variety of sources and is taught today in virtually every school of business. This approach to management may be called the *prevailing* or *traditional style of management,* and organizations that practice it may be said to be in the first stage of total quality management (TQM), the traditional stage.

## What Is the Traditional Style of Management?

Five concepts form the foundation of the traditional style of management.

1. Investors expect a reasonable return for the financial risks they assume.
2. The best way to manage human enterprises is with a hierarchical, or wedding cake, organizational structure.
3. Human enterprises are best managed according to the principles of management, such as the division of labor, unity of command, scalar chain, authority and responsibility, and span of control.
4. The biological and economic concepts of scarcity and competition work when applied in human enterprises.
5. Employees at every level do a better job when they've been promised an incentive.

Of course, far more is contained in books on traditional management than these five concepts, but what they contain springs essentially from these concepts or from the assumptions they make.

### Good Results

There's no denying that many good things have been accomplished by traditional organizations. For instance, military units of the free world, organized and managed strictly in the traditional style, have preserved world order long enough that governments may be able to establish a framework for lasting peace. Industrial and commercial enterprises organized and managed in the traditional style provided jobs, made many people wealthy, and contributed to an improved standard of living for all. Roads, bridges, and dams were built, swamps were drained, railroad tracks were laid, diseases were conquered, and products and services were produced and mass distributed, all by enterprises organized and managed in the traditional style.

But, the question is not whether traditional organizations can produce results. All styles of management, even the worst, can produce results. Examples include Attila the Hun, the Roman Empire, and the Third Reich. These styles of management, by some perverse standards, such as square miles conquered or number of people subjugated, produced results. The real questions are what were the costs of the results, and could a different style of management have achieved more?

## Bad Results

Most accomplishments of traditional organizations came at a high cost. The history of business in the United States, where practically all organizations are managed traditionally, is paralleled by a running account of legislation to protect labor, natural resources, food and drugs, and the environment from exploitation. Throughout the decades, there has been a stream of legal interventions to stop utterly shameless abuses of all kinds by traditional organizations.

For instance, by 1914, every state had passed child labor legislation, and two federal laws were passed in 1916 and 1919 which prohibited the employment in mines and factories of children under 14 years of age. (These federal laws were later declared unconstitutional, but the Fair Labor Standards Act of 1938, which forbade the employment of children under 16 in the production of goods for interstate commerce, largely accomplished their aim.) The point is that legislation was required to stop the exploitation of child labor by traditional organizations. Furthermore, the development and growth of unions was a response, in major part, to the need to curb the ruthless exploitation of labor. Historians will decide whether the achievements of traditional organizations are worth the exploitation of virtually everything they touch.

Today, there is evidence that when traditional organizations come up against offshore competition they are often unable to provide what is expected of them by their stockholders, customers, employees, suppliers, and even by their own chief executive officers (CEOs). Offshore producers, mainly the Japanese and so-called new Japanese, do not, for the most part, practice the traditional style of management. In the early 1950s, W. Edwards Deming taught them to do things differently. And, as a consequence, more and more markets once dominated by the United States have been captured by the Japanese. For proof, look at any parking lot in the United States, and about 35 percent, on the average, of the vehicles there will be foreign made, mainly in Japan. But, automobiles is not the only market in which the United States has lost share. The list is long and includes electronics, computers, audio equipment, color televisions, VCRs, machine tools, semiconductors, telephone equipment, apparel, industrial machinery, household appliances, tires, nuts and bolts, ball and roller bearings, cement, sports equipment, and zippers.

I heard a speech recently by the CEO of an American company that won a famous prize for quality achievement. He said the major barrier to making the improvements that led to winning the prize was the company's own senior management. This astonished the audience, but he didn't mean that their senior managers were a bunch of bad people. He meant they had simply inherited a lot of wrong ideas about how to run a business. As people, they were okay. They were honest, decent people doing their best. It was the style of management they practiced that was wrong. He said this style of management was their main barrier to improvement. And, this style of management had to be changed before the company could successfully compete for the quality prize. The style of management he was referring to is the traditional style of management practiced by virtually every organization in the Western world.

More and more CEOs are understanding the need to move away from the traditional style of management. To better understand what they're up against in trying to make this move, consider in more detail what the traditional style of management is all about.

## Investors and Reasonable Returns

It is well accepted that investors may risk their money as they see fit. They search for opportunities that offer the best returns in relation to the risks involved. Companies need investor money and compete for it in financial markets. As a rule, those with good earnings and good prospects get capital; those with weak earnings and few prospects do not.

To check on the safety and growth of their investments and to search for new opportunities, investors continually evaluate how well companies are doing. They do this mainly by monitoring company financial statements. The law, in fact, requires public companies—that is, corporations—to publicly disclose their earnings every quarter. Investors and their financial advisers search through stacks of these statements as well as financial newspapers, where summary financial statistics are published, in the hope of identifying companies that offer what promise to be good returns. If the prospects of a company look bright, investors may buy its stock. If the prospects of a company look gloomy, they probably won't buy its stock, and they may sell any of its stock they own. What could be more reasonable from the point of view of investors than to restrict their investments to companies that look like they'll pay a good return on an investment?

With owners always looking for companies with good financial numbers, it's no wonder CEOs feel pressure to produce favorable quarterly earnings. If they don't, the owners won't like it, and the CEOs may find themselves in the street looking for a job. In fact, hardly a day goes by that newspapers don't carry stories about stockholders booting out another CEO. But, to investors who are depending on good returns, say to put their kids through college or to provide for their retirement years, this pressure on CEOs is perfectly reasonable. "If you can't run the company at a profit, we'll get someone who can!"

This pressure to demonstrate good performance quarter after quarter dramatically affects the way CEOs manage and plan for the future. One of the main effects is to make them think hard about producing a favorable earnings statement for the current quarter. And, after that quarter is taken care of, they think hard about producing a favorable earnings statement for the next quarter. They are under pressure to think short run, from quarter to quarter, and many of them, in turn, push for short-term results throughout their organizations. It's no wonder so few CEOs show great interest in opportunities that promise to pay off only in the long run, such as new product research and development. They feel they can't divert dollars spent in the hope of short-run achievements to projects that may pay off in the long run. If they do, they know they may not be around long enough to see the result.

## The Hierarchical Form of Organization

Another feature of the traditional organization is the almost universal use of the hierarchical form of organization. The hierarchical form of organization, also called the *pyramid of authority* and *wedding cake* or *functional organization structure,* has been around for centuries in military, government, and religious organizations. There were magazine articles on this form of organization at least as early as the mid-seventeenth century. For instance, see writing on the hierarchical organization by Daniel Craig McCallum, a superintendent for the Erie Railroad Company in 1849.[1] But the person credited with documenting the hierarchical organizational structure in the late twentieth century was a German social scientist named Max Weber. He believed the hierarchical organization, or bureaucracy as he called it, to be the superior way to organize and manage human enterprises.

The hierarchical form is recognized today as the organizational chart, or wiring diagram, in which organizations are arranged into a set of vertical functional hierarchies, or stovepipes, each of which is a distinct division of labor (all the salespeople over here; all the production people over here; all the finance people over here). Within these stovepipes, jobs are arranged into a hierarchy of authority and responsibility resulting in a chain of command, and the authority and responsibility of each job is carefully defined. Or, as Weber explained, "the organization of offices follows the principle of hierarchy; that is, each lower-level office is under the control and supervision of a higher one."[2] Thus, formal authority is virtually zero at the lowest level of the hourly employee, and it increases at each successive level of supervision until it is greatest at the highest level with senior management, trustees, or the board of directors.

Communication follows the same pattern. For purposes of control, communication as orders and directions flow from higher levels to lower. Communication as feedback on results flows from lower levels to higher. But, little of these flows of communication takes place across functional areas.

## Communication in Hierarchical Organizations

In use, the hierarchical form has two main effects that go largely unnoticed by traditional managers. The first is that workers in one functional area, or stovepipe, have little reason to talk business with anyone in a different functional area. In an automobile plant, for instance, an engineer in the product design department doesn't ordinarily talk to anyone on the assembly line. In a hospital, nurses don't usually talk to anyone working in the dietary department, except maybe to complain about a missed meal tray. When a chain of command like this exists, workers are expected to take orders from their supervisor and no one else. This emphasis on vertical authority and communication causes a lot of trouble for managers of traditional organizations, as will be explained later.

## Authority in Hierarchical Organizations

A second unnoticed effect of the hierarchical form of organization is the basis of authority which it assumes. Another way to say this is with a question: What is the source of authority in organizations? This question has been debated for centuries, and the way this question is answered in an organization has much to do with its success or failure.

If one goes back far enough, there was a time when kings had authority over everything. Their authority was believed to come from God. Refusing a request from a king was like refusing a request from God. Kings could wage war, collect taxes, chop off heads, and tell everyone in the kingdom what to do. When the era of kings ended, the ownership of private property became the basis of authority. Owning property today sort of makes you a king, except you can't chop off heads, and you must pay taxes rather than collect them.

To a large extent, authority in traditional organizations has its basis in private property. Authority based on private property works like this. Suppose you own a business, and you hire me to help out. You have the right to tell me what to do because you own the business. You can do with it as you like. And someone you hire certainly can't tell you what to do with your own business. That wouldn't make any sense. That's one kind of authority. In a large organization, the owners (maybe stockholders) delegate the authority to run the business to professional managers, and, therefore, they can tell the workers what to do. Thus, the authority of a frontline supervisor can be traced back up the hierarchy through middle managers and senior managers to stockholders, the owners of private property.

*The Ultimate Source of Authority.* In addition to its basis in private property, authority can come from two other sources: (1) from understanding what customers want, and (2) from knowledge of what needs to be done to provide what customers want. Consider an example. Remember, you hired me as a new employee. At first, I won't know anything about our customers and their needs. And, I won't know much about what needs to be done to take care of our customers. On the other hand, you own the business and have been running it for a long time. You have a pretty good idea about customer needs and how to satisfy them. From my standpoint as the worker, I recognize your superior knowledge of these matters, so I'm willing to do what you say. I accept your authority. Note that I accept your authority, not so much because you own the business, but because you know more about the customers and how to please them.

Notice that who has this second kind of authority can change, as I explained in my first book.[3] Knowing customer requirements and what needs to be done to provide them can get away from you, as the owner, as your business grows. When your business was small, you knew every customer by name. And you knew what it took to satisfy each customer's needs. Back then, you had both kinds of authority: You were the owner and you knew your customers and what it took to satisfy them. But, as the business grew, details here and there began to get away from you. You didn't have time to know customers. You didn't have time to know how to satisfy their needs. At a certain level of growth and bureaucracy, you found you had to delegate some of your responsibilities to your spouse. At a further level of growth, you had to delegate to your spouse's brother. Eventually, however, the business got too big for you, your spouse, and all your spouse's brothers, so you had to delegate to people you hired as employees. Now, you still own the business and still have the authority that comes from the ownership of private property, but lots of other people know many details about your business that you don't know. They know the customers better than you do, and they know better than you how to provide what customers need. So now they have some authority—the kind of authority that comes from knowledge of customer requirements and how to meet them. You're spending most of your time now with your tax accountant anyway.

When it gets to the point where you don't know everything about your customers and how to meet their needs, you have the potential to make errors if you tell employees what to do. This is because you've lost direct touch with the customers and their requirements. Thus, you may tell subordinates to do things you think are right. But, in reality, they are entirely wrong. And, unless you've created the right environment, employees won't say anything about it. To keep from confronting you, they'll keep quiet. And, you'll make a blunder.

As your employees' authority grows through knowledge of customer requirements and how to meet them, you should trust employees and rely on them more and more through delegation. Thus, as an organization grows, there should be a corresponding shift in authority from the top (where authority comes from ownership of private property) to the bottom (where employees know customers and how to meet their requirements). Unfortunately, most traditional managers are unfamiliar with this concept. And those who know about it are often reluctant to accept this shift in authority.

| *Old Style* | *New Style* |
|---|---|
| Direct | Support |
| Dictate | Facilitate |
| Judge | Assist |
| Discipline | Counsel |
| Compete | Collaborate |
| Talk | Listen |
| Quantity | Quality |
| Fear | Trust |
| Secrecy | Openness |
| Work for | Work with |

**Figure 1.1.** Old and new leadership styles.

This shift in authority is the basis for a fundamental shift in leadership style. Sometimes this shift is called *inverting the pyramid*. The idea is that organizations get so big that owners lose touch with the needs of the customers. Owners who understand this can't justify directing employees about how to take care of customers. Instead, insightful owners wisely get into the role of facilitating employees in their efforts to take care of the customers whom they understand. Thus, the role of owners should transition as authority shifts.

There are many ways to express this shift. Figure 1.1 shows one way from the old style on the left to the new style on the right. But the best description of the new style of leadership is provided by Deming in his book, *The New Economics for Industry, Government, and Education.*[4]

## The Principles of Management

Knowledge of the so-called principles of management evolved over centuries in political, military, and religious organizations and, since the Industrial Revolution, in industrial and commercial organizations. References were occasionally made to one or more of these principles in autobiographies and histories written many centuries ago, but the first books about them were written around the turn of the century by people like Frederick W. Taylor, an American mechanical engineer, inventor, and so-called Father of Scientific Management, and Henri Fayol, a Frenchman trained as a mining engineer who rose to the position of CEO of a large mining company.[5] Taylor focused on how to increase the productivity of individual workers, and Fayol was concerned about organizational processes and structure. Many of the ideas of both men went against the prevailing management practices of their time. In any case, Taylor and Fayol proposed 14 and four principles of management, respectively.[6]

## *Taylor's Contribution*

Taylor had a good classical education, but worked his way up from the ranks. Having been a worker himself, he understood that workers are not in control of their output. He understood that when workers don't work hard it's management who's to blame for not designing the work properly and not providing the right training, tools, and incentives. Taylor sympathized with workers because when things went wrong he knew it was the system that was to blame. He was also a strong proponent of cooperation, rather than competition, among managers.[7] Taylor is widely misunderstood by those who haven't read his books.

Despite the fact that Taylor did *not* believe there is only one best way to do things, it is widely believed that he advocated the use of what are now called *methods engineering* and *work measurement* to discover the "one best way" to do a job.[8] The truth is, he was very interested in innovation in the interest of efficiency. He said the best person to do the job should be carefully selected and trained to perform it. Because he advocated separating the planning of work away from workers to functional foremen, he is accused of advocating a cadre of supervisors to ensure that workers do each job in the one best way. This separation of planning from doing the work is the origin of the notion that "all the brains are at the top of a traditional organization." Taylor also advocated using financial rewards to encourage workers toward their maximum output.[9]

Some of Taylor's ideas have not stood the test of time, but many management techniques based on the misconception of his ideas are uniformly followed in every traditional organization. For instance, traditional organizations have job descriptions, policy and procedure manuals, and regulations that explain in detail the one best way to do each job that needs to be done. These one best ways are seldom reviewed for possible improvement. "We've always done it that way, and it seems to be working okay. So why change it?" is the prevailing attitude. Vocational aptitude tests are used to select the right persons for jobs. And, to get the right person–job match, job features remain constant, as they represent the one best way to do things. The trick is to sift through the applicant pool to select the person who can do the job the one best way. New hires are carefully trained to do jobs just as called for in job descriptions and to behave according to policies, procedures, and regulations, and supervisors ensure that the required performance takes place. It is virtually impossible to find an organization in the United States that does not tie compensation to performance. This odious practice is consistent with what Taylor taught, but there is no evidence that he originated the idea. More is said later in this chapter about the connection between pay and performance.

## Fayol's Contribution

Fayol's principles of management have come under criticism, but many of them are uniformly followed in every traditional organization. But, like Taylor's work, much of Fayol's work is misunderstood and misapplied. In any case, he saw management from the viewpoint of the CEO of a large-scale, fully integrated organization. Many of his ideas are similar to those expressed by Weber in his writings on the hierarchical organization. (Fayol and Weber lived at the same time, late 1800s and early 1900s, but there is no evidence that they knew of each other.) Many of Fayol's principles of management had, no doubt, been in practice for decades, yet he was the first to suggest that management is a body of knowledge that can be studied and taught. Among the most widely followed principles cited by Fayol are (1) unity of command, that each employee should receive orders from only one source, (2) unity of direction, that there should be only one plan of action, and (3) centralization, that authority should be centralized to the extent appropriate to the circumstances.[10]

Many of Fayol's ideas stood out in stark contrast to the prevailing management practices of his time. Among these was the "gangplank" amendment to the scalar chain. The scalar chain, an idea proposed by Weber and others, established a chain of command from the senior manager to those at the lowest ranks, and it requires that this chain be followed for all communication. In practice, it virtually forbade horizontal, cross-functional communication. Fayol's gangplank allowed communication to move horizontally from one functional area to another, provided the supervisors in both areas were kept informed. It was thus that an engineer could speak to someone on the assembly line, or a nurse could talk to someone in the dietary department. One notable aspect of the gangplank idea is that it shows how much pressure there was in traditional organizations *not* to communicate horizontally. There was so much such pressure in Fayol's day that he saw fit to propose a means of making some cross-functional communication possible.

Another of Fayol's ideas that was ahead of its time was that individual or departmental ambition and selfishness could work to the detriment of the organization. There are those, today, who suggest that these were early thoughts about optimization and suboptimization or a systems view of organizations.

## Scarcity and Competition

The concepts of scarcity and competition evolved over many centuries through the thoughts of philosophers (such as Aristotle), social philosophers (David Hume, Adam Smith), economists (David Ricardo, John Stuart Mill), theologians (Thomas Malthus), and biologists (Charles Darwin). Many books have been written about what they said about scarcity and competition. The concepts of scarcity and competition underpin the way most organizations have been managed since the Industrial Revolution. And, these concepts apply as strongly today as they did 150 years ago.

A Scottish minister named Malthus (1890) formalized the concept of scarcity with the reasoning that world resources can only be expanded arithmetically while human population grows geometrically.[11] An English biologist named Darwin applied Malthus' thoughts to the entire living nature. He suggested that the struggle for existence is nothing more than competition for scarce resources in which only the strong survive. A Scottish social philosopher named Adam Smith (1937) said it plainly, that the general good is ensured if each individual is allowed to pursue his or her own selfish interests.[12]

The concepts of scarcity and competition began to catch on and were applied in a variety of fields. It seemed to make sense that practically everything is scarce. There is never enough food, housing, medical care, top-paying jobs, expensive cars, large-screen televisions, and money to go around. And, because people are numerous and resources scarce, it makes sense that people must compete to get a share. Because there is usually not enough to go around, it makes sense that the strong will wind up with the biggest share, and the weak must settle for the smallest share. For many people, this reasoning explains much of what happens in life. For instance, there are only a few top-paying jobs, so only a few people can have them. Others must settle for the more numerous, but less-attractive and less-lucrative jobs. The same is true of fine cars, beautiful homes, the best schools, the best vacations, and so on.

Competition is known to have a negative side. Some people don't get to drive fine cars or stay at the Ritz. They have to live on the "wrong side of the tracks." Their kids don't get the kind of education that will help them reach their full potential. But, competition's positive features are thought to more than make up for these negatives. For instance, competition ensures that the most capable people rise to the top to lead, and the weak and inefficient are pushed to the rear to follow. This idea fits in nicely with the concept of the hierarchical organization: The most capable get the few jobs at the top and the many weak and inefficient get the more numerous jobs at the bottom. To many, this is as it should be. Because the success of any kind of undertaking is more likely when its leadership is in the hands of the strongest and fittest, competition is almost universally thought to be a beneficial force because it brings the best people to the top.

Who would want to be in the hands of someone who is less capable? For instance, who would want to have their gall bladder removed by a fumbling, clumsy surgeon who can't remember the names of the body parts when directing surgical assistants during an operation? No one. You want your surgeon to have great hands. You want your surgeon to be capable of memorizing the names of hundreds of bones and muscles in college anatomy class. Not everyone has great hands. Not everyone can memorize all those body parts. Only the fittest can. And that's the kind of person you want to remove your gall bladder. And, who would deny such a person a $300,000-a-year salary, a big home on the right side of town, a fine car, and the wherewithal to stay at the Ritz? He or she deserves it. The same reasoning can be applied to virtually any job that is well paying, whether it's a CEO, certified public account (CPA), labor leader, general, judge, master craftsperson, computer expert, or whatever. Who would want a person of less ability in any of these jobs?

In the animal world, only the strongest, fittest creatures survive the harsh winters and competition with rivals. Spreading their genes ensures the greatest chances of survival of their entire species. Similarly, competition ensures that only the best players make the cut to get starting positions on teams. And a series of competitive events from sandlot baseball through the minor leagues ensures that only the best players make it to the big leagues. Competition, thus, ensures that only the best players are in the ballparks for fans to enjoy on summer afternoons and that only the two best teams make it to the World Series. Similarly, society benefits when the competition of the free market ensures the survival of the most efficient and most effective companies. It is they who provide the best products and services at the lowest prices to the benefit of all.

Most people believe competition brings out the best in everyone, and competition made this country great. This belief is so strong that when competition is absent from an event or circumstance, it is often created artificially. Traditional CEOs dream up awards, such as technician of the year, airman of the quarter, and salesperson of the week to encourage competition among employees. Even education in our schools is based on the belief that competition is good and brings out the best in everyone. For instance, how often are students encouraged to cooperate, say on a term paper, on homework, or on a test? Never. In fact, what is such cooperation called in school? It's called cheating. Teachers don't want students to cooperate. They are always saying, "Do your own work. Work independently!"

Suppose a certain teacher has a room full of exceptional students. They all deserve to make an A. Yet, the school policy is to grade on the so-called normal curve; that is, to have a certain percentage of A's, a certain percentage of B's, and so on, to include a certain percentage of failing grades. Despite the abundance of exceptional students, the school's policy artificially creates a scarcity of high grades. The alleged benefit of the policy is that it brings out the best in the students. Students are thought to study harder in a competition for good grades than they would for the sheer joy and fun of learning. This school policy also creates the inevitable failure and humiliation of a number of exceptional students who get average, poor, and failing grades, but this outcome is thought to be a small price to pay to bring out the best in all students.

Consider an example of scarcity and competition in business. One year, a particular business designated a certain amount of money for salary increases. Instead of allocating the money on the basis of equal shares all around or on seniority, increases were determined on the basis of individual performance. Department heads were required to rate subordinates on a scale of –3, –2, –1, 0, 1, 2, 3, such that the average for each department was zero. This meant that for employees rated on the positive side, there had to be a corresponding number of employees rated on the negative side. Despite the abundance in this organization of exceptional employees, this policy created a scarcity of money for salary increases and a competition for it. This competition was justified on the grounds that it brought out the best in everyone. Employees were thought to work harder for salary increases than they would for the joy and sense of accomplishment from doing a good job. Never mind that the policy created the failure and humiliation of a number of exceptional employees who got no salary increase or maybe got put on probation or fired.

# The Behaviorist's Model of Human Motivation

The behaviorist's model of human motivation was described in the early part of this century by John B. Watson, the father of behaviorism, and more recently by B. F. Skinner. However, the fundamental thinking behind it has been around for centuries: All behavior is caused by external forces, namely punishments and rewards.[13] To train a puppy, give it a treat when it does right and spank it when it does wrong.

Many CEOs have never heard of behaviorism, but they practice it every day in its rawest, most calculating form. If workers get out of line, there's a policy in place to see that they are counseled, reprimanded, docked some pay, suspended, or fired. And, to get them to work hard, there are various pay-for-performance or variable pay plans. These plans range from "a little something extra in your pay envelope" for hourly workers who lift their output to fat bonuses for CEOs who achieve gains in corporate results. Such plans have been in place for decades for senior managers, hourly workers, and the sales force, and recently they have become popular for middle managers. Moreover, most CEOs believe in management by objectives (MBO), and they routinely use bonuses as incentives for individual business units. Traditional managers who use teams provide rewards on two bases; first, to the best individual team members and, second, to the best team. With all these pay-for-performance practices in effect, many traditional organizations in the United States pay more in incentive compensation than in salary increases.

Traditional managers believe rewards and punishment are necessary for one fundamental reason: People don't like to work. They believe most people wouldn't work if they didn't have to. They'd rather watch television, fish, or play golf. What does the bumper sticker say? "The worst day fishing is better than the best day working!" Managers believe the only reason most employees work is for the pay. If they could get paid to watch television, fish, or play golf they wouldn't work at a company. If it weren't for the pay, they wouldn't show up for work at all. Many traditional managers reason that no one in his or her right mind would do the jobs in companies if he or she didn't need the pay. Sometimes the work is dirty, sometimes it's out in the rain and cold, sometimes it's under a house with the spiders, and sometimes it's dangerous or downright embarrassing. Or, "Who would face our complaining customers hour after hour if they didn't need the money?" managers say. And when they overhear employees exclaim "Oh boy, it's hump day!" (Wednesday) or "TGIF" (Thank goodness it's Friday), managers become even more convinced that employees really don't want to work and are only at work for the pay.

Because people don't like to work, traditional managers believe a big part of their job is to motivate, inspire, influence, cajole, control, or coerce employees into it. And because managers believe people work for the money, the basic management tool of motivation is the paycheck: fear of losing it and the hope of increasing it.

Despite the belief that rewards and punishment are successful tools of motivation, at least to gain temporary compliance, there is enormous evidence that gaining employee cooperation in this way is entirely wrong. Behaviorism in the workplace does not work. Virtually every dollar spent on books and management seminars on employee motivation has been wasted. Furthermore, rewards and punishment are not benign or neutral. There is evidence that their effects are harmful because they sap whatever intrinsic motivation employees may have for their work. Details of why behaviorism does not work are presented in chapter 3.

## Moving Forward

In the next chapter, we will consider what CEOs who run their organizations with the traditional style of management think about. We will then consider, in chapter 3, the consequences of these thoughts and how CEOs steer their organizations into the ditch by faithfully following the teachings of traditional management.

## Notes

1. Thomas Weber, *The Northern Railroads in the Civil War* (New York: Columbia University Press, 1952).

2. Max Weber, *Economy and Society*, trans. Guenther Roth and Claus Wittich (New York: Bedminster Press, 1968), pp. 218–219.

3. Charles N. Weaver, *TQM: A Step-by-Step Guide to Implementation* (Milwaukee, Wis.: ASQC Quality Press, 1991), pp. 223–224.

4. W. Edwards Deming, chapters 5 and 6 in *The New Economics for Industry, Government, and Education* (Cambridge, Mass.: MIT Press, 1993).

5. Frederick W. Taylor, *Shop Management* (New York: Harper and Row, 1903); ———, *The Principles of Scientific Management* (New York: Harper and Row, 1911); and Henri Fayol, *General and Industrial Management*, trans. Constance Storrs (London: Sir Isaac Pitman and Sons, 1949).

6. John B. Miner, Timothy M. Singleton, and Vincent P. Luchsinger, *The Practice of Management: Text, Readings, and Cases* (Columbus, Ohio: Charles E. Merrill Publishing Company, 1985), pp. 58–62.

7. Daniel A. Wren, chapter 7 in *The Evolution of Management Thought*, 4th ed. (New York: John Wiley and Sons, 1994).

8. Ibid., p. 131.

9. Taylor, *The Principles of Scientific Management*.

10. Fayol, *General and Industrial Management*, pp. 20–41.

11. Thomas Robert Malthus, *An Essay on the Principle of Population* (New York: Ward, Lock & Company, 1890).

12. Adam Smith, *An Inquiry into the Nature and Causes of the Wealth of Nations* (New York: Modern Library, 1937).

13. John B. Watson, *Behaviorism*, rev. ed. (Chicago: University of Chicago Press, 1930); B. F. Skinner, *About Behaviorism* (New York: Knopf, 1974); and ———, *A Matter of Consequences* (New York: Knopf, 1983).

# Chapter 2

# The Traditional Stage: What CEOs Think About

Most CEOs never doubt that the traditional style of management is the right way to do things. After all, this is what they were taught in high-priced business schools and in professional military education if they were in the service, and it's what they see their peers practicing. How could they know there is a better way? Yet, for most of them, the results of doing things this way are not usually positive.

This chapter discusses what CEOs of traditional organizations think about, and the next chapter deals with what happens as a result of their thoughts.

## Owner Expectations

CEOs are only too aware of the cold eyes of the owners (stockholders, board of directors, or trustees) peering at their quarterly earnings reports. They know owners look at them the same way owners of professional sports teams look at coaches. Sports team owners hire coaches and give them authority to run teams for one purpose: to win games. If coaches win games, they keep their jobs; if they lose games, they get fired. And CEOs know it's the same for them. They're hired for one reason: to make money. If they make money, they keep their jobs; if they don't make money, they get fired. And like the firings of coaches, the firing of CEOs happens all the time. Practically every day the newspaper has a story of another CEO getting fired.

CEOs react in different ways to the pressure from the board to make money. In corporations, some CEOs lobby their stockholders to vote their friends onto their board of directors, and some provide exceptional perks, such as large annual fees, to board members. They hope this will provide a friendlier board environment. But, just like the coaches of professional teams, CEOs react to this pressure by doing the best they can. And, doing their best means trying to do what the owners want. The owners of professional teams want their coaches to win, season after season. And the owners of businesses want their

CEOs to make money, quarter after quarter. This causes CEOs to spend their time thinking about two things: how to make money and how to avoid losing money.

## How to Make Money

Traditional managers think a lot about how to make money. And, these thoughts lead them to do the only thing they know how to do: to practice the traditional style of management. It is doubtful that they know that the origin of their style of management stretches back to people like Weber, Darwin, Fayol, Taylor, and Skinner, but they practice it just the same. They carry out the functions of management—they plan, they organize, they staff, they direct, and they control—within each functional area, as they were taught in business schools.

The most serious error in practicing the traditional style of management is the belief that if each functional area, or department, carries out its responsibilities, the entire organization will prosper and grow. This reasoning can be expressed as an equation: The whole is equal to the sum of its parts. For organizations, this equation does not apply. It is not true, and believing it leads to a world of trouble. The whole is not equal to the sum of its parts because this equation does not consider the *interactions* that take place between the parts, in this case between the functional areas or departments. The equation that does fit is the whole is equal to the sum of the parts plus the interactions. When organizational interactions, or cross-functional processes, are not understood and systematically managed, it leads ultimately to great harm for all stakeholders.

Instead of considering the important interactions in their organization, traditional managers practice what they've been taught. That involves cycling through the functions of management: planning, organizing, staffing, directing, and controlling.

*Planning.* Traditional managers are taught to begin all management activities with a plan. At the senior level, CEOs go through lengthy strategic planning sessions with their senior managers. They talk about social responsibility, the environment, obligations to employees, and ethics. But, most CEOs feel restless in these sessions. They know a lot of momentum and valuable time is burned up talking about these topics. They know planning really boils down to just one thing. "How do we make enough money to meet the owners' expectations and keep our jobs?" They know surviving really means meeting the owners' expectations for money. In the final analysis, planning means setting some goals and objectives to make the kind of money that will keep the stockholders and board off their backs.

*Organizing.* After putting together a plan, CEOs organize. If a CEO takes over a company that is already organized in a particular way, what's the first thing he or she does? Reorganize. CEOs organize or reorganize into some permutation of the functional hierarchy per Weber. The CEOs never mention Weber's name, and they probably wouldn't recognize Weber's name if someone said it, but they organize according to his directions just the same. They arrange jobs and people into some kind of hierarchy of functions in line with the principle of division of labor: all the salespeople over here, all the bookkeepers over there, and so on. They place many more people at the bottom than at the top, where they think the brains are.

In the hierarchy, Fayol's principles of management are observed. Most CEOs won't recognize Fayol's name either, but they follow his teachings just the same. For instance, according to the principles of unity of command and unity of direction, CEOs have authority over a few select managers each of whom has authority over a separate functional area. These managers, in turn, have authority over other managers who run the underlying components of the functional areas. This pattern continues down to the level of supervisors who have authority over hourly workers.

In traditional organizations, it is taken for granted that the hierarchical arrangement is the best way to organize and manage. This assumption is seldom doubted. According to the principle of the scalar chain, authority comes down from the top through ownership. Communication flows down as directions and up as feedback, and accountability for results is thereby presumed to be ensured. Horizontal communication must be approved by the managers at the next higher levels. The actual work to be done throughout the hierarchy is carefully planned, designed, and written up in thick manuals as job descriptions, just as Taylor is thought to have suggested in 1903, according to the one best way.

*Staffing.* In staffing, the director of human resources advertises the available jobs. Applicants are carefully screened for their suitability for the jobs described in the thick manuals. Applicants are hired for these jobs on the basis of simple criteria: ability or potential to do the job, dependability, and subservience. Hiring in a traditional organization is preceded by two investigations: first, vocational aptitude testing to determine if applicants have the inherent talent to do or learn the job, and, second, extensive checking with former employers and personal interviews to assess dependability and subservience.

The unspoken message to personnel is "Check your brains at the front gate, and do as you're told." The best ways of doing things around here were determined by methods engineers or from years of experimentation. What's the sense of considering other thoughts on the matter, especially from someone who hasn't been working here for 20 years?

*Directing.* To direct, CEOs execute their plans for the organization to provide the kind of return that will keep the stockholders off their backs. To execute their plans, they expect from their subordinates exactly what the stockholders expect from them. If the stockholders expect 6 percent, CEOs ask their functional managers for a level of performance that will result in 6 percent to the stockholders. This will translate into sales of so much, production of so much, purchasing of so much, staffing of so much, and so forth. This approach seems so logical and reasonable. It's such a clear, clean model for running an organization. If everyone will just do his or her share to meet his or her separate objectives or goals, everything will come out right every financial quarter. This approach is known as management by objectives (MBO); to others, it is management by results (MBR). MBO is a favorite tool of traditional managers. It assumes the whole is equal to the sum of its parts. It is difficult to think of a management practice that has caused as much damage to organizations and those who depend on them as MBO.

*Controlling.* The same MBO-type reasoning that underlies the direct phase, just discussed, also applies to the control phase. CEOs hold their functional managers responsible for meeting goals just as they themselves are held responsible for meeting goals by the stockholders. What could be more fair and reasonable? To make this happen, CEOs compare what they planned to happen for each functional manager with what each manager made happen. This reasoning is so simple and clear.

> *You know what your job is. All I expect is that you do your share so I can provide the 6 percent expected by the stockholders. And, if you don't meet your goal, it's no one's fault but your own.*

Thus, managers at every level, from CEO to line supervisor, must think about how to meet the performance objectives and goals for their areas of responsibility. Along with his or her objectives and goals, each manager is provided resources (a budget) and personnel and is expected to produce results. What could be a more reasonable, fair, and natural way of organizational life? How could anything that seems so right be so wrong?

# How to Cut Costs

An outsider once remarked that the traditional approach of setting goals and monitoring results, described earlier as MBO, could be very dangerous. The outsider's reasoning went like this: Suppose the board wants a 6 percent return, and that translates into $X$ amount of sales. To try for this level of sales, managers build inventory, hire staff, and commit capital in a variety of ways. To get these sales, managers bring out a new product model and introduce it with a big sales campaign. It looks like everything is going well, but suddenly there's a turndown in the economy. Or, suppose the competition does something tricky. Maybe the competitor brings out an innovative product. Or suppose the market simply can't absorb the targeted level of sales. Under these unforeseen circumstances, how do managers make the 6 percent for the board? How do they keep from losing their jobs?

The answer to this question is easy for any CEO experienced in the traditional style of management. Nothing to it. When things don't go as you planned, all you have to do is cut costs. Remember, under pressure from the board for a return on investment, CEOs think about two things: how to make money and how to keep from losing money. If they can't make money, then they try to keep from losing money. This means cost containment and cost reduction. The CEO of any traditional organization will explain this concept with a simple equation: Earnings equals revenue minus expenses. If you are taking a beating on the revenue (sales) side of this equation, you can keep earning up by slashing expenses (costs) on the other side of the equation. It's simple arithmetic. Nothing to it. Thus, when revenue doesn't work out, CEOs of traditional organizations can be expected to come out with a memorandum like this to their managers: "Because of the current turndown in the market, each department is directed to reduce expenses by 10 percent, beginning with the next accounting period."

## *Hitting the Easiest High Cost Target: Labor*

The biggest cost target on a profit and loss statement is labor. Every CEO knows cutting labor costs goes straight to the bottom line. The morality of laying off innocent employees is seldom discussed in the boardroom, but it is the source of sleepless nights, ulcers, prematurely gray hair, psychiatric consultations, confessions, and suicides among many CEOs who have feelings. The sad fact is that the history of traditional management is a shameless account of the indecent and immoral exploitation of labor. Laying off innocent employees is another theme that runs through that history.

There are many strategies for cutting labor costs. They include holding back on employee salary increases, whether earned or to offset the effects of inflation; using more contingent employees, that is substituting part-time for full-time employees to save on health care and retirement costs; hiring more minimum wage employees; not replacing personnel after normal attrition and expecting remaining employees to do more work; relocating overseas; and replacing workers with machines and robots.

Perhaps the most severe way to cut labor costs is with layoffs. For the outside world, a pretty face is often put on layoffs by calling them *restructuring, realigning the labor force*, or *outplacement;* but insiders cynically refer to layoffs as *housecleaning.* Hardly a day goes by that the newspapers don't carry a story of an organization doing some housecleaning. These news stories go like this: "XYZ Corporation announced Monday it will take a $368 million pretax charge in the fourth quarter for a restructuring that includes eliminating 3800 jobs, or about 8 percent of its work force, over a few years."

Contrary to what some would say, the CEOs responsible for layoffs are not cruel, unfeeling people. They go to church or synagogue. They have homes and families. When they put people out of their jobs, they know the hardship they're inflicting on the workers and their families. They feel guilt, remorse, and shame. Many lie awake nights wondering how these people will get by and if their kids will have enough to eat.

Layoffs are another management blunder. Layoffs are an admission for all to see that a CEO is unable to predict the organization's economic future. If the CEO could predict the organization's future, why couldn't he or she see the upcoming force reduction and accomplish it through attrition? The fact is that the CEOs were blinded by the figures, relying on traditional accounting methods, assuming the future would be a simple extension of the past. As will be explained in chapter 3, monitoring the past is no guide to the future. How managers can see into the future will be explained in chapter 11, when innovation is explained.

Every CEO knows yet another approach to reduce labor costs. This approach is not part of the revenue equation, but a concept out of economics: The more output you can get from a fixed-cost resource, the lower the cost of each individual unit of output. This is a simple matter of efficiency—output divided by input. If you can't increase output, keep output the same and reduce input. In traditional organizations, labor is seen in simple, unemotional terms as an input. And, because of such factors as union contracts, labor is often a fixed-cost input. When the cost of labor is fixed, the important question for CEOs is how to get the most output per unit of labor input. In other words, how can we get the most work out of our labor force?

CEOs know an easy way to get more work out of their employees: Create competition among them. Competition is thought to bring out the best in people, and traditional managers believe competition brings out the best efforts of their employees. They believe employees will work harder if they are competing with their peers and have something to win than they will for the simple joy of learning and achieving in an important, meaningful job.

## How to Motivate Employees

CEOs will tell you they read somewhere that it's better to use intrinsic motivation than extrinsic motivation. This advice has been around for decades, and most traditional managers have given it serious consideration. They understand that intrinsic motivators come from within a job, like how satisfying the work is. Extrinsic motivators, on the other hand, are not in a job; they have to be added on. They include such factors as pay, promotion, short hours, security, and awards.

Over the years, many CEOs have experimented with intrinsic motivation in one form or another. Although many are reluctant to reveal their thoughts on this question in public, when all is said and done, they almost always come up with one of two answers to the question of whether intrinsic or extrinsic motivation is best.

They begin their answer by explaining that there are *positive* extrinsic motivators, such as merit pay and various performance awards, and there are *negative* extrinsic motivators, such as reprimands, not getting a raise, the fear of getting fired, and getting fired. Then, they identify intrinsic motivators as job factors that appeal to an employee's sense of self-esteem, pride, and natural desire to do important, meaningful work. They then assert that their experience shows that either one of the extrinsic motivators, positive or negative, has a far more powerful influence on employee behavior than softer, intrinsic motivators.

There is a second answer CEOs give to the question about whether intrinsic or extrinsic motivation is best. This answer is that even if intrinsic motivation were more powerful, which their experience shows is poppycock, it is far more difficult to implement and manage intrinsic motivation. They argue it's easy to use extrinsic motivation— such as setting up a performance goal, like a 6 percent increase in sales or a deadline on a project—and to reward or punish based on the achievement or nonachievement of the goal. It's much more difficult, on the other hand, to use intrinsic motivation. For instance, exactly what is intrinsic motivation? Its meaning is not clear, even among psychologists. But, if it means something that appeals to an employee's sense of self-esteem and pride, what is self-esteem and what is pride? How do they work? What buttons must managers push to get the self-esteem and pride of employees involved in their jobs? Does this involve restructuring jobs, educating employees, or what?

It may be easy to get employees of health care organizations excited about the meaningfulness of their work because they can see how their efforts help patients get well. But how do you get someone to feel proud of their work if they are cooking hamburgers that they read in the newspaper are full of salt and fat and are actually harmful to their customers' health? How do you get someone to feel proud of their work when they know customers are being overcharged or have to wait on hold 15 rings before their call is answered by the help desk attendant? How do you develop pride in the work of a single parent who is a part-timer and whose job doesn't provide health care coverage for his or her kids? Because of these issues, virtually all CEOs opt for using extrinsic motivation.

## Competition

For CEOs who practice the traditional style of management, competition fits in well with extrinsic motivation. CEOs start out, as explained earlier, with the belief that it's easier to motivate employees with extrinsics than with intrinsics. They then strengthen the effects of extrinsic motivators with something employees are used to, something they are widely thought to like, and something that is thought to bring out their best and make them work hard: competition.

Traditional managers think long and hard of ways to get employees to compete among themselves for extrinsic rewards. In fact, they even stretch things by getting employees to compete for things they are entitled to as a matter of seniority or by learning additional skills, such as promotions, raises, and recognition. If they ever have doubts about the ethics of this practice, they justify it by remembering how much employees like competition. They say, "Competing in the plant and warehouse comes as naturally to our employees as it does to players in a football game. Competition brings out their best."

Many CEOs search for situations that can be made the basis of competition among their employees. Where there once was no competition—only everyone trying his or her best in cooperation, harmony, and justice—CEOs identify something that can serve as a basis for competition. Examples are the lowest absenteeism, the fewest keystroke errors, the best overall turnaround time on emergency repairs, and the highest sales figures.

The results of competition show, of course, that one employee wins while others lose. One data entry clerk gets a plaque and many don't. One repair unit gets an award and many don't. The CEOs behind these programs don't mind that many employees lose and may feel humiliated. To the CEOs, bringing out the best in everyone more than makes up for the fact that many hardworking employees lose and may feel humiliated. Some CEOs go so far as to say privately, with grins on their faces, that there is a certain justice in losers being identified and humiliated. It's Darwin's idea of the survival of the fittest, a natural law of life. They say the reason some employees didn't win is simply that they didn't deserve to win.

Competition is justified by some CEOs on the grounds that it forces losers to study the methods of winners; so, losers will be better people for the experience of losing. It will strengthen their characters. For instance, the data entry clerks who lost in the competition on keystrokes will admire, study, and emulate the methods of the clerk who won a plaque. Similarly, the repair units that lost on overall turnaround time will admire, study, and emulate the methods of the unit that won. CEOs see peer competition—or peer comparison, as some have softened the wording—as a good thing. In this way, they believe everyone improves in performance, and the organization, as a whole, is the better for it. Unfortunately for the stockholders of organizations managed by CEOs who believe this, nothing could be further from reality.

## Moving Forward

We next consider what happens to organizations when their CEOs believe the mythology of the traditional style of management. It is impossible to design a philosophy of management that would be any worse for everyone concerned than the traditional style, the style of management prevalent in the United States today.

# Chapter 3

# The Traditional Stage:
# The Misunderstandings

After you read chapters 1 and 2, you may suspect things don't always run smoothly for traditional organizations. If that's what you suspect, you're right. Traditional organizations are plagued every day by fierce problems and crises that work their CEOs to a frazzle; give them ulcers, gray hair, and heart attacks; and divert them from their real responsibilities. CEOs who practice the traditional style of management are so used to this stressful way of life that they think resolving crises and fighting fires is what management is all about. It is not.

But management's main troubles are not caused by the intensity of the marketplace. Nor are they caused by the rigidity and insensitivity of the government. Nor are they caused by the managers themselves. The main cause of the managers' troubles is the style of management they practice.

Most managers who practice the traditional style of management think they know what management is all about. They think they know what it takes to successfully run an organization. They think they learned it in schools of business, in professional military education, from someone whom they regard as a master manager, or from the school of hard knocks. They are simply mistaken. In reality, they weren't taught what they need to know, and much of what they were taught does more harm than good. Many organizations are better off when their CEOs are off somewhere giving a speech or playing in a golf tournament. In fact, many employees would like to see their CEOs and their other senior managers stay away permanently.

Much is wrong with the traditional sytle of management. The best way to see what's wrong is to read the books used to teach in business schools. Chapter after chapter, teaching after teaching, inaccurate and misleading information abounds about how employees learn, employee motivation, goal setting and feedback, contingency leadership, MBO, decision making, and job satisfaction. Virtually everything said about these subjects and others is wrong. For the purposes of this book, however, several of these teachings are especially harmful and require exposure.

# The Mistake of Monitoring Results as a Guide to the Future

One part of the traditional style of management is particularly harmful. This is the belief that monitoring the past is a sound basis for planning for the future. CEOs plot accounting, financial, and market share data as points through time on run charts. They fit straight lines to these points and extend them into the future. These extended lines are the basis of their future plans.

## *The Future Is Not a Repeat of the Past*

The flaw in the "extrapolate a straight" approach to planning is that the future will not be like the past. Years ago, the past may have been a guide to the future, but it no longer is.

To clarify this point, consider a personal example. Years ago, parents' advice to their children was useful because there were few differences between the experiences of the generations. Years ago, parents' experiences when they were children were much like what their own children would encounter. But, things have changed. Today, children face problems their parents never faced or even imagined facing. For instance, was there a danger of being shot by a gang on the way to public school 25 years ago? Were drugs available in schools? Did students use computers? Were there so many single parent families? With changes like these and many others, how can today's parents offer advice based on their own childhood experiences?

The same is true of organizations. The world is changing so fast that most of what happened in the past will never happen again. For instance, was there a global economy 25 years ago? Were there offshore competitors and multicountry trading blocks competing vigorously in local markets? Did neighborhood businesses have to be the best in the world or go broke? Was the world open to instantaneous communication? Were information technologies and computer networks virtually everywhere? Was the U.S. work force multicultural? How valuable are the experiences that occurred before these changes took place to those who must compete today?

It is a similar mistake to believe you can learn from past mistakes and do a better job next time. On the surface, this seems to make sense, but its value depends, again, on how much the future will be like the past. When the world is changing quickly, past situations in which mistakes were made may never occur again. To the extent that this is true, knowledge gained from mistakes made in the past is of no benefit to you now.

Consequently, managers who work in a fast-paced industry must quit relying so much on postmortem accounting reports and market share information a quarter or more old as a basis for plans for the future. They need to realize that these data are the organization's history books. By the time events are recorded there, it's too late to do anything about them. And they are no guide whatsoever to the future.

There is a better way to plan for the future, and it is explained in chapter 11 as the principles of innovation. In a nutshell, the way to plan for the future is to build knowledge of how customers' processes work and forecast the effects on these processes of environmental changes. Monitoring the environment can provide an early warning of changes that are about to influence customer processes. This provides a window to the future. Looking out this window is how CEOs steer their organizations, by looking into the future instead of by looking into the past with history books.

## The Negative Effects of Hierarchy

Another harmful aspect of the traditional style of management is the almost universal belief that the best way to organize human enterprises is with a hierarchical, or wedding cake, organization structure.

### Why the Hierarchical Structure Is Used

The hierarchical organization is popular because it is thought to ensure control, especially over personnel and costs. This is because it provides everyone with a boss who keeps an eye on what everyone does. There are numerous reasons why traditional managers think it is necessary to keep an eye on employees. For instance, personnel must do their work as specified in job descriptions and behave appropriately, in the sense of conforming to organizational policies and procedures, such as not abusing leave. Some employees will take advantage of the organization and their coworkers if given the chance. Controls ensure that this doesn't happen.

After all, many people are in jail for thefts ranging from the pilfering of tools by hourly employees to the embezzlement of millions of dollars by CEOs, chief financial officers (CFOs), and CPAs.

### The Impact of Hierarchy on What Managers and Employees Think

It is necessary to ensure order in organizations, but the obsession with achieving order through control and compliance has caused the real aim of hierarchies often to become misunderstood. Managers are often trained to think their main job is to hold employees' feet to the fire for more output; to ensure they meet their quotas, work standards, or objectives; and to ensure they don't overrun their budgets. And, employees think their job is to do what managers expect them to do. This is all wrong. It casts managers in the role of dictator, overseer, judge, and disciplinarian. Employees must never ask questions, never make waves, always act respectfully, play politics, say only what's safe, and accept blame.

The real job of employees is to know they have customers, both internal and external to the organization, to strive to discover what these customers want, and to work hard to give it to them. The real job of managers is to teach employees to look at things this way and to assist them in providing what customers want. In other words, employees should not look for guidance to their bosses, but should look for it from their customers. And, when they know what customers need, they should look to management for assistance in providing it. "My customers need such-and-such, Boss. What can you do to help me provide it?" This requires a different kind of employee; one who will ask questions on the customer's behalf, one who will make waves when customers aren't getting what they want, one who will stand up for the customer's rights. It also requires managers who see their roles entirely differently.

We will continue to need organizational hierarchies, but they will become flatter through reengineering, as explained in chapter 12. But the real issue is that advocates of the traditional style of management misunderstand the aim of hierarchies. They see hierarchies as *vertical* structures aimed at ensuring order through control and compliance. In reality, order is only a coincidental function of hierarchies. Hierarchies should be viewed as *horizontal* structures aimed at marshaling an organization's resources on satisfying customer needs. There is so much misunderstanding about the aim of organizational hierarchies that I offer a law to clarify the issue. I call it the *iron law of the hierarchy*.

> *99.9 percent of the work of any successful organization occurs horizontally; only 0.1 percent occurs vertically.*

Micromanagers of traditional organizations behave as if these percentages are reversed.

### Hierarchy Leads to Stagnation

As anyone who has worked in a large organization knows, there is a virtually irresistible tendency toward tighter and tighter controls as organizations grow more complex. Growth means hiring more employees, and hiring more employees means more supervisors, managers, and controls of all kinds. Growth also leads to an ever-increasing requirement for documentation (paperwork), and taller and taller hierarchies, sometimes with as many as seven or eight levels. This tendency is aggravated by outside pressures, such as increasing reporting requirements of various governmental and private oversight, regulatory, and taxing bodies as their jurisdictions increase. As reporting requirements increase, there is a corresponding reduction in the percent of employee time spent on core responsibilities. And, as the size of an organization increases, there is an increasingly disproportionate ratio of management and staff to workers and a tendency to overemphasize procedure. Staff redundancy often develops as management and approval authorities become multilayered. Many economists are convinced bureaucrats add negative value to organizations. Often, too, there develops a tendency toward dilution of single-point authority and responsibility with an emphasis on passing the buck. Thus, organizing and managing within a large hierarchical structure can lead to inflexibility, slow decision making, and eventual organizational stagnation.

Further evidence of the inflexibility of large traditional organizations can be read in the frequent newspaper stories of how *Fortune* 500 companies become sluggish and eventually get tripped up by their own growth and size. These news stories tell of how the companies lose market share to smaller, more agile organizations.

## The Evils of Competition

Many experiences in life teach us to compete, and most of us accept competition as a normal part of life. Most of us also accept the idea that competition brings out our best and promotes the overall good. In some situations, such as sports activities with certain aims, this may be true; but in organizations, competition is disastrous. Competition in organizations almost always works directly *against* the very purposes for which organizations are intended. Competition suboptimizes organizations. The truth is that organizations are far better off when the work there is based on cooperation.

Many traditional managers have bought heavily into the myth that competition brings out the best in their subordinates. They deliberately encourage competition among employees, teams, departments, and divisions thinking they are doing the right thing. Yet, it is difficult to think of anything management could do that would be any more harmful to the very purposes they are seeking to achieve than to encourage competition.

## The Evils of Competition Among Managers

Managers in traditional organizations are forced by company policy to compete for promotions and raises. Managers at one level compete for positions that become available at the next level. They also are told there is only so much money available for salary increases this year and that shares will be allocated on the basis of performance. When faced with situations like these, it is only natural that managers think about how to make themselves and their departments look good. And, that's exactly what senior management wants them to do. But, the catch is that if they can't make their own department look good, at least they can try to make the other managers' departments look bad. That thinking goes back to sports. In sports you have two aims: try to score and try to keep the other guy from scoring. But keeping other departments from scoring is not what CEOs want managers to do.

Competition reminds many managers of an earlier period in their lives, perhaps in high school or college, when they were involved in sports. They learned there that the object of competition is to beat the other team, and many of them carry the same thinking over into their organizational life. In fact, competition becomes so ingrained in them, many deal with all parts of their lives this way. Unfortunately, many can never be taught otherwise. Much of the vocabulary of organizations is made up of sports terms, such as *hit a home run* or *score* for an important achievement; *knocked out, struck out, dropped the ball, TKO'd*, and *took it on the chin* for a setback or dramatic failure; *put on the sidelines* for being transferred to a staff or headquarters job; *get in the game* as a reprimand to concentrate on the moment; *time out* for a break; and *team* for an organized group of employees. It comes naturally for many managers to try to beat other managers like they used to try to beat their opponents in sports.

Of course, managers pay lip service to cooperating with other managers if subjects, such as teamwork, ever come up in staff meetings, but a voice from deep inside tells them they must beat the other managers like they used to beat sports opponents. In the back of their minds, they hear their old coach shouting, "Suck it up, dig in, and fight, fight, fight!" Somewhere from the dim past they can remember the spirited music of the school band and the shouts of cheerleaders. They want to hear the coach shout, "Way to go!" In business, the boss plays the role of the coach. And, managers want to look good for the boss like they used to want to look good for the coach. The last thing many of them want to do is help other managers. It is impossible for many of them to get out of the competitive mode. For them, having weak managers running other departments is an advantage because it makes it easier to beat them and look good to the boss.

## Is Competition Good or Bad?

After a careful review of the research on competition, Alfie Kohn found strong proof that competition is not an inevitable part of human nature, that it does not lead to greater productivity, that it is not more enjoyable than cooperation, that it does not build character, and that it poisons our personal relationships.[1]

Competition, in itself, is neither good nor bad. It all depends on how it is used. To evaluate the effects of competition, one simple rule should be followed. I call this the *rule of when to use competition.*

*If using competition limits or prevents us from achieving our aim, don't use it.*

Consider some situations in which we can think about how this rule applies.

*Competition in Sports.* At some period in our lives, we have all been involved in sports. Suppose, for instance, that our aim is to determine which team or player is best, to identify winners and losers. Competition is perfectly suited for this aim. Competition can determine who is best at something, and participants know before the game starts there will be winners and losers. Next, consider a different aim: to provide entertainment. Some people like to play; others like to watch. Sports are very exciting and, again, competition is perfectly suited for this purpose. Next, suppose the aim of a sports activity is to develop a sense of competitive spirit in the players or to teach players to lose gracefully. The players know before the event starts there will be winners and losers. Then, again, competition is okay. Winning and losing doesn't hurt the aim in each of these illustrations; in fact, it ensures their accomplishment.

But, suppose the aim is education. For instance, consider a high school gym class where students want to learn how to play a sport, develop some skill at it, and come away with a feeling that playing the sport is fun. Is competition right for this aim? Suppose the coach decides to use competition. The coach tosses softballs, bats, gloves, and other equipment out onto a ball diamond and instructs students to choose up sides and play softball for the class period. Let's see what can happen. Suppose a certain child has no experience playing softball.

Knowing of this child's lack of experience, the other children choose this child last as they set up the teams. At the beginning of play, this child is told to sit on the bench on the pretense of being a substitute if someone gets injured. Later, the child is allowed to play but is sent to right field where few balls come his way. Suppose under the pressure of competition the child makes a fielding error on the one attempt he gets, and he strikes out his one time at bat. His teammates are disappointed because their aim is to win, and he didn't help achieve that aim.

This little boy comes away from gym class feeling frustrated and humiliated. He comes away thinking how awful gym class is and how much he hates softball. Suppose the memories of this experience are so bitter that they keep him from being involved much in sports for the rest of his life. With these unpleasant memories, suppose he never watches professional baseball. He never has the thrill of watching the Cubs win in Wrigley Field, seeing an exciting World Series on television, or taking his own kid out on a sunny day in early spring to see a local class AA baseball game. In this case, did competition work? It may have worked for the children who were winners, but did it work to achieve the aim: for all these children to learn to play softball, develop some skill at it, and come away with a feeling that playing softball is fun?

If the aim of a sports activity is education, there needs to be a better way to accomplish it than with competition. The coach needs to show some brains, to think about the aim, and organize an activity that will provide the maximum amount of education each child is capable of absorbing. Competition is not the best way to accomplish this. Maybe the rules of the game need to be modified so the emphasis on winning is lessened or removed. Maybe this means rotating positions and sides so that everyone fully participates. Maybe this means establishing a buddy system whereby the aim of experienced players is to help beginners. Maybe it means requiring that each player on a team must come to bat at least twice and play in the field at least two innings. In any event, an activity needs to be developed whereby competition doesn't defeat the aim. If the aim of sports is education, every child should learn how to play the sport, develop skill at it, and develop a love for the sport that will be a source of joy throughout his or her life as a participant and a spectator. If the aim of a sport is education, there is no reason to allow a bitter competition to take place where some children win and feel great, and some children lose and feel humiliated. It all depends on the aim. Every kid deserves to be a hero.

***Competition Among Your Kids.*** Speaking of kids, consider the best case I know against competition. Suppose you are lucky enough to have children. As you bring them up, would it be a good idea to encourage them to compete against one another? Would competition bring out their best: trying to beat each other in sports, for the best grades, for the best-paying part-time jobs, for the best clothes, for the best looking dates, and for the sharpest car? Or, would it be a good idea to encourage them to cooperate, to support each other, and to be friends? What aim would you have for the relationship between your kids? And, would that aim be helped or harmed by competition?

Before answering this question, think about this. Imagine that many years have now passed, and you're dead. What would you prefer the relationship between your kids to be like then, competitive or cooperative? Remember, life is tough. Everyone has to travel down the long, hard road. When you're not around to look out for them, how do you want them to treat each other? How do you want them to respond when one hears of the misfortune of another? Do you want them to respond in the spirit of competition with a smirk and a wisecrack like, "It serves you right! You should have been more careful." Or maybe, "Hey, tough break, pal. But, you're on your own! Good luck!" Or, do you want them to be a source of support and comfort to each another? "I'm so sorry to hear of your misfortune! What can I do to help? I'll be right over." Parents should think about the aim of the relationship they are encouraging between their children. This is a serious question. Are you teaching and modeling cooperation or competition?

*Competition Among Repair Units.* Consider another example of the negative effects of competition on an aim. A certain airline had repair units at more than 150 locations throughout its traffic area, and its aim for these units was to optimize repair support for aircraft. However, to bring out the best in these repair units, the well-intentioned airline CEO gave a performance award to the repair unit of the year.

The award brought recognition to employees at the winning unit and a 5 percent salary increase to the unit chief. In this competition, do you think any unit chief was enthusiastic about giving up spare parts to help another unit? Do you think any unit chief was enthusiastic about sharing information about a way to improve operations or about how to more effectively perform a certain repair? Do you think any unit chief was enthusiastic about seeing a good mechanic transferred to a unit at which he or she was needed more or promoted to become a master repair trainer at the headquarters? The answer to these questions is no. These unit chiefs worked in an environment, created by management, that was not conducive to cooperation. In this environment, cooperating was not in the best interests of the unit chiefs, and its absence undermined the airline's aim for its repair support function.

Spare parts did not always move to where they were needed; the flow of vital information was often impaired; talented mechanics were not always transferred to where they were most needed; and a large, but unknown number of other acts of suboptimization took place every day in this airline. The key question is whether the CEO's policy of giving a performance award for best repair unit contributed to the airline's aim. It did not.

*Competition Among University Faculty.* Consider yet another example of the adverse effects of competition on an aim, this time at a university. The well-meaning administrators of this university gave salary increases, promotions, tenure, and other awards on the basis of competition among faculty. They believed hard work should be rewarded, and that it was unfair, even immoral, to reward lazy, uninspired faculty members. "If you don't produce, you don't share in the benefits" was their philosophy.

Salary increases, promotion, tenure, and other awards were based on the results of the appraisal of a professor's teaching ability, counseling skills, university service, community service, and articles published in scholarly journals. There was no formal statement of how many articles were expected, but word got around that two per year would keep you out of the doghouse and get you rewarded. The effects of evaluating professors on the number of articles they wrote is shown in the following illustration.

A new, inexperienced, but enthusiastic faculty member approached a senior faculty member who was well-known for publishing many articles. In their conversation, the new faculty member expressed admiration for the senior member's publishing ability and inquired if the two might write an article together. Bearing in mind that rewards were based on individual achievement, do you think the senior faculty member was willing to cooperate with the new colleague? Many faculty are intrinsically motivated and happy to mentor a new person, but the faculty member in this illustration reasoned differently.

*This new guy is pretty sharp. It's too bad his graduate training didn't teach him how to do publishable research. I wonder why he was hired in the first place if publishing is what the administrators expect. Maybe I should help him out. On the other hand, what happens if he really gets involved in research and starts pumping out the articles? What if he gets so good that he does more than the required two per year? What if he starts doing four? What will the dean say? The dean may come to me and say, "Hey, if this new guy can do four articles a year, you should be able to do four instead of your usual two. Have you been sandbagging me all these years?" If that happens, can I do four? What about the afternoon a week I play tennis? And what about the afternoon a week I spend with my family?*

The senior faculty member had second thoughts about cooperating with the new person. In the end, she said, "Gee, I'd like to help you, but my plate is full right now. Let me get back to you when things loosen up a little." But she never got back.

The university's policy created competition among faculty and sub-optimized its aim, to encourage the publication of scholarly research among faculty. In addition, promotion, salary increases, and tenure came easier for faculty who knew how to write articles. But faculty who were willing to write articles but were unable to find mentors didn't write them and didn't get their share of the rewards. Consequently, the turnover rate among new faculty was high. In fact, at the faculty meetings which began each academic year, many new faculty members were always introduced. The audience of existing faculty applauded to welcome their new associates, but most of them saw these introductions as a fearful sight. They knew many new hires really meant many terminations the previous year, and they wondered if they might be the next to go.

Competition among faculty for salary increases, promotion, tenure, and awards may explain why there is so much collaboration on research articles between professors at different universities and so little collaboration between those at the same university. It may also explain, at least in part, why many professors go into administration. Perhaps when they were new, no senior faculty member was willing to mentor them so they could learn to do research for publication. For them, the only way to advance was to go into university administration. The sad part of this is that the hearts of many faculty members are in teaching and research, and they are forced, from lack of cooperation with senior faculty as mentors, to go into administration.

## What Improvement Is Really All About

Another harmful aspect of the culture of traditional organizations is the misunderstanding of improvement. To understand improvement, recall in chapter 2 how CEOs cycle through the functions of management and often find themselves in the control function. To control, they compare what they planned to happen with what actually happened. When there is a difference, they find out why and take remedial action to correct the deviation. The popular names for correcting deviations are *fighting fires* and *resolving crises.*

On a day-to-day basis, CEOs spend much of their time fighting fires. They carry beepers or "bricks" (cellular phones) to alert them when something doesn't go as planned. Their beepers go off, and they rush off to solve the "crisis du jour." After that crisis is solved, a period of calm follows, but soon the beeper goes off again. For most CEOs, their working days are filled with an unending series of crises. Many CEOs pride themselves in their ability to resolve crises, which they call *challenges.* They believe meeting challenges and resolving crises is what management is all about. It is not.

Rather than being proud of the ability to resolve crises, CEOs should be embarrassed. Think of it this way. Carrying a beeper for the purpose of being alerted to another crisis is really a confession for all to see that the wearer doesn't understand an important part of his or her job. No enlightened CEO would permit the continuation of an organizational environment that produces an unending series of crises. Of course, crises can be expected from time to time, even in organizations where TQM is fully implemented, but organizations should be managed so that crises become increasingly infrequent. Operations should run smoothly. To survive and prosper in today's competitive environment, CEOs can't afford to devote so much of their valuable time to resolving crises. In today's competitive environment, there are more important things to think about. These things are continuous improvement and innovation.

## Misunderstanding the Meaning of Improvement

Traditional CEOs misunderstand the meaning of improvement. They think improvement is restoring something that's gone haywire to its original state. Restoration is a kind of improvement, but it is not the kind of improvement we're talking about here. To demonstrate the difference between restoration and improvement, consider an example.

Suppose a CEO gets a report that a certain process isn't working right; say it's producing higher than average costs. This CEO starts up an effort to improve it. After some time, the costs move back down to where they were before, and things are pretty much under control. Would the typical CEO continue improving this process? Most would say, "No. It's working perfectly, so why keep messing with it? I've got better things to do with my time."

The error in this kind of reasoning is that, for most organizations, you can be sure the original state of processes is pretty bad. Few processes, especially those that cross departmental boundaries, were well designed in the first place. Remember, traditional CEOs conceive of organizations as vertical structures and pay little attention to cross-functional processes. For the most part, cross-functional processes just happen. They fall into place as best they can between carefully managed functional areas which are vertical. When a deviation, or spike, occurs in the performance of a process that was not working well in the first place, CEOs get into an improvement frenzy. But then all they do is restore the process to its original adequate state, which was never really very good.

Another important aspect of process improvement is to remember that a customer sits at the end of every process. The aim of every process must be to make this customer's life better. Therefore, rather than evaluating the health of processes strictly with costs, it's better to consider their impact on customers. The real test of how good a process is is whether it's taking care of its customers, and customer expectations are continually increasing.

## How to Teach Continual Improvement

The concept of continual improvement is difficult for many CEOs to grasp. Continual improvement is like outer space or the concept of infinity. It has no end. CEOs can't get their arms around it. It confuses them. They need structure in their lives, and goals and work standards provide it. To them, goals and standards are real. They're something tangible to shoot for. Consequently, there is enthusiasm among some traditional CEOs for approaches to improvement like benchmarking and performance standards, such as the heavy documentation requirements of ISO 9000. "Let's find out who does this job best, and see if we can come up to that level!" Once they meet this level, what next?

One problem with the "What next?" question is that, historically, management has always raised the standard. Thinking of their annual bonuses, CEOs reason "Now that we've reached that level, let's see if we can do better." Employees, on the other hand, see this as a game management plays, another way to turn the screws down on them. It creates the we–them adversarial relationship between management and employees that's older than the era of scientific management. In this struggle, employees reason, "If we meet the current standard, management will only raise it. So why try to meet it? If the standard goes up, it will only mean more work at the same pay." And, historically, this belief is founded in fact. To avoid this kind of resistance, it's better to get everyone into the spirit of continual improvement in the first place rather than improving with a stair step approach where every additional step is a surprise and creates resistance. In other words, don't use goals and work standards.

One way to get people to think about continual improvement is to ask them how it applies in their personal lives. For instance, who doesn't try to put his or her best foot forward? Who isn't looking for the right shirt, blouse, or tie to go with a certain suit? Who isn't looking for a better color of makeup or a better razor blade? Who's still wearing the pastel colors of the 1970s, such as lime green double-knit leisure suits? Who's still wearing his hair exactly like he did when he graduated from high school? A few people do; they think the old ways are best. But most people are continually improving in their personal lives.

Another part of our personal lives which most of us are trying to improve is our health. Consider the increasing popularity of health magazines and the recent higher sales of exercise equipment. And what about what people eat? Most people are interested in eating right. Red meat consumption is going down, and the consumption of fish and poultry is going up. And what about the role of continual improvement for people who participate in sports? What golfer doesn't want to perfect his or her swing? What tennis player doesn't consider different tennis rackets, string, tension, and grips? What jogger doesn't think about the benefit of higher-technology jogging shoes?

These are examples of continual improvement in our personal lives. What we need to do is get the same kind of thinking into our jobs. In our personal lives, everyone is trying in one way or another to improve. The same attitude should apply in organizations, and discussions and illustrations with employees to this effect can have a positive impact on the way they think about improvement. With a little imagination, facilitators and trainers can design some entertaining group activities for employees which show, through examples, the practice of continual improvement in everyone's personal lives and how it applies in the workplace.

When employees hear talk about improvement, they are conditioned by past events to see it as another sneaky effort by management to get more work out of them. It is important, therefore, to stress that, to make continual improvement happen, no one will be asked to work harder than he or she does now. Instead, employees will be asked to identify the useless, wasteful ways work is being done. When these useless, wasteful things are identified and stripped out of the work processes, everyone will be able to concentrate on his or her core responsibilities. And, everyone will be able to work smarter, but not harder, while completing more real work. When this argument is presented to employees, a loud cheer will be heard a mile away. They know what they do is made up of two parts: (1) the real work, and (2) the useless, wasteful part, such as unnecessary documentation and storage, delays because of what is late from upstream suppliers, and meaningless inspection. They know the work processes have never worked well and have prevented them from taking joy in their work. When things are explained in this light, they will be enthusiastic for continuous improvement. The problem then becomes management making good on its end of this commitment.

## Blaming Employees for Problems

Consider this question. What's the first thing traditional CEOs think about when they hear about a crisis or problem? The answer is they want to know who's to blame. "Who's responsible for this problem," they ask. Do they ever think the problem could be in the system or environment surrounding the work? Very seldom. "Our system is the one best way! How could it be the source of the problem?" they declare. They almost always think it's the fault of an employee. They mutter to themselves, "If so-and-so would just do his jobs as we taught him, this problem would never have happened!" This reaction is another harmful feature of the traditional style of management.

The truth is that employees are not the main cause of problems. Many studies show that only rarely are employees to blame. Virtually all problems and crises are caused by barriers and obstacles in the work environment itself, almost always the result of cost-ridden and ineffective work processes. Anyone familiar with the writings of Taylor knows he said more than 90 years ago that employees are not to blame for problems of output. He had been an hourly employee himself, and he knew management was to blame. Management is to blame for not providing the support systems in which first-class employees can do a good job.[2]

Furthermore, employees can do very little to remove the barriers and obstacles that stand in the way of their doing a job of which they can be proud, at least on the scale required to bring organizations to the level of effectiveness needed to compete in today's marketplace. This kind of improvement requires action by management. Unfortunately, CEOs trained in the traditional style of management do not understand this. Bringing about this kind of improvement is in the third stage of TQM, process improvement, explained in chapters 5 through 10.

### The Consequence of Blaming Workers for Crises and Problems

There is an extraordinarily damaging consequence to blaming employees for crises and problems. This consequence is that CEOs who blame employees don't look elsewhere for cause. All they have to do is resolve the crisis or solve the problem and mutter something ugly under their breath about the darn employees. After that, they may think about giving some employee "a good talking to" or, at best, some additional training. But that's the end of it. Then these CEOs grab a cup of coffee and wait for the next crisis.

As a result, improvement never gets started on the real causes of crises and problems, and they continue to create trouble. The real cause of crises and problems lies in the work processes for which CEOs are responsible. Only they have the authority to improve and innovate them.

## Performance Appraisals and Other Punishments

Most of the changes required in the TQM journey are relatively easy for almost everyone to accept. But two changes are resisted by virtually every CEO and provoke questions from every audience that hears them discussed. These two changes would eliminate organizational practices that represent the traditional style of management at its worst.

The first change is ending the use of performance appraisals. There is no doubt about Deming's teaching on this subject. He lists performance appraisals, merit ratings, and annual reviews as *deadly diseases*.[3] And, despite the fact that it's difficult to find a person who doesn't think performance appraisals are worthless, invalid, a meaningless ritual, and a profound waste of time, few people see any alternative to them.

The second change is to quit using rewards to motivate employees. Again, Deming's position is clear. He says the idea of merit pay is attractive, and it seems like merit pay would motivate employees to do their best. But its effect is the opposite.[4] When CEOs hear these words, however, they wonder how you get employees to work hard if you don't pay them for it.

The good news is that performance appraisals and merit pay shouldn't be eliminated early in the TQM journey. In fact, removing them before management understands what to do in their place is a blunder. However, as employees learn more about Deming's teachings, there gradually builds a tidal wave of interest in seeing these changes made. By the time organizations are into the third stage of TQM, the process improvement stage, employees will see the failure to make these changes as the CEO not "walking the talk." Employees will have been taught that you can't select what you want from Deming's teachings and reject the rest. They will have been taught that Deming's teachings form an integrated management philosophy and, if any piece is left out, the entire structure will collapse. It is important, therefore, that CEOs begin early to build knowledge about how to get rid of performance appraisals and merit pay.

There is more good news. There is an easy-to-understand literature on performance appraisals and merit pay, and it provides sensible, straightforward ways to abolish both. Before CEOs throw up their hands about making these changes, it is wise to read this literature.

## *How to Eliminate Performance Appraisals*

Deming has much to say about the evils of performance appraisals and what to do instead.[5] Others also offer valuable information on this subject. They show what's wrong with performance appraisals and offer reasonable alternatives. Their writings on this subject are identified in the suggested reading section in this book.

Ripping out a performance appraisal system should be an open endeavor, not conducted behind closed doors. There are countless illustrations of the closed-door method producing results that are touted to be in harmony with Deming's teachings, when, in fact, anyone trained in Deming's teachings will see them as the same rotting fish wrapped in a different newspaper. When Deming says abolish performance appraisals, he doesn't mean to recast them as peer evaluation, 360 degree evaluation, or internal and external customer evaluation. He says it plainly, abolish them.

Among the alternative ways to make the abolition of performance appraisals an open process is to organize a multidisciplinary team. The membership should be representative of an organization's work force, including management and the personnel (human resources) department. This team's aim is to abolish performance appraisals by finding alternative ways to produce their necessary results (outcomes) that are in harmony with Deming's teachings.

For a period of time, this team should build knowledge about performance appraisals. This includes reading the early books on the subject, such as *Management by Objectives*,[6] reviewing the history of the practice in the organization, understanding Deming's viewpoint on the subject, and reviewing alternative methods of abolition as described in the materials cited here. A next step can be to use the enhanced nominal group technique (ENGT) and consensus to identify the outcomes of performance appraisals as they have been practiced by the organization. (See Appendix C on the use of consensus.) For instance, the team's facilitator could pose the question, "What do we get from our use of performance appraisals here at XYZ Organization?" The results will include such outcomes as a basis for employee feedback; identifying training needs; determining salary increases, bonuses, and promotions; and establishing a documentation trail of counseling for use if an employee sues after being terminated.

When the team is satisfied that its list of outcomes is exhaustive and mutually exclusive, it begins the second part of its work. Here the team takes each outcome, in turn, and finds a way to achieve that outcome that is in harmony with Deming's teachings. Some outcomes will be found to be contrary to Deming's teachings, and, therefore, will be dropped. Examples include salary increases, bonuses, and promotions based on ranking employees. Other outcomes will be dropped because, in the light of Deming's teachings, they are no longer needed. For instance, using performance appraisals to ensure that employees get annual feedback will not be needed after managers assume their new roles in a supportive, collegial relationship with subordinates. Then two-way communication will be taking place every day. A further result of this new closeness between managers and subordinates is that there will be no need for annual appraisal to learn of training needs. Managers will already know of these needs. In fact, managers who need performance appraisals to learn of the training needs of their subordinates haven't been taught their jobs.

### How to Eliminate Merit Pay

Deming has much to say about merit pay and about the larger issue of extrinsic versus intrinsic motivation. Additional information on these subjects is available in books by Rafael Aguayo and Henry R. Neave.[7]

When Deming says that pay is not a motivator, people are surprised, are often amused, and almost always doubt the truth of his assertion.[8] They overlook that he adds to his assertion that people must have enough money to live a decent, respectable life, and, beyond that, pay is not a motivator. Sure, pay is a motivator for the person who is desperate for a job and needs an advance to buy groceries so his or her family can eat that evening. And pay is a motivator to the millions of U.S. workers that are routinely exploited with minimum wages, inadequate or no retirement benefits, and inadequate or no health care coverage.

With the recent publication of Kohn's work, knowledge on the subject of merit pay expanded dramatically. His work is an exhaustive review of the psychological and management research on merit pay, or incentive plans. His review shows that while incentive plans are prevalent throughout the United States, they not only don't produce any lasting improvement in performance, they can undermine any intrinsic motivation employees may have. He explains why incentives fail and offers an alternative.[9]

# The Misuse of Figures

CEOs have been taught much that is incorrect and that restricts their ability to manage effectively. But the emphasis they have been taught to put on figures, or data, to bring a sense of objectivity to their decisions is not misplaced. While figures can be misused, as will be explained, they can make a valuable contribution to the movement of an organization toward TQM. Using figures is far better than using pure judgment for decision making.

Long ago, CEOs got into the figures game in reaction to the expectations of owners for a reasonable return on their investments. This reasonable return was expressed as a figure, say 6 percent, and that kept CEOs thinking about figures. They, in turn, use figures to determine whether their organizations achieve the appropriate mix of revenue and expenses to meet owner expectations for a certain percentage return on investment. Virtually everyone trained in the traditional style of management, whether he or she is from a background in accounting, finance, managerial economics, engineering, human resources, or operations research, has a strong orientation toward figures. Some can do serious computations quickly in their heads. Some know the multiplication tables through 15.

## Pressures to Use Figures

Across time, certain forces have strengthened the emphasis CEOs place on figures. One such force makes providing certain figures a requirement. It is the burden of governmental regulatory and taxing bodies. Organizations must provide certain figures, such as tax information, or suffer penalties, and uncooperative CEOs can be jailed.

Another force exerting pressure for the use of figures is the practice in most industries of CEOs moving from job to job to get ahead. The CEO positions in many organizations are nothing more than revolving doors. As a consequence, many CEOs find themselves in new positions where they don't have the time or see the need to learn the details of the work they're expected to manage. In such cases, they rely on figures to set numerical goals and quotas for their subordinates.

There's a popular management myth that anyone who understands figures can use them to manage anything. According to this myth, CEOs don't need to know the details of the work they manage, provided they understand how to use figures. How many examples can you recall of CEOs moving from one job to another entirely different one? Such movement into almost unrelated fields is possible, it is thought, because of this myth. Such a CEO can start off running a corporation, then run a bar and grill for a while, then move on to manage a CPA firm, spend some time managing a professional baseball team, then take a job as a colonel running a munitions depot for the Army, and go into retirement teaching management in a school of business. According to this myth, a manager who understands figures can manage anything.

It may be obvious from the string of examples in the last paragraph that it's absurd to believe that knowing figures makes a CEO. In fact, knowledge of the details of the work is mandatory for anyone who expects to manage any enterprise. Developing such knowledge takes years. Deming refers to the mobility of management as a deadly disease that afflicts most U.S. organizations.[10]

## *Dangers in the Overreliance on Figures*

Figures are an important management tool. But relying on figures instead of genuine knowledge of what's going on in an organization is foolhardy and can bring about unintended, pernicious results. Let's see how this can happen.

Many CEOs are on the alert for better ways to measure. New ways to measure is a favorite topic of conversation, and many organizations publish booklets on measures, such as *The Metrics Handbook*, or *Measurement at XYZ Organization*. In any case, as CEOs accumulate better and better measures, the practice of managing with figures can become a cycle of increasing loss of control through increasingly incorrect information. This cycle begins when a CEO introduces a new measure which many employees see as another effort by management to hold their feet to the fire for lower costs or more output. Indeed, employees are correct in this perception because most traditional CEOs see employees as a resource, like timber, oil and gas, and coal, to be worked for all it's worth. The ultimate aim of measurement for many CEOs is to get more out of their employees.

When employees see a new measure as another in a long series of management tricks to get lower costs or higher productivity, it will almost certainly be met by employee efforts to fudge the figures, in subtle or blatant ways. There are many illustrations of this. Perhaps the best known are in the area of performance appraisals where there usually develops what has come to be called the *halo effect* (everyone gets high scores). In any case, CEOs eventually realize the current measure is losing its value to fudging, and they start looking for a better measure. When another measure is found and applied, the worried employees again think about how to fudge it. And, so, the cycle continues.

Another unintended, pernicious result of relying on figures in the wrong way is that the more conscientious employees won't fudge the figures but often will do something worse. They will work so feverishly to meet the figures, say as numerical goals and quotas, that they actually harm the organization. For instance, they may rush so much to meet a production quota that they produce errors and waste. Or, they may oversell customers products they don't need, endangering long-term relations with them; for instance, selling a customer the highest-priced product to get the higher commission, when a moderately priced one would meet the customer's need. Or, college professors may give too many high grades in an effort to get their students to give them good marks on student evaluations of their performance. Too many high grades can give a university a reputation as a degree mill.

## The Misuse of Employees

In traditional organizations, employees play distinctive roles. Like their supervisors and managers, they are caught up in a wedding cake organization structure which requires them to focus on pleasing their bosses. The vertical authority and communications patterns portrayed on organization charts show who manages whom and underscore the importance of managers and the unimportance of workers. In traditional organizations, managers are expected to hold their subordinates strictly accountable for results and conduct annual performance evaluations to determine how well they are doing. The idea here is simply "Do what your boss says." Or, in harsher terms, "Do what you're told, and keep your mouth shut. Your boss knows best."

Employees are seldom aware of the horizontal processes of which they are members and in which they have customers and suppliers. They are often discouraged from coordinating their activities with people in different functional areas in these horizontal processes, and, if they do so, they must observe Fayol's gangplank amendment to the scalar chain: Clear it first with the boss, and back-brief the boss afterwards on what happened.

Other forces affecting employees in traditional organizations make it difficult for them to appreciate the need to cooperate with customers and suppliers in horizontal processes. It is made clear to them, usually through the stovepipes shown on the wedding cake organization chart, that each employee belongs to a certain functional area, usually a department, where they are told there are other people like themselves. "We're all in sales." "We're all engineers." "We're all nurses." "We're all auditors." This functional way of grouping activities suggests that people who work in each department are somehow similar to each other and different from people in other departments. And this is true, at least to the extent that their occupations are different, and they may have somewhat different cultures and norms. But, these few differences should not prevent them from cooperating in the best interests of the overall organization.

Employees also see their department managers competing with the managers of other departments, and this suggests that competing against other departments is the thing to do. Of course, CEOs of traditional organizations reduce the natural tendency of people to cooperate by instituting policies and practices deliberately designed to create competition among them. Personnel are forced to compete through performance ratings for promotions and salary increases, and departments are forced to compete on the basis of common measures, such as sales or units shipped, for awards such as shipping department of the year. Remember, traditional CEOs believe the myth that competition brings out the best in people. Unfortunately, they have not been taught that the most important job of any manager is to optimize the system and that competition makes that impossible.

Even though virtually every employee wants to take pride in doing good work and can offer valuable ideas for improvements, he or she is prevented from doing so by work environments filled with barriers and obstacles. The saddest dimension of most employees' organizational life is that they are virtually helpless to do anything to remove these barriers and obstacles, but management continually blames them for poor performance and exhorts them to try for better results. How would you feel if you were trying your very hardest and doing everything within your power, but you got blamed for poor results and problems, both beyond your control?

## The Misuse of Customers

The customers of the worst traditional organizations stand in long lines to pay high prices for products that don't work well or for inadequate, untimely service provided by surly persons who care little for customer feelings. Many customers say if they hear the statement "We appreciate your patience" one more time from a company's so-called service representative, they will kick the responsible manager in the britches! They know the statement "We appreciate your patience" really means "Our boss doesn't know how to manage our resources on your behalf. If he or she did, you wouldn't have to wait. So put up with us until we can find the time to take your money."

Typical of the harsh, unfeeling attitude of some CEOs of traditional organizations toward customers was the practice in American industry of planned obsolescence. This practice reached its height in the 1960s. The thinking behind planned obsolescence goes like this.

*If we produce the very best product we can engineer, it will last a long time. Eventually, everyone will have one, and the market will be saturated. What will we do then? We'll be out of business.*

*Instead, suppose we engineer our product so it will wear out about the time either the warranty runs out or the customer has made the last payment. In that way, we can contribute to a replacement market and stay in business. And, if customers decide against buying new products, just think of the boost it will give our replacement parts manufacturing division and our repair centers.*

A current variation of this practice focuses on warranties. The reasoning behind this abuse goes like this.

*Let's give a 10-year warranty at the time of purchase. Not only will it be a good selling tool, but look what happens if the product fails during the warranty period. Customers will come back to us demanding that we live up to our warranty. Our warranty policy will require us to prorate the remaining years on the warranty and give that much credit toward the purchase of a new product. This will make our customers happy because we lived up to our warranty and, in the bargain, we tie them for life to our product.*

Being a customer in the United States can be so bad that many customers express pleasure at seeing a local business bought out by a foreign company. They think service can only improve. Unfortunately, they are often disappointed because the service from the foreign company is even worse. This is because the CEO of the foreign company was trained, most likely, in the traditional style of management in a school of business in the United States or by U.S. business professors teaching abroad. In any case, the abuse of customers, especially with inferior products, is one reason many U.S. markets have been captured by foreign companies. When American customers have a choice, many take their business elsewhere. When there is no choice, many American customers wish the Japanese would develop products of that type so they could have a choice.

There are many causes for the abuse of customers by organizations in the traditional stage of development. The most important cause is failure to appreciate that every organization is part of a larger system of suppliers, competitors, customers, governing bodies, and others that must be optimized for the benefit of all. In other words, being competitive and self-seeking does not do as much for an organization as being cooperative and working to optimize the overall system.

Instead of exploiting your customers and trying to choke your competitors, think of what you can do to work with your competitors to help customers live better.

*Rather than beating your competition to get a larger share of the existing pie, think how you and your competitor can work together to enlarge the pie so everyone, including the customer, can live better.*

This concept is foreign to CEOs who practice the traditional style of management, but they must learn it if their organizations are to survive to make the transition from customer awareness to process improvement into the innovation stage of TQM. For further discussion of the failure of adversarial competition, cooperation, and a new role for the Antitrust Division of the U.S. Department of Justice, see chapter 3 of Deming's *The New Economics for Industry, Government, and Education.*[11]

## The Misuse of Suppliers

Suppliers whose customers are traditional organizations experience great difficulties. They are seen by their customers as adversaries. CEOs of traditional organizations mistakenly believe it is in their best interests to make their suppliers compete against one another to get the lowest price. Remember, CEOs of traditional organizations believe competition brings out the best in everyone. In this case, they believe it will bring out suppliers with the lowest prices.

Going for the lowest price has harmful effects on everyone concerned because it suboptimizes the system. It can drive suppliers out of business. And few customers can afford to buy the cheapest product. Buying the cheapest product raises costs. This is because of the additional expense of putting the cheaper product into service. Cheap products require more incoming inspection, rework, and time and effort to get suppliers to honor warranties, to name a few additional costs.

The better practice is to purchase the product that represents the lowest overall cost. This usually is not the product with the lowest price tag. Achieving the lowest overall cost requires moving from multiple suppliers to a single supplier for each item to be purchased and establishing cooperative relationships with suppliers. It involves working with sole-source suppliers to continually improve the quality of their input. These thoughts don't make sense to CEOs trained in the traditional style of management.

## Moving Forward

The traditional style of management evolved over centuries, adding something here and something there, so that today it is a hodgepodge of concepts from bygone eras. There is strong evidence that this style of management is not suited to any economic environment, yesterday's or today's. Yet, many innocent people were trained in this style of management in schools of business, professional military education, and the school of hard knocks, by well-intentioned people who didn't know any better.

Persuading practitioners of the traditional style of management that it is the source of most of our organizational and economic woes is extraordinarily difficult. In fact, some say it's impossible. From the standpoint of the long-term health of our economy, two recommendations can be made to deal with this problem. First, we could be patient and let the traditional managers now in the economy simply retire. Give them early outs, if possible. This is not to say that many CEOs and managers who were trained in the traditional style of management can't be taught to see the light. They are the exception, but they do exist, and they deserve the opportunity of education in Deming's way. The second recommendation is to change the educational system so the managers of the future will be properly trained for their work. Fortunately, more and more secondary schools and schools of business around the country, as well as professional military education, are making these necessary changes. Unfortunately, at present, the educational institutions that have made these changes are the exceptions.

We have reviewed the nature of the traditional style of management, the thoughts of those who practice it, and its harmful consequences for those who come in contact with it. We now consider the second stage of TQM, customer awareness.

## Notes

1. Alfie Kohn, *No Contest, the Case Against Competition* (Boston: Houghton Mifflin, 1986).

2. Frederick W. Taylor, *Shop Management* (New York: Harper and Row, 1903); and ———, *The Principles of Scientific Management* (New York: Harper and Row, 1911).

3. W. Edwards Deming, *Out of the Crisis* (Cambridge, Mass.: MIT Press, 1986), p. 101.

4. Ibid., p. 102.

5. Ibid., pp. 101–120.

6. George S. Odiorne, *Management by Objectives: A System of Managerial Leadership* (New York: Pitman Publishing, 1965).

7. Deming, *Out of the Crisis*, p. 102; ———, *The New Economics for Industry, Government, and Education* (Cambridge, Mass.: MIT Press, 1993), pp. 110–118; Rafael Aguayo, *Dr. Deming: The American Who Taught the Japanese About Quality* (New York: A Lyle Stuart Book, 1990), pp. 101–104; and Henry R. Neave, *The Deming Dimension* (Knoxville, Tenn.: SPC Press, 1990).

8. Alfie Kohn, "Why Incentive Plans Cannot Work," *Harvard Business Review* (September–October, 1993): p. 58.

9. Ibid.; ———, *Punished by Rewards: The Trouble with Gold Stars, Incentive Plans, A's, Praise, and Other Bribes* (Boston: Houghton Mifflin, 1993). Particularly, see chapters 7 and 10.

10. Deming, *Out of the Crisis*, pp. 120–121.

11. Deming, *The New Economics*.

# Chapter 4

# The Customer Awareness Stage

Many traditional organizations enjoy protection from serious competition. They have location or price monopolies, or maybe serious competition just hasn't come up against them yet. Long ago, some of these organizations bought what turned out to be the best locations in town. They have monopolies because their customers are willing to put up with abuses—such as not enough clerks to help them find what they want, inferior merchandise, high prices, and long checkout lines—to avoid driving an extra two or three miles to the nearest competitor. And some have monopolies because they charge lower prices. There are many reasons why they can charge lower prices. Some buy in volume, some are more efficient, and many don't pay their employees living wages. Many customers are poor and must put up with anything to get lower prices. But, the history of business clearly shows that monopolies evaporate. The world changes every day. And, every day, another smug CEO who was protected from competition is surprised.

An event can occur for even the most secure traditional organizations that moves them to the threshold of the second stage of TQM—customer awareness. This event can be an announcement in the newspaper by a new competitor.

> *XYZ Corporation announced today at a meeting of the Chamber of Commerce that it has purchased a tract of land in the 6800 block of Northeast Eighth Street, and preliminary construction plans suggest that operations will begin in the spring. They hope their operations will be a model of efficiency, low prices, and customer service.*

True to its word, this vigorous, innovative newcomer begins to pull significant market share away from local traditional organizations.

Unfortunately, many CEOs don't see the need to change their traditional ways until after they're driven to financial ruin. For them, it's only when their accounting figures turn sharply downward that they realize something is wrong. Unfortunately, waiting this long can be too late. By then, sizeable market share has been lost, costs are overrunning revenue, and the business itself is in danger of failure. As explained in chapter 3, accounting records show what happened in the past. In today's world of rapid change, the past is often no guide to the future. By the time trouble is recorded in the accounting books, it's often too late to do anything about it. In today's competitive world, organizations run by CEOs who can't see beyond the figures provided by their accountants often go out of business.

## What CEOs Think as They Move Toward Customer Awareness

As CEOs begin to experience the stress of sharply downward trending accounting figures, they sit up nights worrying that their organizations are headed for the ditch. In many sleepless nights, their worrying goes something like this.

> *Sales are down. Many once-loyal customers don't trade with us anymore. They took their business elsewhere. How could this have happened?*

When customers take their trade elsewhere it hurts CEOs' feelings. Worse, it hurts their pocketbooks. But, given their habit of relying on figures, it's no wonder their worrying leads them to want to see even more figures, this time on customer satisfaction. They wisely reason that to take corrective action they need to find out why their customers aren't satisfied.

> *Which customers left us? Why did they leave? Where did they go? What can we do to get them back and keep others from leaving?*

## Let's Do a Survey

CEOs reason that because customers are the source of sales, they must be important, maybe more important than the CEOs gave them credit for. (Note that the customers they're thinking about are *external* customers. In the customer awareness stage, managers do not realize customers exist both outside and inside their organizations.) When CEOs ask questions about customer satisfaction, it's good news for marketing consultants because it brings more business their way. It is also good news for the in-house marketing staff because it increases marketing's visibility and power.

CEOs meet with their staffs for hours on end deliberating the best way to go about getting figures on customer satisfaction. A major issue they consider is what questions to ask. It is here that CEOs emerging out of the traditional stage of TQM can make a serious mistake. Despite the fact that they read that "quality is defined by the customer," it usually doesn't make much of an impression on them. Instead of getting input from customers to identify problem areas, say through focus groups or a small number of personal interviews, CEOs or their consultants write the questions for their customer satisfaction surveys based on their own notions of what customers want. Examples are such routine questions as "Were you waited on promptly?" "Were our salesclerks courteous?" "Would you recommend us to your friends and relatives?" "What do you like best about us?" Remember, traditional CEOs think all the brains are at the top. They think they know the problem areas around which to write the questions for their customer surveys. They are simply mistaken. If they really knew which areas had problems, why didn't they correct them? The fact is, CEOs often are blind to their real problems, and thinking they know them can only lead to delays in learning what they really are. Delays at this point bring organizations closer to financial ruin.

Because of the gravity of the customer satisfaction survey issue, CEOs often spend far too much time in staff meetings micromanaging the many decisions associated with it, such as what time period to use as a baseline; frequency of surveys; how large samples should be; how to draw samples from customer lists; whether to use telephone, door-to-door, or mail surveys; and whether to interview former customers. While these issues are important, the danger in devoting too much time to thinking about them is that while these deliberations are going on, occasionally up to a year, the sources of an organization's problems remain unchanged and continue to exert their poisonous influences. All this time, competition is eating away at the market.

Sound survey methodology is important, particularly to ensure that samples are *representative*. Methodological issues must be dealt with in a timely manner, but most of this work can be delegated to a competent marketing staff with demonstrated statistical expertise.

As a word of caution, marketing executives often have strong advertising, media, distribution, promotional, creative, or management backgrounds, but are weak in their knowledge of survey methodology. CEOs must take pains to ensure that the samples upon which they are to base their customer-related decisions are representative. The most common blunder here is to accept samples for which representativeness was not demonstrated. My advice is that CEOs should routinely require analyses that demonstrate the representativeness of all samples.

## Acting on Survey Results

Many traditional organizations have histories of insufficient concern for their customers. Therefore, the results from their first customer satisfaction surveys are often negative. Their first surveys show dissatisfaction in a wide variety of areas.

CEOs are usually stunned to see how bad things are. In fact, the news may be so bad they won't accept it. Many dispute the results on the grounds that the surveys weren't conducted properly, such as the sample wasn't representative, the wrong questions were asked, or the analysis of the data was incorrect. They simply cannot believe things are that bad. Sometimes they "shoot the messenger." For instance, precious time is wasted hiring a new marketing research firm to conduct a second survey in the hope that it will show more positive results. Sometimes they hire a new statistician to reanalyze the data, hoping for a favorable interpretation. These delays only allow the wolf to get closer to the door.

Other CEOs conclude from negative customer satisfaction survey results that they must act immediately and decisively to turn things around. "All these delays, abuses, and insults of our customers have got to stop!" they declare. This is the right conclusion to draw; but, at this point, many CEOs stumble by believing they can simply *persuade* customers to come back with heavy expenditures on advertising and promotion. This stumbling block is usually placed in the path to genuine improvement by an influential senior marketing executive who knows no other way of doing business than advertising and promotion. Silly as it sounds, CEOs are persuaded to spend serious money on expensive media campaigns and price discount gimmicks of all kinds, but they don't improve a single thing about the way they do business. They believe advertising and promotion will bring customers back to face the same old delays, abuses, and insults. This approach may do some good at first because the organization's level of awareness among customers is increased by the advertising, and some customers who buy on the basis of price tag alone are attracted by discounts. But in the long run, trying to increase customer satisfaction with advertising and promotions is a foolish waste of time and money. Worse, it delays getting to the heart of the customer satisfaction problem.

## Blaming Negative Survey Results on Employees

There is a second way CEOs can stumble in the face of negative customer satisfaction survey results. Recall from chapter 3 that traditional CEOs believe employees are to blame for all their problems. So, in the face of negative survey results, it's only natural for them to think their employees are to blame. They know all customer contact occurs at the employee level, with salespersons, secretaries, receptionists, service representatives, repair personnel, nurses, delivery personnel, financial counselors, and others. "It must be their fault!" CEOs conclude.

Believing employees are responsible for customer dissatisfaction leads traditional CEOs to want to do something to get employees to do a better job. "If our people would just do their jobs we wouldn't have these customer satisfaction problems!" they declare. This reasoning leads to the conclusion that a better job must be done in the *interfaces* between employees and customers. "We must improve our face-to-face relations with customers. That's where the rubber meets the road!"

To try to improve customer interfaces, what could traditional CEOs be expected to do but create another program. One such program is to come up with a flashy name for employee-customer interfaces, such as "moments of truth," borrowed from the lore of bullfighters. This is followed by an in-house public relations campaign with badges, ribbons, posters, banners, balloons, brass bands, hymn singing, socials, and celebrations exhorting employees to treat customers better.

However, mere exhortation is seldom enough of a program to satisfy most traditional CEOs. They insist on an even more vigorous and aggressive effort to get employees to do a better job with customers. In a great insight, they realize it's unrealistic to think customer service will improve simply by exhorting employees. "What we really need for our employees is a customer service training program!"

## Let's Build a Customer Service Program

After accepting the logic of the "train the employees" solution to their customer service problems, CEOs are comforted to see many books about customer service on the shelves of bookstores. They are also comforted to see the legions of consultants anxious to help build customer service programs. Many marketing research firms have seen this opportunity and begun offering consulting and training in customer service. They reason that they are in the best position to know a client's customers because they conduct surveys on customer satisfaction. It's only logical, therefore, that they should be the ones to train client employees in customer service. CEOs are further comforted to learn from their training departments that the mail is full of brochures from national associations offering conferences on how to improve customer service.

Each of these training sources promises to work with interface employees not to merely satisfy customers, but to *delight* them! They also promise to train employees to provide the kind of service that will not stop at merely bringing customers back for repeat business. Service will be so good, they claim, that customers will brag about the organization to their friends and bring in new customers!

The idea of delighting customers so much that they brag about the organization and bring new customers always sounds good to CEOs who are on the threshold of customer awareness. "There is no doubt," they declare, "that our customers deserve to be delighted." But, as they utter these words, they seldom reflect on why they allowed the abuses, delays, insults, and often outright cheating of customers to occur in the first place. They seldom reflect on their previous assumptions about the customer's importance.

In any case, promises of training employees to delight customers has sold many books and made many dollars for consulting firms and organizers of conferences. And, putting employees into warp drive on customer service has been the theme of many company programs and has dominated the thinking of many CEOs for months, even years.

## What Customer Service Programs Are All About

Most customer service programs aimed at delighting customers concentrate their efforts almost entirely on employees and uniformly promise to build quality into every customer service transaction. These programs promise to include everything needed to turn an organization's vision for unparalleled customer service into concrete action, including classroom training of employees to smile, listen, use positive language, do even more than is required, and use self-scoring assessment tools.

In this training, employees are exhorted to "Go the extra mile!" or to "Take charge of every moment of truth!" Colorful buttons and ribbons with slogans such as "I love my customers!", "I do whatever it takes!", "Ask me!", "The answer is yes!", "I take pride in my work!", and simply "Pride" are distributed to employees so they can display their commitment. Janitors are taught to nod, smile broadly, and say "Good morning!" when they pass customers, now called *guests* or *clients*, in the hallways. And, employees aren't called *janitors, waiters, supervisors, salesclerks, welders,* or *plumbers* anymore. In a bold move to get personnel to feel more a part of the organization, they are called *associates* or *partners!* Highly paid consultants flatter CEOs by telling them theirs is a "legendary" customer service program, or that they are "customerizing" their organizations to retain present customers and attract new ones.

Some CEOs are so enamored with their customer service programs that they offer their training to other local organizations, often under the sponsorship of business clubs or chambers of commerce. They misrepresent this training as a comprehensive TQM effort.

Despite the phony glitter of such false starts, the one positive result of taking this step into the customer awareness stage is that CEOs, managers, and employees begin to understand that there is someone else to please besides their bosses. Executives trained in schools of business begin to doubt the wisdom of the unity of command principle of management. Everyone begins to sense that satisfying external customers is not just a crisis, but a matter of survival. Everyone begins to understand that if customers aren't satisfied, the organization will go broke, and everyone will lose his or her job.

Despite an increased understanding of the importance of external customers, little else changes about the way traditional organizations do business. Many CEOs believe customer service programs are what TQM is all about. They are mistaken. Nonetheless, understanding the importance of external customers is the first important step in the TQM journey.

## The Misuse of Employees

Despite its benefits, there is an unfortunate, even sad aspect of entering the customer awareness stage of TQM. This is the impact it has on employees.

The vast majority of employees are well-intentioned and hardworking. All they ask is an opportunity to do good work and be proud of their employer. But, in the customer awareness stage they pay a high price in mistreatment at the hands of CEOs who mistakenly blame them for the organization's customer service problems. They are forced to endure hours of customer service training which carries with it the humiliating implication that they didn't try to please their customers before the training began. They're forced to wear badges displaying slogans that they see as an insulting suggestion that without the badges they wouldn't do their jobs. As one employee exclaimed, "We don't need no stinking badges!"

### *How to Beat Up Employees with Survey Results*

Many organizations in the customer awareness stage do little more to improve customer service than make things more difficult for their employees. Often with the help of consultants, or with what they learn at conferences, CEOs try to improve customer service by what they see as "working with" their employees. But, all too often what CEOs see as working with their employees turns out to be harsh treatment and is seen by employees as beatings. One way these beatings are administered is with customer satisfaction survey results.

Certainly, nothing is wrong with surveying customer attitudes; the information such surveys produce can be highly useful. In fact, there should be a continual flow of feedback from customers into any organization. The logic of customer-driven quality and quality function deployment (QFD) is sound. But it's one thing to collect customer satisfaction information and quite another to use it correctly. The fact is that customer feedback is commonly misused to beat up employees in the name of improved customer service.

In the first place, many organizations do not share with employees any positive results from customer surveys; but, when something negative comes up, watch out! The impulse of traditional CEOs is to find the guilty person and take corrective action. This corrective action can take many forms, including giving negative survey results to innocent employees who have no control over what caused them; giving negative survey results to innocent employees with an exhortation to do better, but without any training in what to do differently; punitive training; reprimands; probation; suspension; and dismissals. These so-called corrective actions are perceived by innocent employees as beatings. (I refer to employees here as innocent because most customer service problems are in processes, not in the people. Thus, employees are innocent. Unfortunately, this knowledge does not ordinarily come to CEOs until they are in the process improvement stage of TQM.)

In any case, using survey results to beat up employees is entirely wrong. Worst of all, it results in unnecessary employee suffering, and it leads directly to the increased absenteeism and turnover of valuable employees. The only employees who put up with such beatings are those who can't get a job elsewhere. In time, beating up employees leaves organizations only with such employees—not the kind of employees CEOs want working for them.

Fortunately for traditional organizations, many employees stay in their jobs despite the fact that they get beaten up for something they did not do. They love their jobs or customers so much they're willing to put up with such ravages from unenlightened management. They love their jobs or customers, but they do not love the management. This is a common attitude among those who have many years of service in traditional organizations.

There are two especially cruel ways management beats up people with survey results. The first, and most common, is to focus on results about problems employees cannot change. For instance, automobile mechanics at a certain garage were informed of customer complaints about their inadequate repair work on fuel injectors. But, they didn't have access to operating manuals for all types of cars they serviced and were forced to infer that what works on the cars for which they had manuals works on others. They weren't authorized to buy operating manuals, but they had to endure the periodic humiliation of getting customer complaints about their often second-class repair work.

Another example is the customer service representatives at a certain hardware distribution center who were given complaints about customers' inability to get in touch with them. The service representatives were forced to use a telephone system that was completely inadequate for the volume of complaint calls created for them by the company's sales department. (The sales staff was, incidentally, given an incentive of "lightning bonuses" and almost daily sold customers products they didn't need, later called to complain about, and eventually returned.) These service reps were not authorized to purchase new telephone equipment, but got humiliated periodically by feedback about customer complaints for their inaccessibility by phone.

A third example is the clerical personnel of a university business office who got feedback that the financial statements they mail to students were often incorrect and lacked "clarity of language and format." Information about adding and dropping courses was not provided in a timely manner by the university's registration process, and the language and format of the statements, as bad as it was, was designed personally by the university's CFO. The clerks in the business office were convinced that suggesting needed changes was a waste of time. They knew the administrators of the university, and especially the CFO, believed all the brains were at the top. These clerks endured the humiliation of student complaints about unclear and inaccurate statements over which they had no control.

A second cruel way to beat up employees with survey results involves what Deming calls *tampering*. This involves sharing individual customer complaints, comments, or so-called verbatims from customer surveys.[1] Before explaining why feeding back verbatims is tampering, consider what verbatims are. Customer surveys typically contain standard questions asked of representative samples of customer populations. These questions are almost always on what marketing researchers call *verbal rating scales*. Here's an example. "How satisfied are you with such-and-such dimension of our service? Would you say you are very satisfied, somewhat satisfied, a little dissatisfied, or very dissatisfied?"

The psychometric properties (validity and reliability) of survey questions should be assessed, and their means or proportions should be plotted for each wave of surveys (no more often than quarterly) on control charts to separate special from common sources of variation.

Care must be taken to provide survey results only to departments that (with their upstream suppliers) have influence over the customer attitudes being measured, a technique called *rational subgrouping*.[2] When a process so defined goes out of control, according to the well-known rules for making such interpretations, it is appropriate to provide these results as feedback.[3]

In some surveys, respondents who give negative responses are asked for the reason. Sometimes the response rate on these "probes" is low because some respondents hesitate to be specific in their criticism. They may not wish to get someone in trouble. In any case, these negative comments, or verbatims, can be fed back to customer interface departments and their personnel. No assessment is usually made of whether verbatims are representative of the attitudes of all customers who responded to the survey, or even of customers who gave negative responses on the verbal scale questions. However, interface personnel and others can be tormented every quarter with a new set of verbatims. In the first quarter, this was wrong. In the second quarter, something else was wrong. In the third quarter, something still different was wrong. Every time personnel get the verbatims, they attempt to make corrections. Every quarter, new verbatims; every quarter, personnel tamper with their processes.

A customer service representative at a chemical plant was given a copy of the written comments of one customer out of the 1498 she had dealt with over the last quarter. This customer complained that the service representative was abrupt and hurt her feelings. Verbatims are seldom put on control charts to know if they are one-of-a-kind outcomes. Handling customer complaints is a tough job, and getting only one negative in 1498 opportunities is grounds for celebration, not for humiliation. Hardworking, well-intentioned employees should not be beaten up with one-of-a-kind verbatims from customer satisfaction surveys.

Occasionally, CEOs justify the use of verbatims on the grounds that they give employees insight into what they're doing wrong. This is nothing more than a manifestation of the traditional manager's impulse to blame employees for what has gone wrong. CEOs would do far better to understand the horizontal nature of their organizations and monitor tasking memoranda from departments practicing the *"tyranny of the supplier"* process improvement strategy, as explained in chapter 9.

If an organization has control charts in place for the measures on its customer surveys, there are those who suggest that verbatims can make a valuable contribution. One of these contributions is when a measure goes out of control, verbatims can provide information on what may have gone wrong in the process. The other contribution is when a process is in control and information is needed to know how to improve the process to change the center line. In this case, verbatims should be collected over an extended time and portrayed on a Pareto chart to show the most important reasons for customer dissatisfaction. These most important reasons are the basis for initial efforts to improve the process. In neither of these cases, however, should employees be made to feel they are the problem. Nor should individual verbatims be fed back quarter after quarter. As will be explained later, problems are in processes.

Others argue that using verbatims gets the cart before the horse. They say processes should be thoroughly understood before applying control charts to their output. When that is done, employees will be subject matter experts (SMEs) on their processes, and they will have enough insight to know what happened to result in an out-of-control pattern. For these employees, verbatims are unnecessary. It is a serious error, some believe, to set up control charts before having knowledge of the process that produces the output to be controlled.

## How to Beat Up Employees with Performance Appraisals

Beyond using survey results, there is another way managers beat up employees for better customer service. It is to add a new component to their performance rating—how well they satisfy customers.

An especially harsh example of evaluating employees on customer service is a horror developed decades ago called the *mystery shopper*. This popular method works in the following way. Someone willing to play the role of Judas' goat is hired to pretend to be a customer and buy something from a targeted salesclerk or deal with a targeted secretary, receptionist, service representative, nurse, or supervisor. After the encounter, the mystery shopper completes a report card on how well the employee handled the situation. Afterwards, a manager holds a meeting with the employee to review what was done incorrectly and to direct remedial actions. The report card and the manager's review become part of the employee's permanent record. These report cards and reviews are considered in raises, promotions, and other awards. Think for a moment how employees subjected to this kind of mistreatment must feel. Can they be proud of their work knowing this can happen? Can they be proud of an employer who would do this to them?

### The Real Reason for Poor Customer Service

When employees don't treat customers well, it's almost always because something they need to do their jobs is missing, such as operating manuals, an adequate telephone system, or well-designed forms. But, instead of devoting resources to the removal of the real causes of customer service problems, traditional CEOs spend big bucks on surveys to learn what everybody but them knew already—that customers are dissatisfied. They blame interface personnel when the real problems are in the inadequate support provided to interface personnel. Then, more big bucks are spent on customer service training programs. Many resources are wasted on surveys and customer service training programs when the real problem is elsewhere. Experience has taught me the following rule.

> Up to 90 percent of the time, customer interface personnel do not get adequate support from their internal suppliers. (But, they get blamed anyway for customer service problems.)

In chapter 9, this problem will be called the *tyranny of the supplier.* Because these support disconnects are at departmental boundaries in cross-functional processes, CEOs trained in the traditional style of management are unaware of this major cause of poor customer service.

### The Danger in Believing Employees Are Responsible for Customer Service Problems

There's no denying employees play an important role in customer service, albeit a small role relative to the role of their internal suppliers. The record shows that customer service improves when employees who interface with customers are properly trained. As a result, customers will be more satisfied, and sales will go up. But, herein lies a dangerous trap in the TQM journey.

Consider an example. Let's assume for a certain customer interface department that my experience is correct: 10 percent of the customer service problem is in the employees and 90 percent is in internal support. The CEO doesn't know about this 10 percent/90 percent situation but believes employees are the cause of problems.

Therefore, the 10 percent employee contribution is worked by buying a customer service training program. It works, and customer service improves. Customer survey results also get better, and sales improve, too. As this CEO manages with figures, seeing this improvement in survey results and sales leads to the belief that everything is now okay. The CEO concludes that the customer service problem is now resolved. All that's needed is to upgrade training in customer service every six months or so. But notice how this is a trap. Improved figures on customer surveys and sales have lulled the CEO to sleep on the larger, more important dimensions of the customer service problem. Untrained employees is almost always only a small part of the customer service problem. By far, the deeper problems, up to 90 percent of them, are in inadequate support from internal suppliers.

Every day I am in the field consulting I see employees who are willing to do their jobs but can't for lack of support. How can a salesperson do the job if the showroom is too cold, if order books aren't available, or if oil is dripping from the product onto the showroom floor? How can a reservations clerk do the job if the computer is down? How can service advisers please their customers when they have to tell them to take a number and wait?

Employees are only a small part of a vast, interconnected complex of functionally related components that must work together if an organization is to successfully satisfy its customers. CEOs must understand that even when interface employees are fully trained, they cannot do their jobs well unless these other factors are in place.

An example of the helplessness of workers to delight their customers occurred recently in a post office in San Antonio. The postal clerks had obviously been trained to do their jobs. They seemed to like what they were doing. They smiled and chatted briefly with each customer. But the line of customers waiting for service included 20 people and stretched out the front door. Yet only two of the six customer service windows were staffed with clerks, and on the four unstaffed windows were small signs that read "Next Window, Please." But, worse, as we customers waited about 15 minutes for service, we could see a very large banner on a far wall that read, "Every Customer Counts, Every One!" Somewhere behind this situation was a well-intentioned superintendent who was trying to take care of postal customers and thought the best way to do it was to train and exhort postal clerks and to put up a sign bragging about the importance of the customer. But this superintendent didn't know his or her job. This superintendent didn't look beyond the clerks at other factors required for customer service. This superintendent didn't think to measure the flow of traffic through time and staff the windows accordingly. This superintendent thought merely training and exhorting the clerks would do the job. It did not. Think of the humiliation of these unfortunate clerks trying to take pride in their work. All day long they faced customer after customer, each one irritated by the long wait in full view of the empty service windows and the superintendent's sign, "Every Customer Counts, Every One." If customers count so much, why make them wait 15 minutes to buy a stamp?

## The Misuse of Suppliers

Traditional organizations see their external suppliers as adversaries who are to be competed against to get the lowest price. This unfortunate attitude almost never changes for organizations in the customer awareness stage. In fact, it is common for the plight of suppliers to get worse when their customer organizations enter this stage. This happens because organizations in the customer awareness stage often put pressure on their suppliers to treat them the way they treat their own customers. It's sort of "what's good for the goose is good for the gander" reasoning. If we can do it for our customers, why can't our suppliers do it for us? This means they want to fill out questionnaires evaluating supplier service so suppliers will have a basis for improvement. Sounds good. But instead of reacting to this by working to improve *all* parts of what it takes to satisfy their customers, suppliers can fall into the trap laid by most customer service books, consultants, and conference presenters. They work only one small part of the customer service problem, usually by putting the squeeze for better service on their interface employees through exhortation and training.

Suppliers do benefit by getting more orders when their customers transform from the traditional to the customer awareness stage. This is because the sales of their now more customer-oriented customers increase. And, some of the benefit of these increased sales gets passed on to them in the form of more orders.

## Moving Forward

Only after a battering from competitors do many traditional CEOs realize their survival and that of their organizations depends on satisfying customers. The most insightful of these CEOs realize there is more to satisfying customers than exhorting and training employees in customer service. They understand there are other pieces to the customer satisfaction puzzle, and these other pieces must be identified and put in place if their organizations are to survive and prosper. When they understand this, CEOs are ready to move their organizations into the third stage of TQM, process improvement. Process improvement is the subject of the next six chapters.

## Notes

1. W. Edwards Deming, *The New Economics for Industry, Government, and Education* (Cambridge, Mass.: MIT Press, 1993), p. 199.

2. Donald J. Wheeler and David S. Chambers, *Understanding Statistical Process Control* (Knoxville, Tenn.: Statistical Process Controls, 1988), pp. 111–120.

3. Michael Brassard, ed., *The Memory Jogger: A Pocket Guide of Tools for Continuous Improvement* (Methuen, Mass.: GOAL/QPC, 1988), pp. 55–56.

# Chapter 5

# The Process Improvement Stage: CEO Thinking and Barriers

For most organizations, traveling from customer awareness to process improvement is the most important part of the TQM journey. It is important because many competitors—especially in the Far East and Europe, but many in the United States also—are beyond the customer awareness stage of TQM. These vigorous, innovative companies are entering new markets all over the world, many of which were once safely monopolized by organizations operating under the yoke of the traditional style of management. Thus, there is no time to waste in building on the knowledge gained in the customer awareness stage and getting into process improvement.

Moving into process improvement is difficult because almost all of it goes directly against the traditional style of management. Explaining process improvement requires six chapters. The current chapter explains how CEOs arrive at the decision to move their organizations into process improvement. This chapter also identifies the main barriers CEOs encounter as they bring this change about. Chapter 6 explains how CEOs get process improvement underway by establishing a quality council and improvement teams. Chapters 7, 8, and 9 explain what it takes to make improvement teams successful: how teams impact organizational culture, how to train for process improvement, and how to use process improvement strategies. Chapter 10 deals with the little-known but vital subject of team tasking. Tasking is at the heart of successful process improvement activities.

## How CEOs Decide to Improve Processes

In the customer awareness stage of TQM, many CEOs come to realize there is far more to satisfying customers than establishing a customer complaint department and exhorting and training employees. They realize it's foolish to hold employees responsible for the organization's problems. They accept the voluminous research that shows that few employees are 100 percent responsible for their own output. Of course, employees have much to do with their own output, but the part under their control is small compared to the part in the *processes* around them. And only management can improve these processes. When CEOs understand this, it's a sure sign that transformation into the process improvement stage of TQM is beginning.

A small number of employees do their jobs despite the inadequate support in their environment. They are adept at getting the job done despite the barriers in their way. We've all heard stories of wartime situations where rare people, called scroungers, were skilled at going around the notoriously inadequate military supply system to get the equipment and supplies their units needed to fight effectively.

To ensure that it's clear that employee performance is governed largely by work environment, take the time to consider some examples. Could Babe Ruth hit a home run with a cracked bat? Could Michael Chang or Aaron Krickstein rip a cross-court backhand winner with a cracked racket? Can anyone play well at bridge or 42 without a full deck, if the room is too cold, if the lights are flickering, or if the coffee is stale? Similarly, can a nurse provide good patient care if housekeeping hasn't cleaned the patient's room, if pharmacy hasn't provided the right medication, or if the ward clerk doesn't maintain order and provide support on the unit? Can a worker on the loading dock do his or her job if the forklift is inoperative 25 percent of the time? Can an inspector correctly check things if his or her instructions are unclear? Can an accountant complete an audit if the computer system doesn't provide access to needed screens? And what is the effect on all the players and employees in these examples of not having good support? They can't do the job and may become frustrated trying. It's that simple.

## Appreciation for Horizontal Relationships

When CEOs realize people can't do their jobs without support, they begin to think about where the support for their employees comes from. This leads them to an important realization: The departments in their organizations are far more interdependent than they ever imagined. They realize their departments are not merely separate stovepipes in a hierarchical structure, as suggested in traditional management theory, where the most important work takes place vertically in the hierarchy. They realize the whole is not equal to the sum of the parts. They realize there are important interactions between departments. They realize much of the important work to produce what customers want takes place horizontally, across departmental boundaries.

How do CEOs get their minds off their preoccupation with the vertical nature of organizational work to appreciate the horizontal nature of work relationships across departments? It happens in a series of steps. The first step occurs in the customer awareness stage when CEOs accept the importance of external customers. The importance of the customer may seem obvious, but this awareness is a giant step in the right direction for many CEOs. The second step is when CEOs realize there is more to customer service than exhorting and training employees. They realize that pleasing customers requires not only well-trained, conscientious employees, but good products, sound policies, clear instructions, and a myriad of other components. They realize all of these components are interrelated in processes. And what exactly is a process? Simple: All work is a process.

CEOs realize processes produce the products and services customers receive. They realize these processes are not limited only to the departments that come into direct contact with customers. Processes cross over a number of different departments ending in the one that has direct contact with customers. In other words, they realize that one department does something, such as receives and inspects incoming materials from external suppliers, and hands the materials off to the next department. The next department does something else, such as assembles the material to make something, and hands the assembled product off to yet another department. And the process continues. Some CEOs prefer to think of this as a chain of small departmental processes laying end-to-end across many departments that, collectively, make up one big process. Or maybe they call the large process a system. Others think of the way departments work together simply as one horizontal process. In any case, the processes eventually produce the organization's product or service which goes out the door to the customer.

To some CEOs, the concept of horizontal relationships among departments comes easy. To others, it is difficult to grasp. To further clarify this concept, consider an illustration of a manufacturer of red wagons. The purchasing department in this firm buys wheels, strips of wood, paint, bolts and nuts, and other materials from vendors. The loading dock receives these materials, uncrates them, and passes them over to the inspection department where 100 percent are checked. These materials are then transported to two assembly departments where the various materials are glued and bolted together to create wagons. These two assembly departments then pass the wagons off to another department where they are painted. From there, the wagons are checked over and put in inventory. When the sales staff and business office do their jobs, the names and addresses of customers are sent to the shipping department where, in one instance, a boxcar order of wagons is sent to a customer, a big hardware wholesaler in the Texas panhandle.

If the wagon manufacturer CEO thinks hard about what it takes to produce red wagons, he or she sees that only part of the work in the organization takes place vertically within the various departments. There's no denying that this vertical work is important. The vertical part is what each department does within itself, including unloading, inspecting, assembling, painting, selling, and bookkeeping. These activities are work, so they, too, are processes within departments. But this thoughtful manufacturer realizes other important work takes place horizontally as departments work together handing things off among themselves, like materials, unpainted wagons, customer names and addresses, share parts, cross-trained workers, and communications of all sorts. Furthermore, the manufacturer realizes these horizontal processes must be understood, planned, and controlled if customers are to get what they want. The CEO realizes these horizontal processes were not well designed or managed properly in the past.

The wagon manufacturer may realize that when key horizontal processes are not well managed, terrible things can happen. In fact, the CEO realizes that the mismanagement of these processes has probably been responsible for many of the crises and problems that have plagued the company for years.

The wagon manufacturer may think of these horizontal processes as flows. Any failure upstream in a flow will have negative consequences somewhere downstream. Upstream failures are like polluting a stream. The pollution may be overlooked where it enters the stream because it quickly disappears downstream or because the polluter doesn't know he or she is creating pollution. But, regardless, the pollution flows downstream where it invariably causes trouble. For instance, how can the assembly department (downstream) do its job if purchasing (upstream) bought parts that won't fit? How can the paint shed (downstream) concentrate on its job if the wheels keep falling off because faulty cotter pins were used by assembly (upstream)? How can the business office (downstream) mail bills to correct customer addresses if the sales staff (upstream) doesn't collect the right addresses? How can the sales staff meet customer expectations if the wagons are not good quality? Or if the company doesn't stand behind its service policy? Or if the company doesn't offer convenient financial arrangements? Even the secretarial staff (upstream) cannot provide good support to managers (downstream) unless the data processing department (further upstream) keeps word processors in working order.

The list of examples of horizontal relationships between upstream and downstream departments can go on endlessly, and horizontal relationships are not limited to manufacturing. They are in every organization you can name, including law firms, educational institutions, insurance agencies, military units of all kinds, taverns, pool halls, farms and ranches, hospitals, police and fire departments, fraternal orders, religious facilities, Italian restaurants, trucking firms, firearms retailers, governmental units at all levels, tennis ranches, and hotels.

## Appreciation for Internal Suppliers and Customers

As CEOs think more about the horizontal processes that flow from upstream to downstream across the departments in their organization, they come to another insight. Their departments are really internal suppliers and customers of one another. In other words, all the customers aren't outside the organization walking around in the street. And, all the suppliers aren't over in the warehouse district. CEOs realize many customers and suppliers are right there inside their organizations. For instance, the sales department is the internal customer of the production department. This is because the production department provides products for the sales staff to sell, just as the organization itself provides products for an outside customer, say a hardware wholesaler, to sell. The sales staff is an internal customer; the hardware wholesaler is an external customer. They are both dependent on their suppliers for good products. Continuing this example, the production department is itself an internal customer of the inspection department. If the people in inspection let shoddy material through, how can the production department do its job well? In a hospital, the nursing staff is an internal customer of the pharmacy. The pharmacy is an internal customer of the admitting department because the pharmacy needs to have correct information on the location of patient rooms to send medications to the right place.

## Realizing Processes Need Improvement

The more CEOs get to know about their horizontal processes, the more they realize these processes are in terrible condition and in desperate need of improvement. Often, this realization is simply a matter of putting two and two together. For instance, for years, there may have been rework in the assembly department, and the CEO used to look at it as a normal cost of doing business with excuses such as "Well, nobody's perfect. At least they get out 90 percent. I guess 10 percent rework is not so bad. Things could be worse. It could be 15 percent. And, anyway, the guy at the trade association told me 10 percent rework is about right for assembly departments in this industry."

With his or her thinking confined to the vertical viewpoint, that the organization is a collection of vertical stovepipes, this CEO doesn't know to look for the cause of the rework problem beyond the walls of the assembly department. Maybe the CEO calls the assembly department manager on the carpet periodically, and maybe the assembly manager spends time fighting fires when the rework rate gets too high. But neither the CEO nor this manager ever think about looking across into another department for the cause of the rework problem. Is the CEO to blame for his or her nearsightedness? No, not at all. This CEO, like most other CEOs, is merely following what's taught in traditional management theory. Remember Weber's hierarchical organization structure? Remember Fayol's principles of management, in particular unity of command and the scalar chain? According to these teachings, everything of real consequence in an organization happens vertically. The fact is, however, that this is simply not so.

As CEOs learn more about horizontal processes among internal customers and suppliers, they realize most of their problems are caused by something that went wrong upstream. When they accept this fact, they don't have to live with a 10 percent rework rate. They can fix whatever is wrong upstream and bring down the rework rate. In chapter 9, a powerful strategy for dealing with upstream problems will be explained as the tyranny of the supplier.

Remember how customer surveys usually show that external customers don't get what they want? Research also usually will show the same is true of internal customers. They don't get what they want either. And, this is true despite the fact that internal customers and their internal suppliers are in the same organization and work for the same CEO. Does this happen because internal suppliers are bad guys? Not at all. It's because they work in traditional organizations in which they have been taught to look upward to the boss rather than outward to their internal customers. In any case, many CEOs realize the abuses, delays, and insults of external and internal customers they have been blaming all along on their employees, as explained in chapter 4, are really the fault of flawed horizontal processes. This represents an enormous improvement in what most CEOs think.

# Doubts About the Value of Competition

As CEOs think more about the need to manage horizontal relationships, their common sense leads them to doubt the value of another aspect of the traditional style of management: competition. Most CEOs think about whether competition is good or bad. They wonder if it isn't really humankind's basic nature to compete. They wonder if competition in school is good or bad. They think if competition works well in sports it should also work well in organizations. Such questions are interesting to CEOs for a time, and the topic makes good after-dinner conversation.

For most CEOs, the competition–cooperation question comes down to one basic question. Does competition help an organization accomplish its aim? Specifically, can employees cooperate with one another, as they must do if horizontal process are to work well, when management is constantly encouraging them to compete? For instance, can production units compete for performance awards and, at the same time, help one another by sharing spare parts, knowledge of better ways to work, and cross-trained engineers? Can salespeople compete for bonuses and, at the same time, cooperate by sharing leads? Can college professors compete for salary increase, promotion, and awards and, at the same time, help one another in team teaching and as collaborators on research papers? There is no doubt some employees are big enough, emotionally speaking, to overlook the competition barrier that CEOs place in the pathway to cooperation. But these employees are exceptional.

Many CEOs realize that it doesn't make sense that departments and employees can compete and cooperate at the same time. But, they must cooperate if they are to produce the best products and services. Therefore, CEOs who have thought this question down to its core simply throw out competition. Many later observe that they thought getting rid of competition would be difficult, but in retrospect it turned out to be pretty simple. It's just a matter of thinking the competition–cooperation question through to its logical conclusion. To get at the essence of this question, CEOs need to ask themselves one question: "Does competition promote or detract from the accomplishment of the aims of my organization?"

What CEOs throw out about competition includes many time-honored policies and practices of the traditional style of management. For instance, they know employees and departments cannot cooperate when they are caught up in personnel policies and practices that encourage them to compete for salary increases, promotions, and performance awards. So these policies and practices go. Employees still get promoted and still get salary increases. But the methods used to identify employees to promote and to award more salary are deliberately and carefully designed to avoid creating competition. For instance, promotions and salary increases can be based on seniority or skill acquisition. There are many examples of the success of this approach.

CEOs know employees cannot cooperate when they are managed with numerical standards and quotas. So these practices go, too. And, they realize that the same reasoning about the need to cooperate applies to external suppliers and customers. They realize it's not smart to force suppliers to compete against each other to get the lowest price. It is better to think about total cost; that is, the overall cost to get a product into service. So, they move toward sole-sourcing to build cooperative relationships with one supplier for each product bought, and work cooperatively toward the lowest overall cost and best quality. In addition, because they are suppliers to their own customers, they strive to build long-term, cooperative relationships with them in which they strive to constantly improve their products and services.

## Obstacles in the CEO's Way

As CEOs move their organizations into the process improvement stage of TQM, they almost always run up against a variety of obstacles. These obstacles include such problems as how to organize and manage process improvement activities, how to reallocate resources to support employee process improvement teams, and how to find good training in process improvement team skills. Each of these obstacles can be overcome, and the way through these obstacles is explained in this book. Yet, the most serious obstacle to process improvement always seems to be the CEO's own personnel. Because this obstacle is the most important one, it deserves comment.

### Employee Resistance to Process Improvement

Employee attitudes toward moving into process improvement vary from mild reluctance to stubborn resistance. These attitudes are present in one form or another in virtually all personnel, be they salaried, hourly, managerial, or nonmangerial. These employee attitudes can be summarized as follows:

1. Employees are rigid and unwilling to change. They are set in their ways. They are reluctant to learn anything new.

2. Employees are uncooperative. They are out for themselves and reluctant to work with members of other departments for the overall betterment of the organization.

3. Employees are unwilling to think for themselves or to show initiative. They want to be told what to do.

4. Employees are impatient to see results from their efforts. When they are involved in any undertaking, they look for feedback to gauge how well they did.

CEOs see these attitudes reflected in the faces of their subordinates any time they try to change their organizations, beginning, for instance, with movement into customer awareness, but certainly with movement into process improvement. In the face of these attitudes, CEOs ask themselves "Why are my people like this? Why are they so unwilling to change? Why must they make my life so difficult? I'm trying to do something here that will keep this organization solvent and ensure their jobs. But, will they go along with me on this? No. I have to drag them along, kicking and screaming, every step of the way. Incredible!"

There is a simple answer to these questions. It lies in what I call the *third law of organizational development:* People are the way they are because the system made them that way. Said another way, employees are what the traditional style of management made them.

In their hearts, people are willing to be cooperative and are actually anxious to try out new things. Think about your own attitude when you took your first job. You wanted to please. You wanted to fit in. But, when you took a few chances you got your fingers burned. When you went out on a limb for someone or to try a new idea, someone cut the limb off behind you. After this happened a few times, you learned to be careful and guarded about what you said and did. The prevailing style of management was teaching you the organizational ropes. It was teaching you organizational survival skills. You learned to be careful of whom you trusted and in whom you confided. You became hesitant to try anything new; old ways are safe ways. Management really didn't want you to change from the old ways. Remember, we manage with Taylor's idea that there is a one best way to do things. In a manner of speaking, we tell employees to check their brains at the front gate and do things in this one best way. Is it any wonder people become rigid and set in their ways? The prevailing style of management taught them to be that way.

Consider the second attitude listed: Employees are uncooperative and they are out for themselves and unwilling to work with people in other departments for the betterment of the organization. What have we been teaching them all along? Do we teach them cooperation, or do we teach them competition? Ever since they were children, they've been taught to compete because we believe competition brings out their best. In sports, in school, and in our organizations, people are taught competition. Most employees learned this lesson well. Is it any wonder they're out for themselves? Is it any wonder they're reluctant to cooperate with people in other departments? On the contrary, they want to beat the other department to win the annual department of the year award established by management. Is it any wonder they try to make themselves look good and others look bad? They want to get the salary increases and promotions management makes available to winners. Is it any wonder they want to make their numerical quota even if it means suboptimizing the larger organization? They want to get the production or sales bonuses management makes available to winners.

Consider the third attitude: Employees are unwilling to think for themselves and show initiative, and they want to be told what to do. Remember how we've always told them in so many words to check their brains at the front gate? And remember how we have these so-called principles of management about authority and unity of command. "I'm your boss. I sign your paycheck. So, I'll tell you what to do." Now, after all these years of training in this way of doing things, we want them to change. We want them to think for themselves.

The fourth attitude really has two parts that are tightly woven together. The first is the intense need employees have to see results, to get feedback from their work as a measure of how well they're doing. Where did this need for feedback come from? As people grew up, they were involved in many activities in which there was feedback to tell them how well they were doing. In school, they got numerical grades on homework, examinations, and report cards. In sports, there was feedback, too. You won or lost. You got three hits in four times at bat. You bowled 215 or shot 97. As people grew up, many of them got used to relying on feedback to tell them how good or bad they were.

As time went by, they left school and joined the labor force. In their jobs, management continues what school and sports began. Management provides more opportunities for people to get feedback to measure how well they are doing. As employees, they are given production and sales targets, numerical quotas of all types, objectives, and performance reviews as a basis of feedback to tell them how they're doing. So, because of a lifetime of this kind of training, it's only natural for people to look for results to measure how well they're doing.

The second part of the fourth attitude is impatience. In some ways, impatience comes from people's hunger to see results of how well they're doing. They don't like to wait around for these results. Remember how impatient a classroom of students became when homework or an examination wasn't graded and returned promptly? The same is true in organizations. Employees want to see feedback on their work, and they want to see it quickly. If they have to work for a long time without some feedback on how they're doing, they become impatient and frustrated. They need to see successes for reinforcement to make them feel good.

It's important to recognize people's need for immediate feedback from their work. When we discuss employee teams in the next chapters, as a part of process improvement, special consideration must be given to satisfying employee needs to see results from their improvement efforts. If this need is not met, teams will not be as successful as they could be.

*How to Change Employee Attitudes.* The CEO will be faced with changing the attitudes of people who grew up in Western culture and Western organizations. It's important to understand that these are attitudes the employees have been taught, and that these attitudes are among the most serious obstacles any CEO faces in trying to move an organization into process improvement. Thus, to bring about substantial improvement in any organization, CEOs must change these attitudes.

Considered from a broader perspective, trying to change employee attitudes is the same thing as trying to change an organization's culture. This is because an organization's culture *is* its employees' attitudes. Culture is defined as the shared view of what is important and how things should be done. So, to bring about organizational improvement, the specific aim of CEOs must be to change two things: (1) what employees think is important and (2) how employees think things should be done.

Changing an organization's culture is not easy. Imagine, for instance, how difficult it would be to change what you think is important and how you think things should be done. Imagine how difficult it would be to make this change for all the people in an organization. Not an easy task. In fact, the record over many years shows that the vast majority of attempts to change the culture of organizations has failed. Ask yourself how much change you have seen in organizational life since you began your career. You'll probably conclude that today we manage our organizations pretty much as we managed them in the 1980s, 1970s, 1960s, or even 1950s. There have been some organizational changes because of laws and technology, but the traditional style of management has pretty much dominated organizational life for decades.

Correspondingly, the attitudes of employees in organizations have stayed pretty much the same, too, across these decades. They continue to think the same things are important and continue to think things should be done the same way. For instance, we still treat our suppliers as we did 50 years ago, basically with competition to get the lowest price. We continue to mistreat our employees, thinking competition for salary increases, promotions, and bonuses brings out their best. We still abuse and mistreat our external and internal customers. And, we still believe there is a one best way to do things.

## Moving Forward

Western organizations have failed time and time again to bring about serious, fundamental changes in their cultures. To some, this is a reason to be pessimistic about the future. But, knowledge is available now that was never available before to help us make this change. This knowledge is the road map away from the traditional style of management. This road map consists of the famous 14 points taught by Deming, the man responsible for the Japanese economic miracle. In the next chapter, we discuss how CEOs take action to implement the 14 points to transform the culture of their organizations.

# Chapter 6

# The Process Improvement Stage: How CEOs Take Action

Over the years, CEOs have made many gallant efforts to bring about improvements in their organizations. In fact, almost every employee can tell you about the veritable parade of these efforts that marched through his or her organization, few of which achieved anything really worthwhile. Except for gains from technological advancements, organizations of today are pretty much like those of yesteryear. Because such efforts failed so often, they picked up the name *programs*.

## A Running History of Programs

For most organizations, a new program is introduced about every two years. Examples of programs of the past include work simplification; job enlargement; job enrichment; orthodox job enrichment; zero-defects (ZD); participative management; zero-base budgeting; quality of work life (QWL); feedback; goal setting; goal setting and feedback; goal setting, feedback, and incentives; organizational behavior-modification (OB-mod); quality circles; shared governance; customer service; theory Z; empowerment; and reengineering. Each time, CEOs promote their new programs with enthusiasm and fanfare. (I was in an audience once when a new program was being introduced, and a drummer had been hired to do a drum roll as the CEO walked to the front of the room to speak on the program's behalf.) CEOs proclaim how the new program is different and how it will benefit the organization, such as by improving human relations, making jobs more enjoyable, reducing turnover and absenteeism, improving communications, increasing sales, improving scheduling, reducing employee or customer pilfering, or reducing costs. Everyone in the audience knows this is just another program, and, like its predecessors, it will last only a couple of years. Like its predecessors, when its results don't meet expectations, it will fade and eventually disappear.

As a consequence, most employees only appear to be enthusiastic about new programs. In their private thoughts, they know this is really another waste of time away from their usual jobs. Some employees react to programs in terms of what they call the *foxhole complex*. When a new program is introduced, they slide down into their foxholes and wait for the program to pass over, like a dark cloud full of thunder and rain. After a period of time, the program does pass over, and they come out of their foxholes and get back to work as usual.

# The Second Law of Organizational Development

Over the decades, few improvement efforts, or programs, have resulted in lasting gains in effectiveness. These failures occasionally occurred because the effort was conceptually or technically flawed, but usually there was another reason. That reason is that organizations seeking to make improvements don't change their culture away from the traditional style of management. In fact, any attempt to increase an organization's effectiveness must recognize what I call the *second law of organizational development* (OD).[1]

> *Any attempt to increase organizational effectiveness will eventually get washed out unless it has adequate cultural support.*

To illustrate this law, consider an example of an organization that tried to increase the effectiveness of its staff meetings. The method involved getting the agreement of all staff members before meetings on (1) the agenda to be covered, (2) the time to devote to each agenda item, and (3) whether agenda items are simply informational or require a decision. Participants rotate turns serving as facilitator and timekeeper, and members in these roles encourage participation and ensure that scheduled times for agenda items are adhered to.

The added structure provided by this approach to meetings has improved meeting results and maximized the use of personnel time for many organizations. But, experience shows that it does not work well in organizations that practice the traditional style of management. The spirit of competition in these organizations keeps many staff members from cooperating enough to make the method work, and fear prevents many members from speaking their minds on difficult subjects. But, the most common reason it fails in traditional organizations is that some CEOs feel uncomfortable conducting staff meetings in a way that is different from what they are used to.

In traditional staff meetings, the senior member sets the agenda, which is often unknown to others until they sit down at the table. Most of the meeting time is spent on two activities. The first involves the senior member going around the room questioning each member, in turn, finding out who did or failed to do what he or she was assigned at the last meeting. If someone didn't complete his or her task, the senior member frowns and wants to know why not. The second activity consists of the senior member talking, often endlessly, while everyone else tries to stay awake. Most members stay awake out of fear, not out of interest. Many senior managers believe this is the one best way to conduct staff meetings.

Consider an example of the second law of OD in action. In a certain organization, a new CEO was brought on board. Before the first staff meeting, the organization's method of holding meetings—the nontraditional, participative method outlined early in this chapter—was explained to her in the hope she would continue it. It had been highly successful for the organization in the past. To everyone's surprise, the new CEO slammed her palm down on her desk and exclaimed in a loud voice, "Don't you think I know how to conduct a staff meeting?" Sure enough, she knew how to conduct a staff meeting. She knew the traditional way. She was unwilling to continue the culture that would support this more effective method of conducting staff meetings. As a consequence, the new way of conducting meetings grew wings and flew out the window, never to return.

Because of the effects of the second law of OD, it is essential that CEOs who wish to increase their organization's effectiveness must first bring about supportive changes in its culture. As discussed in the first three chapters, the culture that must be changed, at least in Western organizations, is the one that results from the practice of the traditional style of management.

Many CEOs recognize the need to support their OD efforts with the right kind of culture, but few of them understand precisely what's wrong with their existing culture or how to change it. Until recently, guidance in how to successfully move away from the traditional style of management did not exist. Fortunately for everyone, this guidance is now available.

# Changing Organizational Culture with Deming's 14 Points

Judging from their writings, seminars, and videotapes, many TQM philosophers recognize the need to move away from the ruinous effects of the traditional style of management. But the emphasis they place on this important dimension of OD is meek, indeed, compared to the well-thought-out, comprehensive, and emphatic approach of Deming. In the preface of his book, *Out of the Crisis*, Deming says it plainly, "The aim of this book is transformation of the style of American management." In even more emphatic terms, he continues by saying, ". . . the style of American management is unfit for this economic age. . . ." Later in his book, he suggests that his ". . . 14 points are the basis for transformation of American industry."[2]

Not only does Deming emphasize the need to change the culture of American organizations, but he provides a road map, the 14 points, to follow in making the transformation. It is clear from his recent writings that the transformation also requires what he calls a *system of profound knowledge*.[3] Thus, education in Deming's teachings can be the guidance for changing an organization's culture. Let's examine how this education can be accomplished.

## A CEO's First Step

The first law of OD is that attempts to change an organization's culture will fail unless its CEO is directly involved. (This person is not always a CEO. He or she may be a principal owner, a director, or trustee. He or she may be an elected official or military commander. This person is the individual in ultimate authority. Because this person is often a CEO, I shall use that designation to mean the person in ultimate authority.)

The first law of OD states that the CEO must be directly and continually involved if any cultural change is to take place. After all, the CEO owns the culture of the organization. This culture cannot be changed unless the CEO desires it to change. As a consequence, the CEO's first step in changing an organization's culture is to decide whether this is really what he or she wants to do. Thus, with feet propped up on a coffee table and a cold soda pop in hand, the CEO must think about the effects of the traditional style of management on the organization. Simply said, the CEO must decide whether continuing to run the organization with the traditional style of management is right or wrong. A CEO's thoughts along this line might be as follows:

*Is our tall, hierarchical structure, supposedly with all the brains at the top, the right way to do things? Does competition really bring out the best in my employees, or do I want to change the system to promote cooperation? Do I want my employees to continue to wait to be told what to do? Do I want them to do things the way we original-ly designed them, or do I trust them enough to get them into the spir-it of continual improvement? And, most important of all, am I capable of making the required changes in myself?*

## The Impossibility of Faking the Transformation

It is impossible to fake transforming an organization to Deming's phi-losophy. It is easy for anyone to see when a CEO talks TQM but keeps the traditional style of management in place. There are literally dozens, if not hundreds, of ways to know if a CEO is serious about making this change. For instance, is the purchasing department required to make suppliers compete against one another for the low-est price? Are customers still abused, delayed, insulted, and cheated? Have personnel policies and practices been revised to bring them into line with Deming's teachings? Or, are employees still harassed with performance appraisals and pay-for-performance schemes? Is the CEO visible or hidden in some obscure part of the building and main-ly at the country club romancing the board? If such issues are not addressed, the transformation to Deming's way is not really taking place, and few employees will be fooled by a CEO's claims to the con-trary. Employees will chalk up TQM as "just another program." They will be right.

## Personal Change Is Required

CEOs who want to change the culture of their organizations must change their own attitudes and behavior. Why is this so? There are two reasons. First, it is the CEO's management style that is most in need of transformation. CEOs are the biggest supporters of the tradi-tional style of management. It is they who have required their organi-zations to practice it.

There is a second reason why CEOs must change their personal attitudes and behavior. Through the ages, philosophers have said human beings think and behave in pretty much the same way in all parts of their lives. According to this view, it is impossible to be one way in one part of your life, say at home, and another way in another part of your life, say at work. In other words, your culture (what you think is important and how you do things) is pretty much the same regardless of where you are. And, psychologists who have studied personal change say it must take place throughout all parts of your life. CEOs must understand that embarking on the TQM journey requires significant and broad changes in personal life as well as in professional life.

*How to Decide Whether to Make the Change.* CEOs should spend a lot of time thinking about whether to make this professional and personal commitment to Deming's way. Some suggest this decision is easier when it is discussed with another CEO who faced the same decision. For instance, a CEO of a 550-bed critical care hospital may feel better about this decision after talking to a CEO of a similar hospital who faced the same decision. In any case, when CEOs think this question through, more and more of them are deciding to make this journey of cultural transformation for themselves and their organizations.

To better understand what's involved in transforming to Deming's way, CEOs should learn as much as they can about Deming's teachings. Deming says the way to make the transformation to his style of management is to follow what he calls the road map. This road map is his famous 14 points. Knowing more about the 14 points will help with the decision. There are a number of books that explain the 14 points. My favorites are Deming's own books and *The Deming Guide to Quality and Competitive Position*, by my friend, Howard S. Gitlow, and his wife, Shelly J. Gitlow.[4] There are others included in the suggested reading list at the back of this book.

CEOs must carefully consider the 14 points, the deadly diseases, obstacles, and the system of profound knowledge which comprise Deming's teachings. Then CEOs can decide whether this is the path they want to take to transform their organizations away from the traditional style of management.

## A CEO's Second Step

Once they commit to Deming's way, CEOs wonder "What's the next step?" What should they do to bring about the transformation of their organizations from the traditional style of management? In the last of his 14 points, Deming indicates what should be done.

*Management in authority will struggle over every one of the . . . 13 points, the deadly diseases, the obstacles. They will agree on their meaning and on the direction to take. They will agree to carry out the new philosophy.*[5]

When I first read these sentences, I interpreted them to mean that the CEO and senior managers of an organization should discuss the 14 points, diseases, and obstacles and come to a consensus on whether to change the organization's culture with Deming's philosophy. As I gained more experience in how this actually happens for organizations, I began to interpret these words differently. Now, I think Deming means this: The person in authority has already made the decision that the organization is going to make the journey away from the traditional style of management. So, in this meeting, the issue is not whether to make the journey. That decision has already been made.

If that's the case, what is the aim of the meeting? The first aim is that the CEO and the senior managers must determine the exact meaning of the 14 points, diseases, and obstacles as they apply to their organization. Said plainly, they need to use Deming's 14 points, diseases, and obstacles, to understand what's wrong with their existing culture. The second aim is to agree on the direction to take to bring about the transformation. In other words, how exactly will they use Deming's teachings to get their organization away from the ruinous effects of the traditional style of management?

Let's think again about this meeting. Think about it from the perspective of the first law of OD, that the CEO must lead any organizational change, or it will fail. From this perspective, this meeting should be seen by the CEO as his or her first effort to transform the organization's culture. Remember, culture is defined as a shared view about what's important and how to do things. So, in this meeting the CEO must begin to change what senior managers think is important and how they think things are to be done. You can be sure that the existing culture will be based on the traditional style of management, and it must be changed in the specific ways suggested by Deming. After all, the culture of the senior managers is the most important part of any organization's culture, second only to the culture of the CEO. If the CEO and the senior managers have been working together for a period of time, their cultures are probably pretty much the same. Culture is, after all, a shared view. So, in this meeting, the senior managers are asked by the CEO to consider each of the 14 points as a way to change their attitudes and behavior from the traditional style of management.

The CEO must make it clear in this meeting that he or she has committed the organization to make the TQM journey, but there is an unwritten part of the agenda. Beginning in this meeting, and in other early phases of this undertaking, the CEO needs to get a sense of where each senior manager stands in his or her commitment to the journey. Is each willing to make this transformation both professionally and personally?

It is important for CEOs to realize that most people simply cannot think through complex issues like those contained in the 14 points in a single meeting, or even at a two-day off-site meeting. Of course, most politically wise senior managers will pledge their commitment to something they may privately think is "just another program" because they know it pleases the CEO, but their genuine commitment can come only with knowledge. Therefore, to further each senior manager's knowledge of the 14 points, diseases, obstacles, and profound knowledge, more education than a two-day off-site program is required.

Each of the 14 points contains information about (1) the old way of thinking or doing things and (2) the better way of thinking or doing things. Said another way, reading the 14 points tells you two things: first, what not to think or do in a certain situation and, second, what to think or do in that situation. Consider several examples of how this works.

Point 3 is "Cease dependence on inspection to achieve quality." In the traditional style of management, the old way, inspection is relied on to achieve quality. If an inspected product doesn't meet specifications, rework it or throw it out and make another one. This is like making 50 cookies by baking several batches and tossing out the burned ones every time until you have 50 good ones. Deming says this approach is wrong. To achieve quality, continually improve the process that produces the product you've been inspecting. Fix the oven, watch the cooking time more carefully, or do whatever it takes to improve the baking process.

Point 4 is "End the practice of awarding business on price tag." In the traditional style of management, business is awarded to the lowest bidder. It's in the regulations of traditional organizations; they must do it. They must buy the cheapest product. Using the cheapest product limits the quality of work and ends up costing more. The better way is to consider total cost, the cost of getting the purchased product into service. In any case, at the meeting referred to at the beginning of this section, the senior managers must go through each of the 14 points and learn how the ways they now do things are wrong and begin to map out how they are going to find the better way through Deming's teachings.

Deming's teachings are not a cookbook on how to implement TQM, but rather a set of dos and don'ts on how to get free of the traditional style of management. This is a little understood point. However, his teachings are meant to be taken quite literally. For instance, he says "the customer defines quality." He does not mean that the customer defines quality so long as the customer's needs can be handled with our present staffing and resources. He means the customer defines quality! Period. If you do not have the staff and resources to provide what the customer wants, get them. If you don't, someone else will, and you'll be out of business. And so it is with his other points. They should be taken literally. Consider his teaching that we "improve constantly and forever the system of production and service." This does not mean fix things so they're working right again, and then everyone quits improving. Improving constantly and forever means just that: improve constantly and forever.

## *Senior Manager Training by Teaching*

To acquire more knowledge of Deming's teachings, the CEO can ask each senior manager to prepare a presentation on one of the 14 points, diseases, or obstacles or on some aspect of the system of profound knowledge for presentation to others in the organization. The CEO should ask that the length of these presentations be at least 45 minutes. Why 45 minutes? Any manager worth his or her salt can skate through a short presentation, and he or she won't learn much by preparing for it. Most managers will slap together a few notes and for 15 or 20 minutes they will look very good in the presentation. But few can look good with this limited preparation for 45 minutes. If 45 minutes are called for, managers know the CEO wants a serious, substantive presentation. They'll put in the preparation time and benefit greatly from the experience.

This presentation should first be made at a senior staff meeting and later to groups of other employees. And the old saying applies, "Nothing helps people learn better than teaching something themselves." This works best when a series of seminars is established by the training department so everyone in the organization can hear the senior managers, including the CEO, explaining the 14 points, diseases, obstacles, and profound knowledge as these subjects relate to the organization. The result is not only a deeper understanding among senior managers of the road map to the new culture, but it helps create the required understanding throughout the organization. This is what Deming calls *creating a critical mass.*[6]

In addition to making presentations before the organization's personnel, senior managers also should be asked by the CEO to take turns doing a 15-minute review of a quality topic for weekly staff meetings. Topics to be covered should include the many issues in Deming's teachings, perhaps with an interpretation by a different writer on the subject, such as Gitlow and Gitlow, Aguayo, or Andrea Gabor.[7] Or, these presentations can be reviews of a related article from the American Society for Quality Control's magazine, *Quality Progress*. Care should be taken that all assignments are on materials that are consistent with Deming's teachings. There are theoretical and practical differences between Deming's teachings and those of many other quality philosophers and writers. Some of these differences are so great that they can run an organization into the ditch when added in with Deming's teachings by some well-intentioned manager. To underscore the importance the CEO places on TQM, these presentations should be the first agenda items at staff meetings.

It is important that senior managers not always present the same part of the Deming message, say the same point over and over. They must be asked to rotate through all of his teachings, making presentations on each part. It is inadequate for each senior manager to know one piece of the Deming message. All of them must know all of the message and know it well.

# The Changing Nature
# of Staff Meetings

As learning about Deming's way increases, an interesting change takes place in senior staff meetings. At first, the agenda items dealt with at these meetings won't seem to have much to do with Deming's teachings. But, the more managers learn about the 14 points, the diseases and obstacles, and profound knowledge, the more relevant the points will become to the items on their agendas. For instance, before the senior staff members begin their education in the 14 points, an agenda item on the organization's sick leave policy might be dealt with in a fairly routine manner. The discussion then might be confined to meeting legal requirements. But, as knowledge of the 14 points grows, management will call into question its own assumptions about the motives behind employee sick leave behavior, and the policy on sick leave will be revised. The policy will change substantially from what it was before the staff members became knowledgeable of Deming's teachings. They will realize, for instance, that their sick leave policy is not independent of employee behavior but actually causes (or forces) employees to use sick leave in certain ways. In fact, the personnel policies in organizations that practice the traditional style of management are almost always based on faulty assumptions about employee motivation, and they need to be revised.

The more senior managers learn about Deming's teachings, the more their deliberations take on a new meaning. They begin to see the implications for TQM in more and more of the agenda items they once dealt with routinely, probably on the basis of MBO consideration. They begin to realize that the extent to which they can make these decisions according to Deming's teaching will determine whether the transformation of their organization to TQM will succeed or fail. Eventually, issues related to managing for quality absorb so much of the team's time that the CEO may decide to change the management group's name from senior management or executive council to the *quality council.*

Quality councils are part of what is a transitional organizational structure. Quality councils are transitional in the sense that they represent a part of the organizational structure that is intended to help bring about culture change. The decisions made by quality councils help an organization make the transition from the traditional style of management to the philosophy of management proposed by Deming. The aim of quality councils, in other words, is to be one of two vehicles for bringing about a transition, or transformation, away from the traditional style of management. (The other vehicle is employee teams, which will be explained later in this chapter.)

## Quality Councils

I first learned of the concept of a high-level steering committee for quality transition more than 10 years ago while working with Dr. Steven L. Dockstader and Dr. Chandler Shumate, scientists at the Navy Personnel Research and Development Center in San Diego. It is my understanding that the steering committee component of TQM, or TQL (total quality leadership) as the Navy calls it, originated in the writings of Juran and was modified by the Navy for its use. My favorite of Juran's many books that include discussions of quality councils is *Juran on Leadership for Quality: An Executive Handbook.* In this book, there is a comprehensive explanation of how quality councils work.[8] My view of what quality councils must do in the TQM transformation parallels, in large part, what Juran says about this topic, including their membership, responsibilities, and how they select processes for improvement.[9] But, I see Juran's emphasis on the role of quality councils in changing organizational culture to be far less than what I have found necessary in my work with organizations. I also differ with Juran's teachings in a number of other ways, such as with his apparent endorsement of the use of performance appraisals.[10] Juran has made an inestimable contribution to knowledge about quality, and I recommend that his handbook be read, especially the pages about quality improvement councils.

A quality council is composed of the senior members of an organization. In fact, for an organization new to the TQM journey, this council can be seen as the senior staff who, for the first part of its regular weekly staff meeting, puts on its quality hat and discusses TQM issues, both for the purpose of self-education and for the applications of TQM to the issues on the agenda for that meeting. In other words, at the start of staff meetings the CEO may say, "Okay, let's start our meeting today with quality council issues." The staff members work for a period of time to complete the quality issues, and then they move on to other business.

As the months roll by, however, an important thing happens, as explained previously: They find themselves spending more meeting time on quality issues and less time on other business. This is because education in Deming's 14 points, obstacles, diseases, and profound knowledge makes them realize that what they used to think of as routine business is really quality business. Eventually, literally everything they do comes to be seen in TQM terms. When this happens, TQM is becoming a way of life for them. Eventually, TQM is not an extra item on the agenda, nor is it a portion of the agenda. It *is* the agenda! When this happens, the senior managers have made an important step toward their own cultural transformation. Quality is becoming a way of life for them.

## Quality Councils and Improvement Teams

Quality councils must play two major roles in the cultural transformation of organizations. The first is to take the lead in providing long-term education in the Deming management philosophy for themselves and all others in the organization. The importance of this role cannot be overemphasized. The second role is to charter and support employee teams.

*Misunderstanding the Aim of Teams.* Few managers fully understand the aim of teams in a TQM effort. Nor is the aim of teams fully understood by most consultants, even many who have written books about teams. Most people understand the aim of teams as they are used in the traditional and customer awareness stages of organizational development. In these stages, teams have one aim: stomp out a fire, beat back a crisis, kill the snakes and alligators, find the guilty employee for punishment, and get back to business as usual. If work processes are involved, the traditional view of teams is to use them to restore work processes to the one best way.

Using teams to do one-shot process restoration is really nothing more than a manifestation of the one best way from the traditional style of management. Same stuff, different package. It sounds right because it does reduce costs and increase effectiveness, and can save CEOs their jobs. But, for the long-run strength of an organization, it's entirely wrong. (Incidentally, all TQM consulting firms with which I am familiar offer process improvement consulting and training based exclusively on one-shot restoration and holding the gains.)

*The Correct Role of Teams.* Organizations need to change their culture so they get into continual improvement. They need to quit thinking about restoring something to the one best way and fire fighting. They need to think about continual improvement. Teams should not restore processes to a working state and then disband, but should improve the processes forever. That's what the phrase *continual improvement* means. It doesn't mean working on something for six months, then quitting. The first word is *continual,* and continual means forever. It means we've got to make things better and better and better.

There are a number of reasons why processes must be improved continually. One is that customers are fickle. Their needs change, and their expectations are constantly rising. And, when customers' needs change, different process outputs are required. A second reason to continually improve is that new process technologies come along every day. And, to stay competitive, the useful ones must be incorporated. A third reason is that suppliers often modify the character of their output. Sometimes for the better; sometimes for the worse. These supplier changes often happen without warning because few organizations, especially traditional ones, work closely enough with their suppliers to know the suppliers' process capabilities and anticipate changes in them. When suppliers change their outputs, it requires adjustments in their customers' processes.

The point is that teams that improve processes must have two aims. The first aim is well understood: Processes must be improved. The second aim is not well understood. It is that teams can be a training ground where employee culture gets changed. In other words, participating on a team can change what employees think is important and how they think things should be done. And, when you change these things, you are really changing an organization's culture.

Attitudes can be changed when managers and other employees work on teams. First, they can be taught there is no one best way, that what they do is *continually* improve things. A team is not dismissed after six months or a year of work. The team keeps after it. They should want improvement after improvement after improvement. This takes patience. Teams have to work a long time simply to understand how their assigned process works. Having patience is a second attitude that has to be built. A third new attitude is that all the brains are not at the top, but this means employees have to start thinking for themselves. A fourth attitude is cooperation, and team members must cooperate through consensus to decide how to improve processes.

Thus, teams must not only continually improve processes to increase organizational effectiveness, they must also be a force for changing team member attitudes. And changing team member attitudes changes an organization's culture. Teams are, therefore, the second part of the transitional administrative structure spoken of earlier. The quality council is the first part of this structure, and the second part is teams.

## Teams and Culture Change

In his teachings of point 14, Deming says

*Management in authority will explain by seminars and other means to a critical mass of people in the company why change is necessary, and that the changes will involve everybody.*[11]

Many CEOs and their senior staffs work hard at doing what Deming suggests here. They find meaning in the other 13 points and strive hard to communicate it to employees. When employees hear this message, most are delighted that senior management is committed to the Deming philosophy. Although they will worry that this is just another program, they hope management will follow through to change the organization as Deming suggests. They will be happy to see the removal of the barriers to their pride of work, the elimination of work standards and exhortation, and fear driven out. The critical mass of support that Deming requires will have formed, at least in the minds of employees. Now the employees sit back and wait for management to take action to follow through on its commitment. So, here are the senior managers on the spot. What do they do next to bring about the transformation to Deming's way? Sometimes very little.

Unfortunately, the cultural transformation and increased organizational effectiveness the CEO hoped for do not materialize. He or she sees that long-term education for everyone in Deming's teaching is not enough. He or she hoped that education in Deming's teachings would bring about a critical mass that would somehow empower employees so the transformation would take hold. But nothing happened. The TQM effort drifts aimlessly.

This point in the TQM journey is a dangerous one. At this point, the CEO is like an newborn fledgling in the jungle, prey to every hungry TQM consulting firm. Engaging many of these firms has led to expensive and time-consuming detours and dead ends in the TQM journey. It would have been far better for the CEO to return to Deming's point 14 and reread his section on taking action to accomplish the transformation. Here, Deming emphasizes that "every job is part of a process" and that "everyone can take part in a team."[12] For the CEOs who study this section, its meaning often is not understood.

### The Answer Is Teams

Something else, beyond mass education by the CEO and senior managers, is needed to get the TQM effort going. The something else is a way to get people in the organization to actually *practice* Deming's teachings. People learn in different ways, and experience shows that many people simply can't learn the Deming philosophy by hearing lectures or watching videotapes. They learn from real-life, hands-on experiences. They learn by applying the Deming philosophy in real, on-the-job situations. They learn by experiencing Deming's philosophy in action. Rather than listening to someone talk about it, they need to do it. The question is, how can this kind of learning be made available? The answer is to use employee teams in a way that not only increases an organization's effectiveness but has an impact on the culture of the team members themselves and on all others in the organization.

## Moving Forward

It is not enough to use teams as firefighters, although this has some minor benefits. Nor is it enough to use teams to restore processes to their one best way, although this has some major benefits. Nor is it enough to use teams to improve processes constantly and forever, although that has some outstanding benefits. To reach their full potential, employee teams must be used so their work impacts an organization's culture.

To reach their full potential, teams must have two aims: to increase an organization's effectiveness (by improving its processes), and to help change an organization's culture. The next chapter explains how to initiate and manage teams to impact an organization's culture, and chapter 8 explains how teams increase an organization's effectiveness through continual process improvement.

# Notes

1. Charles N. Weaver, *TQM: A Step-by-Step Guide to Implementation* (Milwaukee, Wis.: ASQC Quality Press, 1991), p. 65.

2. W. Edwards Deming, *Out of the Crisis* (Cambridge, Mass.: MIT Press, 1986), pp. ix, xi, 23.

3. ———, *The New Economics for Industry, Government, and Education* (Cambridge, Mass.: MIT Press, 1993).

4. Deming, *Out of the Crisis;* ———, *The New Economics;* and Howard S. Gitlow and Shelly J. Gitlow, *The Deming Guide to Quality and Competitive Position* (Englewood Cliffs, N.J.: Prentice Hall, 1987).

5. Deming, *Out of the Crisis,* p. 86.

6. Ibid.

7. Gitlow and Gitlow, *The Deming Guide;* Rafael Aguayo, *Dr. Deming: The American Who Taught the Japanese About Quality* (New York: A Lyle Stuart Book, 1990); and Andrea Gabor, *The Man Who Discovered Quality* (New York: Random House, 1990).

8. J. M. Juran, *Juran on Leadership for Quality: An Executive Handbook* (New York: Free Press, 1989), pp. 43–56.

9. Ibid., pp. 44–46, 52–54.

10. Ibid., p. 69.

11. Deming, *Out of the Crisis,* p. 86.

12. Ibid., pp. 89–92.

# Chapter 7

# The Process Improvement Stage: How Teams Impact Culture

Through the decades, teams have been used many times in an effort to increase organizational effectiveness. These teams have had various names, such as quality circles, tiger teams, task teams, rapid response teams, self-directed teams (SDTs), employee involvement (EI) teams, innovation teams, and partners-in-action. The record shows, however, that these efforts have met with only limited success. Why is this so? The answer is that most team efforts violate the second law of organizational development.

*Any attempt to increase organizational effectiveness will eventually get washed out unless it has adequate cultural support.*

The culture in which most teams' efforts have been tried is the culture of the traditional style of management. It is difficult to imagine a culture any more unfavorable to team success. Consider several examples of how this culture handicaps teams.

## How the Culture of the Traditional Style of Management Handicaps Teams

First, consider how competition, a favorite tool of Western management, handicaps teams. Competition is justified on the grounds that it brings out the best in employees. Over the years, employees get used to competing, so it's only natural that they compete, rather than cooperate, when they're assigned to teams. They try to maximize their own personal interests and protect the interests of their department, just as they've been taught. They assume the other members of the team are out for themselves, too, just as they are in the rest of the organization. They know that in the rest of the organization everyone seeks to maximize his or her own self interests by doing whatever it takes to get promotions, salary increases, and recognition. This attitude is seldom discussed openly, but it's there nonetheless. Employees reason, "Why would it be different on a team from the way it is in the rest of the organization?" Thus, team members are privately suspicious of suggestions that they should be open, honest, and cooperative on teams. Their experience tells them it's a dog-eat-dog world. It doesn't make sense to be cooperative on a team and competitive everywhere else. They wonder, "How can there be an island of peace in an ocean of war?"

Competitive behavior by members can seriously limit a team's potential. For instance, suppose a team member knows about an unnecessary delay in a certain department in the horizontal process the team is chartered to improve. This member may be reluctant to say anything about the delay for fear a member from that department may use it against him or her later. Who knows when another team member will be appointed to a peer review board or be promoted to supervisor? Then that member would be in a position to get back at the person who broke the code of silence. "The smart thing to do is play it safe. Say nothing that might come back later to bite you." Yet, if teams are to be successful, members must feel comfortable identifying opportunities for improvement.

To reduce the competitiveness in their cultures, organizations spend millions of dollars annually on team building, the major purpose of which is to build cooperation. Professional team builders use psychological tests to identify team member strengths and weaknesses. They show the results to team members and suggest they can accomplish more by working together than separately because together they capitalize on everyone's strengths. Sounds good, and it works. But many team members privately say team building is a waste of time because they don't see the sense of being cooperative for two hours on a team and being competitive the rest of the time at work. Unfortunately, few traditional CEOs are willing to eliminate the personnel policies and awards programs that drive competition every day throughout their organizations. They mistakenly still believe competition is a good thing.

Many CEOs have learned that competition among members of the same team is not good, but they make another kind of mistake. They think competition works between teams. Consequently, they are delighted when they see books and seminars about how to get teams to work harder by creating competition between them. Team competition is based on various compensation and reward schemes. But, creating competition between teams is as much a management blunder as creating competition between members of the same team. It fosters just what we're trying to change with the Deming philosophy. It reduces cooperation between individuals, teams, and departments. It builds barriers between employees and departments. Worse, it reinforces the mistaken idea that competition in an organization is a good thing.

A second example of a cultural barrier to the success of teams in making improvements is that employees are taught there's a one best way to do things. And, they continue to think this way when they're assigned to teams. Despite what may be said in team training about the need for continual improvement, they find it difficult to break the habit of thinking there's a one best way. On teams, this translates into restoring work processes to the best way to do them and being reluctant to work on them any more after that. Employees are programmed, so to speak, to diagnose problems, recommend remedial actions, get their accomplishments recognized by management, and get back to work as usual. To improve things beyond merely restoring processes to the one best way is an attitude they have difficulty accepting.

Competition and the one best way are two of many attitudes employees learn working for those who torment them with the traditional style of management. Other especially harmful attitudes in this kind of culture are impatience and being fearful. As a group, such attitudes represent a cultural barrier to efforts to change organizations and increase their effectiveness. There are a number of ways to change these attitudes, and the most successful one is to charter and manage employee teams with this aim in mind.

## Two More Attitudes that Must Be Considered

Two other attitudes are always prominent in the culture of organizations as they come out of the traditional and customer awareness stages of TQM. One is unique to CEOs and senior managers; the other is shared by all employees, salaried and hourly.

The first of these attitudes was reviewed in chapter 2. CEOs and senior managers feel intense pressure from the owners—whether stockholders, a board of directors, trustees, a commander, a headquarters, or elected officials—to keep things moving. (I'll refer to this group as *the board.*) This pressure can be for a better bottom line, consistent dividends, reduced costs, more effective operations, or all these things and more. Whether CEOs admit it or not, in the face of this pressure they often feel desperate for something they can show to the board at their periodic meetings, usually every quarter. The fear underlying this desperation is real. If they don't do something to impress the board, CEOs run the risk of losing their jobs.

The second prominent attitude in organizations coming out of the traditional or customer awareness stages was explained in chapter 6. Most employees have seen so-called programs of one sort or another come and go over the years. Therefore, when an initiative called *TQM* is announced, employees slide down into their foxholes to wait for what they see as a new program to blow over. From experience, they suspect TQM won't do any more good than the other programs that came before it, and it won't last very long. They see TQM as another way for the CEO to appease or impress the board and thereby get something for him- or herself, such as a fat bonus, by tightening the screws on employees.

Indeed, there is plenty of historical support for this expectation. It's a fact that virtually all CEOs are continually on the lookout for something to show the board and, in far too many cases, they have tightened the screws on their employees over and over again to come up with something. Remember, traditional CEOs believe they wouldn't have all these problems if the employees would just put their backs into their work. So, the typical CEO squeezes employees to do more with program after program. Remember how, in the customer awareness stage of TQM, employees are taught to smile and required to wear badges with words proclaiming their commitment to the organization's legendary customer service program? Customer service efforts of this type are nothing more than another program, an effort to get more work out of employees.

### Actions to Accommodate These Attitudes

If CEOs don't get something to take to the board and everyone isn't brought up out of his or her foxhole, the cold fact is that an entire TQM effort can fail and an organization can slip back into the dark, murky waters of the traditional style of management. In fact, CEO reputations and survival often ride on the success of the first few TQM process improvement projects. If CEOs don't show their boards some early showcase results from process improvements, boards may redirect budget away from TQM, and they may begin to wonder if their CEO is the right person for the job. Similarly, if something isn't done to get employees up out of their foxholes, their support may never be obtained.

Therefore, the first few horizontal processes identified for improvement by teams—I recommend three—must be selected for their impact in these areas: something the CEO can take to the board and something that will get employees up out of their foxholes. The criteria for selecting subsequent processes for improvement can be different, but the first processes must be selected on the basis of the certainty of their impact on these two attitudes.

*A Word of Caution About Selecting Processes for Improvement.* A word of caution must be expressed about which of these two criteria is more important. Many organizations are in perilous financial condition. Some CEOs know they are in trouble, but others think their financial house is in order when, if the future could be seen, the wolf is only a few steps from the door. For financially imperiled organizations, if the color of the bottom line doesn't soon change from red to black, their CEOs will be forced to fall back on their training in traditional management to cut costs with employee layoffs. But, remember, layoffs provide only temporary relief; layoffs don't get at the real cause of an organization's problems. The real cause is that customers have taken their business to competitors simply because they are not getting what they want. And, customers are not getting what they want because of poorly designed and unmanaged cross-functional processes.

It is important to understand that it's the high costs of these poorly designed and unmanaged processes that must be contained and reduced if organizations are to be saved from financial ruin. Laying off employees is not the answer. And, for more organizations than CEOs are publicly willing to admit, there is no time to waste in getting these costs down. If cost-reducing life preservers are not thrown to these imperiled organizations, they will drown in a sea of financial troubles. Here's the point, and it's an important one. Getting employees up out of their foxholes is important, but it is always better in the beginning of a TQM effort to go after high-cost processes. This results in a much improved bottom line and ensures financial viability. Organizations following this advice will be solvent so they can continue their TQM journey. Admittedly, this is a form of fire fighting, and we like to keep fire fighting to a minimum in TQM. But, for many organizations, unless the high costs of key processes are reduced, there simply will be no tomorrow.

# Sure Ways to Select Processes for Improvement

Among the surest ways to identify high-cost processes is to ask for the advice of the CFO. The CFO can be asked to list the categories of an organization's highest costs, in total and broken down by department, and to show how these costs compare to the national averages for similar organizations of the same size. CFOs will know where to find data on national cost averages, probably from trade associations. These analyses usually identify departments or activities where costs are high compared to national averages and point to processes that can be targeted for cost reduction.

If the CEO and CFO don't yet fully understand what is meant by processes or cross-functional processes, they should make these selections in terms of identifying high-cost *problems*, rather than worrying about identifying processes. This is because most problems, and certainly all of the really serious problems, are directly related to cross-functional processes.

Other useful information that CFOs can provide to help identify cost-related processes include various accounting or financial measures. Some of these are ratios that show the relationship of one financial measure to another, such as bad debt as a percentage of accounts receivables. Others show how much time something takes to turn over, such as inventory and accounts receivables. Other such measures show how well organizations use various resources, such as cash, noncash items, various inventories, physical plant, accounts receivable, accounts payable, and travel vouchers. When these measures are out of line with national figures for comparable organizations, they usually point to processes in need of improvement. For instance, most organizations take far too long to mail statements to customers after products have been sold or services rendered. In most organizations, the horizontal process for preparing these statements is the source of concern, but usually no one has been successful at speeding up the process. Improving this process means money is tied up for fewer days in accounts receivables and a faster cash flow. And, a faster cash flow means more money in the bank drawing interest. Speeding up cash flow has been the key to the doghouse door with, or at least good for a temporary reprieve from, the board for many CEOs.

Identifying processes for improvement to get employees up out of their foxholes requires another tactic: finding processes with high visibility. Increasing cash flow, as mentioned earlier, will impress the board, but it will not be visible to the average Joe/Jo on the shop floor. And, if he or she heard about it, it wouldn't have much meaning anyway. On the other hand, improving other processes will be visible to employees. Such processes may include improving the value or healthfulness to employees of menu items at the snack bar; shortening checkout lines in the cafeteria; making it easy to find a parking place in the employee garage; improving security so employees feel safer on organization grounds; improving the business office so employees can easily cash a personal check; making the temperature more comfortable in work areas; and, for employees who use equipment, such as word processors, improving the response time of in-house repair units. When these processes or others like them are improved, employees notice it, and their attitudes toward TQM are favorably affected. It may take a couple of solid, visible examples, but employees will eventually say, "Well, it looks like the old man [or woman] is finally going to do something to improve things around here. It looks like this TQM stuff is actually going to work after all." The only way to get employees up out of their foxholes is with *action*, not talk. Employees have heard all the big talk and empty promises they can stand from "some joker in a three-piece suit," as they might say.

# How Teams Influence Employee Attitudes

Teams are used to some degree by virtually every organization regardless of its stage of development in TQM. Most organizations do not use teams to their full potential, however.

## How Teams Are Misused

Organizations in the traditional and customer awareness stages use teams to fight fires and carry out special projects, such as planning retirement parties. Many teams, commonly called *quality circles*, are used to work quality issues. But, CEOs who initiate quality circles usually don't appreciate the horizontal nature of their organizations, and, for them, the focus of these teams is confined to vertical, functionally related, quality issues. The usefulness of such teams, therefore, is limited.

Unfortunately, few CEOs—even those whose organizations are in the process improvement stage of TQM—use teams to their full potential. The focus of teams is usually limited to merely restoring processes that have broken down or become inefficient. There is no doubt that using teams for this purpose is of benefit to organizations, and this reason alone justifies their use. But teams have considerably more potential which, unfortunately, goes untapped in most organizations.

## A Better Way to Use Teams

Teams have far more potential than merely restoring broken-down processes. But their other use is not widely understood. To be used to their full potential, teams must help change both the way employees do things and what they think is important. In other words, teams must be used to help change an organization's culture. It may not seem that the work of teams has anything to do with changing attitudes and culture, but it can and must if organizations are to survive and prosper.

Using teams to further the cultural transformation of organizations requires new knowledge. This knowledge is that Deming's 14 points, diseases and obstacles, and profound knowledge apply to the work of teams just as they apply to the professional, personal, and family lives of everyone.

*When teams improve processes by practicing and modeling Deming's teachings, they are a significant force for moving an organization away from the traditional style of management.*

No one leading or facilitating a team or providing training in leading and facilitating teams can do his or her job unless he or she appreciates this knowledge and knows how to put it into practice. Consequently, everything said in this chapter and the next about how teams operate is cast in a framework of Deming's teachings. Let's begin by considering what must be done to get teams started.

## The Logic of Continual Improvement

Deming's teaching in point 5 is to "Improve constantly and forever the system of production and service."[1] This point is violated by fire fighting and using teams simply to restore broken-down processes. When Deming says continuous improvement, he doesn't mean fixing something and getting back to usual work. That's how it's done in traditional management. Consider an illustration to demonstrate this point.

Suppose a quality council charters three teams, each with a process for improvement. Over the months, these teams fix some problems that result in improvements the CEO can take to the board and that begin to get employees up out of their foxholes. Eventually, performance measures on these three once-ailing processes begin to fall into line with the national averages or benchmarks, and, eventually, they operate even better than the national averages or benchmarks. Because it is expensive to operate teams, especially in terms of payroll, what are cost-conscious quality councils likely to do when the performance measures on these processes are improved? They are likely to declare these processes fixed and disband the teams. And, if they are sufficiently impressed with their results, they may charter three more teams to fix other processes. In time, these additional three processes get fixed, and even more teams get chartered. Suppose this goes on for four years, and the major processes of the organization are fixed and humming along nicely. At this point, what are cost-conscious quality councils likely to do? They are likely to establish measures to hold the gains on these improvements and go out of the process improvement business. Their reasoning is that they have gotten everything fixed. They now see things running pretty smoothly. They are satisfied.

There is no doubt such improvements do a world of good for organizations. There is no doubt that customers and employees are more satisfied, costs are lower, cycle time is less, expenses are reduced, and the cost of management is less. But let's look more closely at what seems to be a great success story. What impact has all this improvement had on the manager over in the fabrication department? Or on the foreperson of the loading dock? Or on the CEO's secretary? Or on the sales force? Are these employees better able to do their jobs? Yes, no doubt about it. Are they now able to take more pride in their work? Yes, no doubt about it. But let's look a little further.

Are the fabrication department manager, the loading dock foreperson, the CEO's secretary, the sales force, and all the other employees in this organization practicing Deming's point 5? Is everyone constantly and forever improving his or her part of the organization and its relationship with the other parts? Or, are employees merely happily working in an organization that is now vastly better because of the recent process improvement effort, an effort that has now been placed on the back burner? The answer is yes, they are happily working in a vastly improved organization, but they are *not* continuing to improve things. They assume all the needed improvements have been made. Now it's time to get back to work as usual. They are no longer improving anything. All the one best ways have been found or restored. They are not practicing Deming's point 5. Why not?

The answer to the question Why not? lies in understanding the difference between two alternatives: (1) an organization vastly improved by a successful process improvement effort where improvement has stopped with everyone now doing things in the one best way, and (2) an organization vastly improved by a successful process improvement effort where improvement is still going on with everyone constantly and forever improving the system of production and service. In the first case, improvement stopped because the culture was not changed by the process improvement effort from the traditional style of management. The process improvement effort merely restored the broken-down bureaucracy so that things work better.

Teams were used to increase effectiveness, but they had no impact on the organization's culture. Teams fixed their assigned processes and got back to work as usual. It is of great benefit to have things work well again, but having things work well again is not nearly all the improvement that's possible.

In the second case, employees quit thinking about the one best way and learned that improvement is continuous. Continual improvement became a way of life for them. It became part of the culture.

The question is how to use teams not only to improve processes (increase effectiveness) but, at the same time, to help change an organization's culture so continual improvement is accepted by everyone as the way to do business. The answer is to organize and manage teams with both of these aims in mind.

## The Two Kinds of Teams

When I am asked for a source of information about improvement teams, I identify H. James Harrington's book, *Business Process Improvement*.[2] What I learned from his book forms the foundation of what I say in the rest of this chapter about teams.

From the viewpoint of process improvement, there are two kinds of teams. The first is a *process improvement team* (PIT). PITs are chartered by quality councils to improve cross-functional processes, or, as explained in chapter 2, the interactions between departments. A cross-functional process is defined as a series of repeated steps (or actions) that extends across two or more functional areas, or departments, and uses inputs (resources) from suppliers to produce outputs (goods or services) for customers. All work is a process. But PITs work only on processes that cross at least two departments.

### Initiating PITs

Quality councils create PITs by writing charters for them. A charter has three parts, each of which represents a decision by the quality council: (1) the name of the person selected to be the leader of the PIT, (2) a written statement of the aim (or opportunity statement) of the PIT, and (3) a block diagram of the assigned process. Consider next the meaning of each of these three parts of a charter.

***How to Select PIT Leaders.*** The selection of persons to lead PITs can be made in a number of ways. Beyond doubt, the best is to assign the manager who owns the cross-functional process being chartered. This is the person responsible for the resources and decisions in the departments that contain the process. Another way is to assign the middle-level manager who owns the departments either downstream or upstream in the process. This person is not a department manager, but a manager of department managers. Yet another way is to assign any person from senior management, preferably someone in the hierarchy directly above the departments that contain the process. When possible, it is better not to select as a PIT leader the manager of any single department into which the process extends. Unless this person fully appreciates the need to optimize the process, he or she may be overly concerned about justifying and defending his or her department. But, often circumstances dictate a different way to select PIT leaders from those described here. Unorthodox methods of selection can be successful.

In selecting PIT leaders, bear in mind that PITs have two aims: (1) to improve a cross-functional process and (2) to help change the organization's culture. The second aim has important implications for the selection of PIT leaders. Because leading PITs involves managing teams with Deming's 14 points and profound knowledge, as explained in the remainder of this chapter and the next, considerable pressure can be exerted on PIT leaders to change away from the traditional style of management. Hence, an important consideration in selecting PIT leaders is that they be supporters of the Deming philosophy. It is ordinarily not difficult to find candidate PIT leaders with an interest in the Deming philosophy, provided the CEO has made it plain that the organization is going in this direction.

*PIT Opportunity Statements.* In his point 1, Deming teaches that we should know the aim of any undertaking in which we are involved. For instance, organizations and departments should have statements of purpose and mission statements, and families and individuals should write down their principal intended accomplishments. Similarly, every PIT should have an aim. This aim should be to improve a process and to help change culture. Aims are provided by quality councils to PIT leaders in written statements called *opportunity statements*. The effectiveness part of an opportunity statement identifies a cross-functional process targeted for improvement, identifies the boundaries of the process, points to the measurable improvements possible, and identifies those whom the improvements will benefit. The culture part of an opportunity statement refers to how the team will carry out its work in line with Deming's teachings. A fill-in-the-blanks example of a PIT opportunity statement follows:

> *There is an opportunity to improve the process by which* _____ *takes place. This process begins when* _____,

*crosses from _____ to _____ to _____ , and
ends when _____ . This process currently _____
[costs too much in terms of _____ ] and _____ [oper-
ates too slowly in _____ ]. Its improvement will be of benefit
to _____ and to _____ . The team will learn, practice, teach, and model the Deming management philosophy.*

Quality councils must take pains to provide team leaders with
operational definitions of the terms in their opportunity statements.
The word most often not defined and which is the source of later difficulties is *improve.* (See the use of this word in the first sentence in the
fill-in-the-blanks opportunity statement.) The word *improve* can have
many meanings. Does it mean to reduce cycle time (from when a product or service is requested until it is received), or timeliness (when it
arrives in the hands of customers), costs, delays, inventories, or what?
If a quality council and a team have different definitions in mind, mis-
understandings will surely develop.

Let me try to be clearer about this point. One of the errors made by
quality councils in chartering teams is the most serious. Councils fail
to provide teams with opportunity statements that make clear the
aims of targeted processes. Every process must have an aim. In fact,
Deming says, "Without an aim, there is no [process]." His definition of
a process is ". . . a network of interdependent components that work
together to try to accomplish the aim of the [process]."[3] Thus, for a
quality council to charter a team with an opportunity statement that
says *improve* is important but insuffecent. The team needs to know the
aim of the process it is chartered to improve. In my experience, the aim
of every process must be to meet and then exceed the requirements
and expectations of the customers of the output of the process. Consider an illustration of a team's need to know the aim of its chartered
process.

In this illustration, a hospital laboratory PIT was chartered with an
opportunity statement to improve the reporting of lab results to nursing units. After a year of work, the team enhanced the process in
countless valuable ways, such as reducing costs, eliminating duplication, and reducing errors. But the enhanced process continued to
deliver lab results to nursing units at 8:30 A.M. for the use of physicians
who need them at 7:00 A.M. Enhancing this process was of great benefit from the cost and quality perspective, but the team still was not
achieving its aim. This problem is often in the chartering itself.
Because of a vague charter that says *improve,* a team assumes the
important work is reducing costs, eliminating duplication, or reduc-

ing errors when, in fact, what is needed is something entirely different. This confusion can be reduced by including process aims in opportunity statements.

*PIT Block Diagrams.* Quality councils also provide each PIT leader with a graphic picture of his or her assigned process. This picture is in the form of a block diagram drawn on a sheet of paper. A block diagram is a series of usually no more than three to five blocks or rectangles connected with one-way arrows showing where an assigned process starts and ends and what goes on in between. Block diagrams are not intended to show detail. They show a broad overview of a process. They are macro, not micro. They are molar, not molecular. In each block is written some words describing a step in the process. A block diagram of a process reflects the understanding of the quality council about the boundaries of the process, that this process starts here and goes through this department, that department, that department, and ends here. It is within these boundaries that councils expect a PIT to bring about improvements.

Consider two illustrations of block diagrams for a hospital laboratory. Both diagrams might consist of three rectangles with one-way arrows between them. In the first, the three squares contain the words "requesting," "processing," and "reporting" laboratory products. This would indicate a large process that extends from when a physician writes a lab request (the start of the process) to when a ward clerk files the report in a patient's chart (the end of the process). But the part of this large process to be improved could be defined by the council to be much smaller, such as if the three rectangles contained the words "Results are printed in the lab," "Runner delivers results to nursing units," and "Ward clerk files results in patient's medical record." This shows the area for improvement is only in the reporting part of the larger process. Thus, the level at which improvement is to take place can be broad or narrow. In any case, block diagrams show the boundaries within which processes are to be improved.

It is important to understand that the boundaries (the start, end, and both sides) of a process are judgments. Choices of boundaries are based entirely on what councils want PITs to improve. If a council doesn't want something improved, it leaves the item out of the boundaries. If it wants something improved, the council includes the item.

For an example of how judgment is used to develop a block diagram, consider the admitting process at a psychiatric health care facility. In the first block, the process could start in several different places, such as in physician offices when physicians recommend that burned-out executives get some rest and rehabilitation. If so, the words in the first block would read, "MDs recommend rehab." On the other hand, the process could start when an executive walks up to the information desk at the psychiatric facility. If so, the first block would read, "Executive arrives at info desk." The first block shows where a quality council thinks the improvement efforts of the PIT should begin. If part of a PIT's charter is to consider how to get more physician business, the starting point of the process should be the offices where physicians make decisions to admit patients to particular psychiatric facilities. On the other hand, if a council doesn't want a PIT to consider how to get more physicians to use its facility, the starting point should be later in the process. The same reasoning applies to the boundaries on the sides and at the end of the process.

## How PITs Influence Attitudes

Now consider how PITs influence the culture of an organization. When a PIT leader is given a block diagram, one of the leader's first acts is to visit with the managers of each of the departments identified in the block diagram. These are the managers of the departments that contain the process targeted for improvement. Sometimes only two departments are involved; sometimes there are many more.

Bear in mind that PIT activities have been endorsed by the CEO, and the CEO and other senior managers are involved and visible as trainers in Deming's teachings. As a consequence, the PIT leader, who may be a senior manager, and the department managers take these PIT activities seriously. The leader probably knows the department managers, and sits down with each of them over a cup of coffee and says, "Well, you know I got roped into leading this PIT." Here they both laugh because, like everyone in the organization, they think, at least to some degree, that this PIT stuff is just another program.

Each PIT leader is trained to talk to the department managers about Deming's teachings as he or she applies to starting the PIT and as he or she relates to the manager's department. The leader explains how important work takes place in horizontal, cross-departmental ways rather than entirely in vertical stovepipes. The leader extends this idea by explaining that horizontal processes are composed of a series of customer–supplier relationships and asks the manager to identify the customers and suppliers of his or her department. The leader may need to talk about the fact that customers and suppliers are internal just as they are external. Here the leader can get into the issue of how quality is defined by the customer (part of Deming's point 2) and how departments must cooperate with their suppliers (Deming's point 4) to ensure the best for their own customers. The leader must emphasize the need for optimization (Deming's profound knowledge) and that there must be no barriers between departments (Deming's point 9) that share a horizontal process. Otherwise, barriers will prevent employees from taking pride in their work (Deming's point 12).

The need and nature of this training for department managers by PIT leaders varies, and leaders should be prepared to spend more time with some managers than others. Leaders also should be prepared to spend more time on some parts of Deming's teachings than on others. Learning Deming's teachings does not proceed at the same pace for everyone. PIT leaders can expect department managers to be practicing many of the 14 points already, willing to practice many more, hesitant to practice several, and dead set against aspects of one or two. Leaders must remember, also, that their training efforts with department managers are being complimented by a long-term education in the Deming philosophy led by the quality council. In other words, this training is coming at department managers from two directions, from PIT leaders and from the quality council.

## How to Select SMEs

Another important piece of business goes on in the meetings between PIT leaders and department managers. This is the selection by each department manager of a person from his or her department to serve as a member of the PIT. Departmental personnel who are selected to serve on PITs must meet certain requirements. They must be SMEs, pronounced with an *s* (as in source or less) and *me*—on the part of the process that goes through their department. Furthermore, each must be the best person in his or her department for the job. SMEs must be given time off from their regular duties to attend PIT meetings and to do PIT homework. The PIT leader must make it clear to department managers that they must make provisions to have some other department member, or a temporary employee, pick up the work load left by the member assigned to the PIT. It is unfair and demoralizing to ask someone to take on additional duties as a SME while maintaining his or her regular workload. The CEO must visibly endorse this approach and provide additional payroll as necessary.

# The Liaison Role
# of SMEs

A key role of SMEs is that they serve as the liaison between the PIT and their department manager. In this critical but often overlooked role, they report back to their department manager and other department members, as needed, the goings-on at each PIT meeting, especially as they affect their department. In these back-briefings, department managers learn how PITs go about making improvements, and this learning is important because it helps managers change to Deming's perspective how they think things should be done and what they think is important. This is another way PITs affect the culture. PIT leaders practice the Deming management philosophy to run teams effectively, and managers learn how this works through these back-briefings from their liaison SMEs. These back-briefings are an important part of the work of teams, and they should never be skipped.

But, now consider an important question about SMEs. Who selects the persons to represent a department as SMEs on PITs? Are they selected by the quality council? Are they selected by PIT leaders? The answer to both questions is no. SMEs are identified by their department managers. They are the persons whom department managers trust and want to serve as liaisons. It is important that department managers make this selection because it gives them a greater sense of representation, participation, ownership, and control in PITs. To select SMEs in any other way would be to revert back to the traditional style of management: "All the brains are at the top. We'll identify the right person as the SME out of your department. Your job is to keep your mouth shut and live with our decision."

When teams are in operation, there are actually three kinds of SMEs. The first is the SME, already described, who attends every meeting. Then there are ad hoc SMEs. They are persons asked to attend a team meeting for a short time, perhaps 30 minutes or an hour, to provide information not known to members. There are also temporary duty (TDY) SMEs. They are needed for several meetings, or perhaps for several months. They possess special knowledge required by a team, but they need to interact with the team to provide it. It can't just be reported. For instance, they need to be present to observe flow diagraming to ensure that regulatory requirements, such as safety standards, are met. They cannot just say this in 30 minutes; it takes their actual participation for a period of time. But, after that work is completed, they are excused.

## Another Way PITs Affect the Culture of Departments

The activities of PITs affect the culture of departments in another way. This is in the way process improvements identified by PITs are implemented. To understand how this works, consider an example.

Suppose a certain PIT is working on a process that goes through departments A, B, C, and D. Assume all the preliminary work between the PIT leader and the four department managers has been taken care of, and SMEs from the four departments are in place. After meeting three hours a week for several months, perhaps flow diagraming the process, the PIT identifies something in Department A that needs improvement. Maybe a certain machine is down too often, or maybe too many copies of some document are being made or needlessly stored. Suppose the PIT has found a reasonable solution to the problem and has tested it for feasibility. The question is how is this improvement in Department A made? Does the PIT leader file a report with the quality council which directs its member with responsibilities for Department A to get a tiger team together to make the improvement? Does the PIT put together a task team of its own members to carry out the improvement in Department A?

The answer to this question has two parts. Improvements in Department A are sought, but some cultural impact on Department A needs to be made in the bargain. Therefore, the improvement should be brought about like this. All along, the liaison SME between the PIT and Department A has been back-briefing the manager of Department A on the activities of the PIT. The department manager has had frequent and ample opportunity to provide input to the PIT on any improvement contemplated by the PIT for Department A. This could have been done through the liaison SME, or the manager could attend PIT meetings to present the department's viewpoint in person. But now it is time to make the actual improvement. Who should do it? The answer is the department manager, of course.

There is an important reason for asking department managers to make PIT-identified improvements in their own departments. The reason is that one of the PIT's aims is to change how department managers think things should be done and to change what they think is important. Until now, they've been taught that only methods engineers or tiger teams from higher management can make changes in the way things are done. Until now, they have been taught that methods engineers and tiger teams use their stopwatches to find the one best ways, and that, once found, departments must slavishly follow them until directed otherwise. But, now, we want department managers to do things differently. Now, we want them to believe there is *no* one best way. Now, we want them to believe the persons closest to a job are the best persons to say how that job should be done to satisfy their customers. We want them to get into the spirit of making changes.

## A Few PITs Create Many DITs

Now, imagine that some time has passed, and there are a number of PITs operating in the organization we're talking about. As department managers make improvement after improvement in response to requests, or taskings, from PITs, several interesting things happen. First, when the number of taskings increases to a certain point, department managers realize they can't make all these improvements singlehandedly. They need help. So, they get some help within their own departments. They may start out doing the improvements with the help of one subordinate. But as the taskings from PITs grow in number, the help of other department personnel is needed. If a department is small, all department members may eventually be asked to help. If a department is large, maybe half a dozen employees will help. Maybe those asked to help will be the department's supervisors. Sometimes, the department members making the improvements may decide to call themselves a *department improvement team* (DIT).

A second thing happens as PITs task DITs with improvement after improvement. Department managers, or DIT leaders as they may call themselves, sooner or later realize they don't have to wait around for taskings from PITs to improve their departments and their relations with their mainly internal customers and suppliers. Eureka! It dawns on them that their DIT can generate its own improvement initiatives. Through their liaison SME, they learned the tools and techniques used by PITs to identify improvement opportunities, and there is no reason they can't use these methods to find improvements in their department themselves. Before long, DITs are self-generating taskings for themselves. And, as time passes, DITs begin to influence upstream departments to improve their part of horizontal processes to remove barriers to good work they inadvertently cause for downstream departments. Barriers between departments are being broken down as DITs work improvement taskings among themselves.

When DITs start working on self-generated initiatives to improve themselves, their culture has been influenced by PITs. So, the concept of the one best way has gone out the window, and departments are practicing Deming's point 5, continuously and forever improving the system of production and service.

It is important to remember that while PITs are jump-starting DITs into continual improvement and the other parts of the Deming philosophy, the quality council must be providing education in the Deming philosophy, providing plenty of encouragement and reinforcement, and supplying the needed resources for the implementation of recommended changes.

## The Transitional Nature of PITs

Remember, in chapter 6 it was explained that implementing TQM involves a transitional administrative structure. This structure is the vehicle to bring about the transformation away from the traditional style of management. Part of this structure is the quality council. When the senior staff members that make up the quality council understand that practicing Deming's teachings is their full-time job, the name *quality council* can drop off. The council's members may want to take back the name they used to use before they started TQM, except now they understand what their job is. Similarly, when every department is practicing Deming's teachings and feverishly improving everything it does, PITs can drop off and DITs can eventually start calling themselves *departments* again. PITs and DITs don't exist anymore, because now departments understand their jobs. This is how quality councils, PITs, and DITs are transitional. Their aim is to jump-start organizations away from the traditional style of management into following Deming's teachings. After they have done their work, they can drop off.

## Moving Forward

Teams have two aims. The first is to impact the culture of an organization, and how this happens is explained in this chapter. The second aim of teams is to bring about effectiveness gains, such as to reduce costs, eliminate waste and duplication, reduce cycle time, tear out unnecessary bureaucracy, and increase customer satisfaction. How teams get trained to do this is the subject of chapter 8; chapter 9 explains how to do it.

One of the most serious and common roadblocks in the TQM journey is a CEO tampering with the organization by launching several simultaneous TQM initiatives. For instance, an organization commits to the transformation of the traditional style of management using Deming's teachings. But, as this effort is about to bear fruit, the CEO brings in a consulting firm to do some training in the teachings of another quality guru. Afterwards, who do employees listen to, Deming or the other guru? Or, a CEO creates a process improvement infrastructure of PITs and DITs and, a few months later, hires a firm to train in SDTs. Afterwards, do teams operate as PITs or do they operate under self-direction?

Incessant tampering with a TQM effort is a roadblock for many reasons. There are serious differences between the teachings of the quality gurus and between different team training philosophies. Unless these inconsistencies and others are resolved—and they are almost never even understood, much less resolved—management will confuse employees and create TQM roadblocks. There's no telling how much time and money has been needlessly wasted by CEOs who cannot keep from tampering with their TQM effort.

# Notes

1. W. Edwards Deming, *Out of the Crisis* (Cambridge, Mass.: MIT Press, 1986), pp. 49–52.

2. H. James Harrington, *Business Process Improvement: The Breakthrough Strategy for Total Quality, Productivity, and Competitiveness* (Milwaukee, Wis.: ASQC Quality Press, 1991).

3. W. Edwards Deming, *The New Economics for Industry, Government, and Education* (Cambridge, Mass.: MIT Press, 1993), pp. 50–51.

# Chapter 8

# The Process Improvement Stage: Training

Deming says people learn in different ways.[1] But, while some say this is obvious, most organizations teach the Deming management philosophy in only a limited number of ways, usually through some combination of lectures, videotapes, and books. My experience suggests that these teaching methods deny complete knowledge of Deming's teachings to many who would benefit from it.

## How People Learn

Some people can learn from a lecture or videotape, and some people can learn from a book. But, it's difficult to get data on how much learning about the Deming philosophy takes place in these ways. You could get an approximate answer if you knew the number of people who check out library books on the Deming philosophy. You could count the signatures on the due-date cards inside the back covers of these books in your organization's library. Despite the fact that these books are known to be available, and reading them is stressed, my casual investigation in the libraries of perhaps 35 organizations shows that few employees borrow these books.

It may be that fewer people than is thought can learn from a book or even from a lecture or videotape. But, a better explanation may be that few people are motivated to learn in these ways. Learning from books and lectures may bring back unpleasant memories of school. Some employees have the unfortunate attitude that schooling and learning are behind them. But, regardless of the reason for the apparent lack of learning that takes place in these ways, many CEOs are disappointed with the low yield they get from their investment in this kind of training. They feel no critical mass of Deming supporters develops. Despite the high cost of this kind of training, especially of TQM videotapes, it seems to benefit only a certain kind of learner.

### A Better Way to Learn for Some

My background in training suggests that many employees learn best from experience. To learn something well, they need to participate in a practical, on-the-job application of the subject matter. To learn to ride a bicycle, for example, many people don't get much out of a book or lecture on the subject. But, under the guidance of someone who knows how to ride, they will listen to instructions, watch the other person ride, and then they'll try to ride. For them the real learning comes from trying to ride. And, after a few spills, they learn how. For another example, consider how to learn to use the ENGT. Most people will patiently listen to instructions, maybe read something, but they always want to watch someone else do ENGT before they're willing to try it themselves. Then, the experience of actually conducting an ENGT session teaches them the most about how to do it.

There are probably many exceptions to this on-the-job approach to learning, but I don't believe learning Deming's teachings is such an exception. To learn Deming's teachings, most people are willing to listen to lectures on the subject, but many never develop a real understanding of his message until they actually experience his teachings on the job. They need to see his teachings in action. Unfortunately, however, most CEOs seem to be ignorant of this perspective. They almost never provide Deming training in on-the-job experiences. Either they don't understand the importance of this kind of training, or they don't know how to provide it.

## Teams as a Way to Learn

Most CEOs are unaware that teams can be a training ground in which employees get on-the-job experience in Deming's teachings. When used in this way, teams can be a powerful force for bringing about the transformation of organizations away from the culture of the traditional style of management.

Consider how teams can help transform organizations away from the traditional style of management. To be sure, the way PITs work through DITs to jump-start departments into continual improvement, as explained in chapter 7, is an important way teams can change organizational culture. But, there is another powerful way this can happen. PITs can be chartered and managed so that literally everything they do is in line with the Deming management philosophy. When anyone in an organization comes in contact with one of its PITs—whether as a member of the quality council; as a PIT leader, facilitator, or SME; or as a DIT leader or member—some of Deming's way rubs off on him or her. Through time and with the visible, active support of the CEO, Deming's way rubs off from PITs on more and more employees. Eventually, a critical mass of employees begins to think and behave according to Deming's teachings. Understanding this effect of PITs is vital to the successful transformation of any organization to the Deming style of management.

## How to Make Team Learning Effective

One key to successful TQM transformation is, of course, the CEO. He or she must be aware constantly that the aim is to transform the organization away from the traditional style of management to the Deming way. He or she must not only be involved in teaching the Deming philosophy, but must model leadership according to Deming's teachings. For Deming's teachings on leadership, see his most recent book.[2]

Another key to making the TQM transformation is an organization's team leaders. In addition to their other skills, they must be trained in the Deming philosophy and understand that a major part of their role as team leaders is to train and influence team members according to Deming's teachings. They also must be trained to realize that the new norms for employee attitudes and behavior must be modeled in PITs. Furthermore, team leaders must be trained to realize that one of the main ways PITs influence organizations is through their impact on DIT leaders and members. The aim of this influence is to get departments into the spirit and practice of the Deming philosophy, and this influence can be brought about only if every PIT member serves as a model of Deming's teachings for personnel in his or her department. Thus, PITs work hard to continuously improve things and make organizations more effective. But, beyond that, PITs must be agents that affect organizational culture. They do that by being a training ground for all employees in how to think and behave according to Deming's teachings.

One way to understand the role of PITs is to think of them as little organizations that practice Deming's teachings. Consider some of the ways PITs practice and model Deming's teachings. For instance, how do PITs practice Deming's point 1, constancy of purpose? One way is for each PIT to follow its opportunity statement which is its charter or aim provided by the quality council. Once a team knows its aim, it seeks to create constancy of purpose toward achieving that aim. Furthermore, team members learn to state the aim of any activity before they engage in it, whether it is coming to consensus on ground rules for meeting behavior, using a statistical tool, or gathering data. To see the common sense in Deming's point 1, consider how difficult it would be for team members to work together toward an aim if they had not first agreed on what their aim is. Through time, team members learn the power in constancy of purpose, and they will begin to practice it in other parts of their professional lives and even at home.

Next, consider how teams practice Deming's point 2, part of which is adopting a new philosophy toward competition. Teams strive to give up adversarial competition. They seek to learn what it means to be part of a team cooperating to accomplish a shared aim. They learn what it means to make decisions by consensus. Also, according to another part of Deming's point 2, they strive to adopt a new philosophy toward customers, striving always to see quality from the customer's point of view, whether the customer is internal or external. As to points 3 and 5, rather than relying on inspection, teams strive constantly and forever to improve the process that was chartered to them by the quality council.

Appendix A, "How Teams Can Practice and Model the Deming Philosophy," is a guide to team leaders and facilitators in how Deming's teachings relate to teams. Beyond the 14 points, team leaders and teams must model themselves on Deming's concept of profound knowledge. They must continually study profound knowledge and seek to apply it.[3]

# In What Subjects Should Teams Be Trained?

Before teams can successfully increase an organization's effectiveness, their members must be trained. Basically, they must be taught to practice Deming's teachings. In particular, they must learn new ways to make decisions, the importance of cooperation, and the use of statistics and consensus-building skills. Remember, to change an organization's culture is to change what people think is important and how they think things should be done.

## *Training in Decision Making*

One important part of team training is to get members to quit thinking it's okay to base decisions entirely on judgment. Members need to be trained to base decisions as much as possible on data. And, being able to base decisions on data requires understanding some simple statistical techniques. After all, that's what statistics is: techniques for gathering, analyzing, and displaying data. (The statistical tools required by teams are identified under "How to Train in Statistics and Consensus Tools" later in this chapter.) Basing decisions on data can be an important change for most team members. This change alone will increase greatly the effectiveness of any team.

Going one step further, however, many team members will believe basing decisions on data is the ultimate in decision making. And, there is no doubt this is a vast improvement over making decisions solely on judgment. But, the fact is there is a level of decision making beyond using judgment or data. It uses both judgment and data, but organizes them in a scientific way to make decisions. For beginners, however, it's enough to use data to support judgment in decision making. So, let's defer the subject of scientific decision making for the moment. Appendix B of this book deals in detail with the transformation of decision making, and the three approaches to decision making—judgmental, data-based, and scientific—are explained there.

### Training in Cooperation

There is another subject in which team members must be trained. They must learn to cooperate. Remember, we have been conditioned to compete by our experiences in school, sports, and organizations where the traditional style of management is practiced. We have been taught competition brings out the best in everyone. We need to be taught there's a better way. We need to understand there are some places where competition is appropriate, say in professional sports; but in most places, especially in organizations and on employee teams, it leads to disaster. As explained in chapter 3, the value of competition depends on whether it helps accomplish our aim. Usually, competition does nothing to help accomplish the aim; in fact, it almost always creates insurmountable barriers to accomplishing an aim. Fortunately, there are some easy ways to get team members, or anyone, into the spirit and practice of cooperation. It's through the use of consensus-building tools. These easy-to-use tools are identified next.

### Training in Statistics and Consensus-Building Tools

Training in basic statistics and consensus-building tools should be available to all members of teams, including leaders, facilitators, and SMEs of both PITs and DITS; but, this training should eventually include everyone on the payroll. Using these tools is part of the new culture.

## How Should Teams Be Trained?

An important question is how to get training in statistics and consensus building to everyone. A common way is to hire consultants to do it all. That way can work under certain conditions, but there is a less expensive alternative that works far better.

## *How to Train in Statistics and Consensus Tools*

Many CEOs are surprised to learn they have people on their payrolls who can provide training in statistics and consensus building. Employees with college degrees in such fields as engineering, business, psychology, sociology, nursing, and most sciences (such as biology, physics, and chemistry) know statistics because academic training in these fields includes statistics courses. Moreover, the statistical tools required for process improvement are not complicated. The most powerful of these tools are stratification, flow diagrams, and the Pareto principle; but there are other supportive tools, including cause-and-effect diagrams, histograms, run charts, and scatter diagrams. All these tools are simple. In fact, people who have academic training in statistics are overtrained to teach these tools because they know advanced statistics, such as analysis of variance, multiple regression, and log linear modeling. These advanced statistical tools are rarely required in quality improvement.

Candidate in-house statistics trainers should be asked to glance through two books, by Michael Brassard and Kaoru Ishikawa, that cover the statistical tools required of teams.[4] When they see how easy these tools are to use, they may ask for a short review course by an experienced applied statistician from a local college or organization. But, most employees who have an academic background in statistics and are interested in being statistics trainers will feel comfortable teaching these simple tools without any further training. Glancing through these two books, they'll see that the statistics they're being asked to teach are easy compared to the statistics they faced in college.

Perhaps the most demanding part of teaching the statistical tools for quality improvement is making them meaningful to the other employees who are trying to learn. This can be done best by providing exercises in which the tools are applied to realistic problems which employees will recognize. This means the instructor must know the organization and the local vernacular, or how to talk the language of the employees being trained. As an example of not knowing the local lingo, I saw a well-known industrial consultant bomb during a presentation on TQM to an Air Force audience when he referred to their enlisted ranks as *private* and *corporal*. These ranks do not exist in the Air Force, and the trainer's ignorance of the names of the enlisted ranks betrayed his overall ignorance of the Air Force. As a result, his effectiveness as a trainer was reduced to zero. The Air Force wasted the money it spent on this training, and he was never asked to work at the Air Force base again. In-house trainers are more likely than outsiders to know their own organization and its vernacular and, thus, are better able to provide realistic exercises and problems.

The same can be said of the consensus-building tools. Employees with backgrounds in psychology, sociology, organizational development, and some business fields often feel comfortable teaching consensus building without further training. They may wish to glance through some readings on this subject, such as Peter R. Scholtes, Charles A. Aubrey and Patricia K. Felkins, and some may want a short refresher course before they teach these materials.[5]

Although brainstorming is the most well-known consensus-building tool, the most useful such tool is NGT, and it is explained in *Group Techniques for Program Planning*.[6] There is what I regard as a more powerful way to use the original NGT which I call the *enhanced NGT* (ENGT). In any case, in the hands of a skilled facilitator, the ENGT is a flexible and powerful tool for consensus building. Often, but not always, team voting is required in consensus building. When used for consensus purposes, voting must not be democratic, majority wins, or Robert's Rules of Parliamentary Procedure because these approaches create winners and losers. There is an easy way to vote that leads to consensus without creating winners and losers. The use of the ENGT and this voting method are described in Appendix C.

Thus, a reasonable level of expertise in statistics and consensus-building tools can be developed by in-house trainers. I recommend four hour-long tools seminars on each of the following modules.

1. *Consensus-building techniques:* Specific content should include defining consensus, brainstorming, ENGT, team voting methods, and individual and team exercises.

2. *Flow diagrams:* When and how to use this tool, and individual and team exercises.

3. *Cause-and-effect diagrams:* When and how to use this tool, and individual and team exercises.

4. *Statistics 101:* Review of averages, variation, charts, graphs, sampling, data collection, simple experiments, and illustrations.

5. *Variation:* Content should include defining variation, run charts, control charts, and illustrations.

Each of these five modules should be taught on a regular basis, say once a month, so personnel destined for team assignments can attend the entire series for four hours each week for five weeks. Team leaders should take these seminars, but their training must be more extensive, as described in the next section. And, it is important that CEOs and their senior staff members take these seminars and incorporate these powerful tools into their day-to-day activities.

## How to Train Team Leaders

My recommendation for team leader training includes the seminars described in the previous section, but the most important part of team leaders' training takes place on teams. This training is conducted by a master facilitator.

Recall that I recommend starting with three PITs to achieve results CEOs can take to their boards and that will get employees up out of their foxholes. On these first three PITs, a master facilitator plays the role of trainer of the leaders assigned to the teams. Master facilitators are usually outside consultants. They need not be SMEs on the processes their teams are chartered to improve, but they must be masters of the Deming management philosophy and thoroughly understand the statistical tools, consensus building, the logic of PITs and DITs (as explained in chapter 7), and team improvement strategies (as explained in chapter 9). The aim of master facilitators is not only to guide teams in improving their chartered processes and in practicing and modeling the Deming philosophy, but also to train team leaders in these skills. Team leaders need to know much about the Deming philosophy, but they need not be masters in it. Becoming a master in the Deming philosophy takes years. Recall, Deming says "one need not be eminent in any part of profound knowledge in order to understand it and to apply it."[7]

Employees selected to be trained as team leaders are assigned to the first three PITs as understudies to a master facilitator. Two leaders are assigned to each team. Thus, these first teams have two leaders, SMEs, and the master facilitator. During the first few meetings, the master does most of the planning, team leading, and facilitation, with the understudies observing and learning. But, over a period of months, the master turns more and more of the team leading and facilitation over to the understudies. In the last few meetings that the facilitator is with a PIT, the facilitator plays the role of observer, coaching the understudies in strategy and evaluating their meeting-to-meeting management of the team. When the understudies are sufficiently trained, the facilitator drops off the team, but must be available to meet with the leaders to further their education and answer questions.

After the facilitator leaves a PIT, a new employee can be added to the team to serve as an understudy to the newly trained team leaders. Often SMEs on the first three teams express interest in team leading. This interest should be nurtured and accommodated. One of the trained team leaders takes over a newly formed PIT with one or two understudies on the team. The same is true for subsequent generations of understudies. As each one is trained, he or she spins off to another PIT to train others. It is thus that a cadre of experienced team leaders can be created.

*Formal Team Leader Training.* In its purest form, team leader training team leader in succession violates rule 4 of Deming's funnel experiment in the same way a secret gets distorted in the parlor game where people sit around in a big circle and whisper a secret to one another.[8] The secret is whispered to the person at one end of the circle, and that person whispers it to the next person, and that person whispers it to the next person, and so on. When the last person to hear the secret tells what it is, everyone is amazed that the secret is nothing like it was when whispered to the first person. Similarly, when leader trains leader, the training downstream is nothing like the initial training.

In training team leaders, care must be taken to avoid violating rule 4 of the funnel experiment. All understudy team leaders must undergo uniform training and periodic upgrade training from a master facilitator. In addition, the master must be available to team leaders for consultation, and the master must frequently participate on every team.

I conduct a team leader course called the PIT/DIT Leader Training Seminar. The prerequisite for each attendee is solid familiarity with Deming's teachings, and the material covered includes the following:

- An overview of Deming's profound knowledge
- The infrastructure for improvement (membership and responsibilities of the quality council, PITs, and DITs)
- How to find a process to improve (including chartering by the quality council with an opportunity statement and block diagram as well as other methods of finding a process to improve)
- How to organize a team that knows the process (how to select SMEs and SME roles and responsibilities, and how to plan and conduct initial and subsequent team meetings)
- Team strategies for process improvement (discussed in chapter 9)
- An overview of the basic statistical tools (flow diagrams, cause-and-effect diagrams and tables, Pareto principle and

charts, stratification, scatter diagrams, correlation, check
sheets, histograms, and run charts)

- Consensus building (brainstorming and ENGT)
- Group behavior and dynamics (principles of human behavior,
  conflict resolution, situational leadership, interactive behavior,
  dysfunctional behavior, and team building)
- The Deming plan-do-study-act (PDSA) cycle for building
  knowledge before implementing improvements
- PIT- and DIT-related exercises to be done individually and in
  groups of two and five persons

I sometimes find it useful to structure this training around a version of
the FOCUS-PDSA improvement strategy developed by the Hospital
Corporation of America.[9] The acronym FOCUS stands for *find* a process to improve, *organize* a team that is familiar with that process, *clarify* the process, *understand* sources of variation in the process, and *select*
an opportunity for improvement. PDSA, of course, is the Walter A.
Shewhart or Deming cycle, explained as part of Appendix B.

# Training for Management

It is important that management be trained in the Deming philosophy
and in the TQM tools and team strategies. Managers must understand
what they are asking their subordinates to do. They must attend every
training session they ask their subordinates to attend. They must
understand the materials taught so well that they can teach them and
answer questions about them. For instance, they must be able to
answer, without hesitation, any question about Deming's teachings,
from the 14 points, to tampering, to the ins and outs of profound
knowledge. They must know the four kinds of flow diagrams, the
Ishikawa diagram and table, which three tools are used most often by
teams, the three team strategies, the dangers of tasking, and who went
to Japan first, Deming or Juran. They must have so much TQM knowledge they can have fun with trivia questions about it.

Here is a warning to CEOs who would embark on the TQM journey without sufficient knowledge. It is often the case that CEOs fail to
understand enough about the Deming philosophy and the TQM tools
and strategies. They believe a superficial knowledge of these materials
for themselves and a strong training program for their subordinates is
sufficient. They believe the mere fact that they have empowered their
subordinates with TQM is sufficient. They believe their responsibility
is to get TQM training going and bless and exhort the undertaking at
employee gatherings. Aside from that, they devote their time to other

important business issues—whether that's fighting fires, romancing the board of directors, or scouting for new business opportunities—and just let TQM happen. This approach always leads to CEO blunders, leads to CEOs not intervening when they should (especially about taskings, as explained in chapter 10), adds unnecessarily to the cost of TQM, and causes serious delays in TQM implementation.

## Moving Forward

As leaders complete their initial training, their teams get underway. Training makes it possible for teams to bring about effectiveness gains by improving cross-functional processes. They learn how to tear out of processes the waste, abuses, delays, redundancies, and duplication that have so long kept costs high and customers dissatisfied. If these achievements are not brought about on a large scale, many organizations eventually drown in a sea of financial trouble. In addition to their life-saving process improvement activities, teams have a second aim: to help change their organization's culture.

To accomplish both of these much needed aims, what specifically do teams do? What are the strategies by which they achieve their two aims? The next chapter provides the answers to these questions.

## Notes

1. W. Edwards Deming, *The New Economics for Industry, Government, and Education* (Cambridge, Mass.: MIT Press, 1993), p. 111.

2. Ibid., chapters 5 and 6.

3. Ibid., chapter 4.

4. Michael Brassard, ed., *The Memory Jogger: A Pocket Guide of Tools for Continuous Improvement* (Methuen, Mass.: GOAL/QPC, 1988); and Kaoru Ishikawa, *Guide to Quality Control* (Tokyo: Asian Productivity Organization, 1982).

5. Peter R. Scholtes, *The Team Handbook: How to Use Teams to Improve Quality* (Madison, Wis.: Joiner Associates, 1988); and Charles A. Aubrey and Patricia K. Felkins, *Teamwork: Involving People in Quality and Productivity Improvement* (Milwaukee, Wis.: ASQC Quality Press, 1988).

6. Andre L. Delbecq, Andrew H. Van de Ven, and David H. Gustafson, *Group Techniques for Program Planning: A Guide to Nominal Group and Delphi Processes* (Middleton, Wis.: Green Briar Press, 1986); and Charles N. Weaver, *TQM: A Step-by-Step Guide to Implementation* (Milwaukee, Wis.: ASQC Quality Press, 1991).

7. Deming, *The New Economics*, p. 96.

8. Ibid., chapter 9 and p. 202.

9. Executive Learning, *Continual Improvement Handbook: A Quick Reference Guide for Tools and Concepts. Healthcare Version* (Brentwood, Tenn.: Executive Learning, 1993).

# The Process Improvement Stage: Team Activities and Strategies

Once teams get past introductions, team building, and training, three basic activities occur: meeting management, changing team culture, and process improvement strategies.

## Team Meeting Management

Meeting management begins when a facilitator and leader meet privately for 15 minutes before each team meeting. Here the facilitator and the leader finalize their plans for what will take place at the team meeting. They review the agenda and agree on the aims of the meeting. They agree on how each of the planned activities of the meeting will carry the team toward the accomplishment of its aim, or opportunity statement. They agree on who will do what on the agenda. For teams that operate without facilitators, leaders must think these questions out alone before meetings start.

Team leaders begin meetings by asking a SME to read the team's aim, or opportunity statement. Next, they assign to SMEs the roles of timekeeper and recorder; do any necessary team building and training; review the minutes from the last meeting; and begin working through the agenda. As meetings come to an end, they assign homework to SMEs and conduct meeting evaluations. Facilitators monitor the progress of meetings and intervene as appropriate in issues of strategy, tool selection, and group dynamics.

Facilitators and leaders meet for another 15 minutes after each meeting to evaluate how well things went, to make course corrections, and to finalize agendas for the next meetings. Because facilitators have by far the most team experience, they should make constructive recommendations on how leaders can improve their team skills and how they can model Deming's teachings. There are several good references on team meeting management, including Scholtes.[1]

# Changing Team Culture

Team activities should be designed to change the thinking (culture) of team members about how things are to be done and what's important. According to this approach, each chartered PIT, and each DIT as it gradually develops, is a training ground for members in how the Deming philosophy works. In other words,

> *The operation of each team is a continuing example of how organizations of any size should work according to the Deming management philosophy.*

To help affect how teams do things and what their members think, formal training should be provided for them. This training should involve presentations by leaders and facilitators, and the materials to be taught depend on a team's stage of development. Sometimes training needs to start with the basics, especially if members have not seen presentations by the quality council on Deming's teachings. The basics are Deming's 14 points, obstacles and deadly diseases, and profound knowledge. It is always beneficial to have ongoing team training in Deming's teachings. However, as training in Deming's teachings continues, other presentations should be made on the statistical tools, consensus building, and the use of the PDSA cycle in scientific decision making, explained in Appendix B.

The most important kind of training for every member occurs as teams faithfully follow Deming's teachings in the way they conduct their business. Many team members either cannot learn or are not motivated to learn about Deming's way from lectures, videotapes, or books. For them, team activities are the best opportunity to learn Deming's teachings.

At every team meeting, members see the Deming philosophy in action. They learn the importance of cooperation and patience. They learn there is no one best way, as teams improve processes endlessly. They learn how their departments are components of a larger system—the organization. They understand that their departments are evaluated on the basis of their contribution to the larger system. They see the 14 points in action. They see teams work to counteract the deadly diseases and obstacles. They see profound knowledge in action.

Doing things Deming's way comes naturally for many people, and it gets to be a habit. With time, team members will incorporate more and more of Deming's way into their individual jobs. And, as PITs task DITs to carry out various improvements and act as their program managers on those improvements, department managers and their subordinates also get exposure to how things are done Deming's way. In their involvement on PITs and DITs, members get a strong message that things are being done differently. They see that the organization is serious about its commitment to Deming's teachings.

## Process Improvement Strategies

Knowing how to manage teams and change their culture is important, but it is another thing entirely to know the strategies by which teams improve processes and, thereby, bring about increased organizational effectiveness. Team leaders can be taught all the statistical tools, and they can know all about group dynamics. But, unless they have a good working knowledge of the three strategies for process improvement, their teams are certain to flounder.

*Floundering* is a word that strikes terror into the hearts of team leaders and facilitators. Floundering occurs like this. A team is following every teaching in the team handbooks. Every member is actively playing his or her assigned role. Every member is cooperating. Every member is motivated and enthusiastic about making some real improvement in the assigned process. Everyone is doing his or her best. Yet, after all the preliminaries are over, after all the introductions have been made, after all the team building has been done, after all the training in the Deming philosophy has been done, a silence falls upon the meeting. This silence may occur during the third meeting or after three months of meetings. Members look at each other, and then they look at the leader who, in turn, looks at the facilitator. The facilitator swallows hard and feels sweat trickling down the middle of his or her back. The facilitator looks down at the agenda and realizes the team is going in circles. Months of time and expense have gone into the team's efforts, and nothing has come of it. Furthermore, in the deadly silence, no one seems to know how to get the team back on the right track. When this happens, a team is floundering.

It is tragic that so much floundering occurs. Floundering is an embarrassment to everyone on a team and a waste of an organization's resources. The reason there is so much floundering—most of it unknown to management—is that while there is a significant body of literature on how to manage teams and on the improvement tools, there is little to nothing in books and magazines about the *strategies* teams follow to bring about improvements. And, sadly, much of the sparse literature on team strategies is misleading or incorrect.

The cause for the misleading and incorrect nature of what is in print on team strategies may be that most of the writers on the subject haven't spent the thousands of hours on teams to know which strategies work. And, those who know what works don't write books and articles. Sadly, much of what is written about teams is based on the psychological literature written as early as the 1950s or on questionnaire or interview results. Information based on these sources is of no value for teams operating in a culture based on Deming's teachings for one simple and obvious reason. With rare exceptions, this information is designed for teams operating under the traditional style of management. Learning from these materials does more harm than good because they teach how teams work in the old culture. Using these materials merely perpetuates the traditional style of management—just what we want to get away from. Such materials should be stripped from organizations' bookshelves.

Deming has provided all the knowledge needed to make teams successful. Team leaders who don't understand how his teachings apply to teams cannot expect to achieve much success. Management may claim success for its teams operated in the traditional way based on effectiveness gains. But, compared with what they could achieve if they operated under the guidance of Deming's teachings, such teams flounder needlessly, are much slower in achieving results, and their results are not as good. Worst of all, they have no effect whatsoever on the second important component of organizational development—culture change. Remember the second law of organizational development.

> *Unless provided with the appropriate cultural support, effectiveness gains eventually get washed out.*

All of Deming's teachings apply to teams, but three of Deming's 14 points are the foundation of the basic strategies teams use to improve processes. These are point 5, "Improve constantly and forever the system of production and service"; point 2, "Adopt a new philosophy," a key portion of which is "The customer defines quality"; and point 4, "Don't deal with suppliers on price tag alone." The application of these strategies varies somewhat depending on whether a team is a PIT or a DIT, and this variation is explained here.

### Team Improvement Strategy 1: Improve Constantly and Forever

The most commonly used process improvement strategy for both PITs and DITs is based on Deming's point 5 in which he teaches to "Improve constantly and forever the system of production and service."

In *Out of the Crisis,* Deming says any process can be flow diagramed to show how the work is divided into stages. A flow diagram is an easy-to-use statistical tool that uses geometric symbols written on paper to describe the detailed steps in a process. The symbols include ovals for the steps that begin and end processes, rectangles for actions or operations, diamonds for decision points, bullets (or *D*s) for delays, and arrows for the direction of a process flow. There are many books on flow diagraming. For an overview of the method, see Scholtes or Brassard; but for a comprehensive explanation, see Harrington.[2]

*How This Strategy Works.* PITs receive their charters from quality councils in the form of opportunity statements. Opportunity statements must include information about the intended aim of the process targeted for improvement. Once teams complete the preliminaries of getting started, SMEs flow diagram the sections of the cross-functional process for which each is an expert. The aim of flow diagraming is to build knowledge about how processes work, not as teams would like them to work or how they are supposed to work as described in procedure manuals. Once team members understand how a process actually works, they are in a position to assess whether the process is accomplishing its aim. If it's not, the team can begin to consider improvements that will make the achievement possible. If the aim is being accomplished, the team can begin to look at other important features of the process, such as reducing its costs.

In flow diagraming processes, teams usually stay within the boundaries of processes as described in the block diagrams provided by quality councils. But, SMEs are almost always more expert than members of quality councils in how processes work. This is because council members are far removed from most horizontal processes. They may have a vague idea of how processes work, but they rarely have detailed knowledge. It is not uncommon, therefore, for PITs to go back to councils with recommendations that their charters be revised, usually with different boundaries. Wise quality councils are receptive to such recommendations.

*Senior Managers Are Unaware of Process Problems.* I recommend that senior managers be selected to lead the first PITs. When they do so, they are astonished to see that processes that go through their areas of responsibility work so differently from how they thought. Although the senior managers never plan or directly manage these processes, they are astonished that the processes work so poorly. They wonder privately how the organization survived all these years with these key processes working so poorly.

Of course, senior managers are not to blame for the broken-down condition of their cross-functional processes, even though these processes are their responsibility. They were merely practicing the prevailing style of management, managing organizations as if they were hierarchies of largely unrelated vertical activities where these vertical activities, or departments, were managed with MBO. They were taught the management myth that the whole is equal to the sum of its parts. In organizational terms, they were taught that if each department is managed properly, usually with MBO, the entire organization will work well. Of course, this view fails to take into account the interaction between departments. These interactions are the cross-functional processes that PITs seek to understand and improve. The fact is that most organizations prosper or go belly-up based on how well their cross-functional processes work. The exceptions are organizations that are lucky or have monopolies. In any case, for many senior managers, serving as PIT leaders is an eye-opening experience that accelerates their transformation away from the traditional style of management.

As PITs flow diagram cross-functional processes, they discover many opportunities for improvement. For instance, they find machines that don't work as well as they should. They find unnecessary and redundant steps. They find duplicate copies being saved for no reason. They find needless inspection. They find unnecessary inventories. They find barriers and obstacles that prevent employees from taking pride in their work. They find departments following MBO or operating as profit centers with the result of severely suboptimizing the organization.

As they flow diagram processes, SMEs must feel free to "tell it like it is," to point out all the inappropriate things that go on in processes. Make no mistake, countless inappropriate things go on in processes, and SMEs know about them. They have put up with them every day for years. These things have kept them and their coworkers from doing the kind of work of which they could be proud. But, whether team leaders realize it or not, many SMEs are afraid to identify problem areas. They worry the team leader will say, "Why didn't you report this earlier?" or "So you're the person who broke that machine!" Or, they may worry they'll get a coworker in trouble.

To the extent that fear exists on teams, improvement opportunities will not be identified, teams will not be as successful as they could be, and organizations will suffer from not having these needed improvements made. Thus, every effort must be made by team leaders to practice Deming's point 8, drive out fear.

*The Need to Build Knowledge.* Outsiders often remark that it must be difficult for PITs to find something to improve. Actually, finding opportunities for improvement is easy, but it requires a very different perspective. To acquire this perspective, teams should *not* be trained to concentrate on finding opportunities for improvements. This sounds strange because it's contrary to the culture of traditional organizations which encourages fast results. But, it's true nonetheless. Instead of desperately racing to find something to improve, teams should concentrate on *building knowledge* of how their assigned process works. Therefore, team members must be taught patience. They must be taught that if they will commit the time to building knowledge of how a process works, the opportunities for improving it will eventually flow forth.

There is a connection between building knowledge of how processes work and finding opportunities to improve them. I call this connection the *iron law of process improvement.*

> *When a team sees no opportunity for improvement of a process, it is* always *because they have failed to build sufficient knowledge of how it works.*

Unfortunately, this law is unknown to most team trainers, and it is, therefore, the source of much floundering.

Improvement opportunities come from knowledge, not from someone's judgment or from the use of a statistical tool. Judgment and statistical tools play important roles in the improvement processes. But team members should be taught that the role of judgment is to be a source of hypotheses about the causes of process problems that must be tested with data. Statistical tools should be taught as ways to build knowledge of how processes work. Teams should be taught that when they want to improve a process, they need to first build knowledge of how it works. Improvement comes from knowledge. The decision-making style based on building knowledge is explained in Appendix B.

There is an important side benefit to teaching teams to focus on building knowledge of how their process works rather than on desperately racing to improve it. Remember, team members come from our culture where there is great impatience for results. They hunger for accomplishments and like to chalk up a deed at every team meeting. Otherwise, they feel they wasted their time. But, if they accept that the aim of their PIT is to build knowledge of how their process works, rather than immediately improving the process, their hunger for results is easier to satisfy. Their hunger is satisfied every time knowledge of how their process works is built, and this happens at virtually

every meeting. Leaders should stress how knowledge was built when-
ever it is. With this aim, members will feel satisfied with a meeting
if the team used the time to build knowledge. Before long, enough
knowledge will be built so that identifying improvement opportunities
comes easy and fast enough to satisfy even the most impatient team
member.

*The Need to Focus on Improvement Opportunities.* Incidentally, it
is better to refer to barriers and obstacles in processes as *improvement
opportunities,* not *problems.* While it is true that barriers and obstacles
are problems, calling them problems is reminiscent of the old culture.
If this sounds like splitting hairs, consider this reasoning.

In the traditional style of management, barriers and obstacles are
called *problems,* and the word *problem* carries the idea that someone is
to blame and we need to find that person for punishment. In fact, there
is an interesting team exercise that supports this interpretation. A
facilitator identifies an organizational problem familiar to the team
and asks team members to think about it. They are asked to take two
minutes to imagine the source of the problem. They are then asked to
write down the *source* of the problem. Most of them will describe a
person. They will describe someone like a certain associate administrator, the director of the computer center, or some technician supervisor. We all tend to associate problems with people. Of course, the fact
is that problems are in processes, not in people.

We hear the word *problem* used all the time in traditional organizations, and we associate with it blame, guilt, and fear. If your boss takes
you aside and says, "Look, I think we've got a problem. Please see me
in my office this afternoon," your blood pressure will go up, and
sweat will pop out on your forehead. You'll think about what you
might have done wrong. You'll think about your job security and
whether you can get a job somewhere else. On the other hand, if your
boss says, "I don't have a problem with that," you feel a sense of relief,
even relaxation. This is the impact of the word *problem.* To have a better organizational culture, we don't want employees to react in fear.
We need to quit blaming people; problems are in processes. We need
to realize that people are doing their jobs as well as they can under the
prevailing style of management.

In the new culture, there is no place for managers who crush their
subordinates with remarks like "I've got a problem with what you
did." Such remarks are confessions of the ignorance of those who
make them. Those who make such remarks need to be taught the
ruinous effects of the traditional style of management and the need to
adopt a new philosophy.

On the other hand, to refer to barriers and obstacles as *improvement opportunities* creates a positive attitude. Rather than leading us to think about blame and punishment, these words create positive energy to do something—to make more improvements. Suppose your boss has been trained to think this way. He or she comes to you with a statement such as "Look, I've got some data here that suggest we have an opportunity to reduce the cost and increase service on the Looper account. Get your flow diagrams of the Looper processes, and let's get together this afternoon in my office." You would see your boss trying to base decisions on data. You would feel good that the two of you were going to work on the Looper processes as colleagues, not as boss and underling. And, you would feel good about the challenge of an improvement opportunity. You want to do a good job, and you would see this as a chance to improve things and make it easier to do a good job. These remarks from your boss would not make you feel that you were being blamed for problems on the Looper account. Your boss's remarks would not make you feel that your job was on the line, nor would they make you fearful.

As PITs build knowledge by flow diagraming, they encounter a long series of improvement opportunities. "This part here takes too long, that step there is unnecessary, this over here shouldn't be done that way, and that piece there never worked right in the first place." As these opportunities are identified, they are passed off as written "taskings" to the managers of the departments where they exist, according to the procedure explained in chapter 7. These departments take taskings from PITs and carry out the improvements identified. Tasking is an important part of cultural transformation, and it is discussed in chapter 10.

***How to Make Improvements Identified in Flow Diagraming.*** As PITs flow diagram processes, they always face a certain decision. This decision is: Should improvements be made in the order in which they are identified in flow diagraming, or should the entire flow diagram be completed before improvements are selected for action? There are good reasons to make improvements either way. The correct approach depends on the situation.

The argument against making improvements as they are identified is that the first opportunities identified may not be the most important ones. Improving these can result in personnel spending costly time working on comparably unimportant issues. According to this view, it is better to flow diagram an entire process and then go back to prioritize the improvement opportunities that were identified. This ensures that the most important problems in a process are worked first or, said a better way, it ensures that the most promising improvement opportunities are worked first.

The argument for making improvements as opportunities are identified is this. Flow diagraming the details of large or complex processes can take months, sometimes years. For instance, how long does it take to flow diagram a major part of the contracting process at an automobile assembly plant? Through these long times, some PIT leaders, facilitators, and SMEs are almost certain to leave teams for various reasons, and some team members may forget what happened months ago in flow diagraming. They may lose memory on the importance or unimportance of improvement opportunities identified in their flow diagram. Despite taking careful minutes during meetings, PITs can fail to maintain sufficient corporate memory to later correctly prioritize the improvement opportunities identified as they flow diagramed a large or complex process. According to this view, it is better to work on improvement opportunities as they occur, and to use SME judgment to establish their priorities; that is, to know whether an improvement opportunity is important enough to work on now or to defer.

There is a compromise between these two alternative ways to build knowledge to get to action in flow diagraming. Here's how it works. All processes are made up of smaller processes. Therefore, stratify large or complex processes into the smaller, discrete processes that make them up, and prioritize them. Then, take the most important smaller process and flow diagram it. Prioritize the improvement opportunities that result, and work them in order of importance. Then, return for the second most important process in the large or complex process, and flow diagram it, and so on.

Consider an illustration. One large and complex process in hospitals is providing meal trays to patients. The overall dietary process involves three parts, each of which is a sizable process in itself: ordering, preparing, and delivering patient meal trays. Rather than flow diagraming all three parts, a team could begin by breaking off what it regards as the most important piece, say delivering meal trays, and flow diagram it first. They then prioritize the improvement opportunities that result from that flow diagram, and work them off in order of importance. Then, the team members go back to pick up the second most important piece, say ordering meal trays, and flow diagram that process, and so on.

There is another opinion about how to build knowledge to make improvements with flow diagrams. According to this view, a process should always be flow diagramed starting at the head of the stream, in other words, where the process begins. (In our dietary example, in the preceding paragraph, this would be when a diet plan is ordered for a patient by a physician.) This view continues by suggesting that improvements should be made as they are identified, beginning at the head of the stream. The reasoning is that the worst problems in processes are virtually always upstream. In the few cases where this is not true, it makes little sense to improve something downstream first because later improvements upstream will usually make their revision necessary anyway.

*How DITs Use This Strategy.* How do DITs use Strategy 1? The answer is, they use it in much the same way that PITs use it.

It is important to realize that PITs and DITs are virtually identical, except for the level in the organization where they operate. The difference is that PITs deal with processes that cross departments, or functional boundaries, while DITs deal with processes that cross units, usually sections, within a department. Both have members from the organizational elements their processes cross: PIT members come from departments, and DIT members come from sections. But, both improve processes with the same strategies and tools. The success of both is based on the knowledge of their SMEs. Both use the improve constantly and forever strategy to flow diagram processes they wish to improve as a means of building knowledge about them. For both, having knowledge of how processes work leads to the identification of improvement opportunities.

When it comes time to task off an improvement opportunity identified by a DIT, who takes the taskings? Who makes the improvements? If a team is a PIT, taskings go to DITs. If a team is a DIT, as in this case, taskings go to sections. Sections are the organizational units within departments through which targeted processes flow. There are liaison SMEs from each section on DITs. To take this logic a step farther, in sections there are subDITs that have the same relationship to DITs that DITs have to PITs. Occasionally, however, a DIT will establish a subDIT, or task team, composed of personnel from several sections who are tasked to carry out an improvement of interest to the sections they represent. Supervisors of the concerned sections must be kept informed of their activities. Between DITs and subDITs, the formality of written taskings is necessary because it establishes a documentation trail of improvement activities. Tasking is explained in chapter 10.

*A Sure Sign of Poor Training in Improvement Strategy.* There is a sure sign that department managers have been poorly trained in the quality improvement philosophy and have only superficial knowledge of Deming's teachings. When an improvement effort is underway, this sign is revealed in a department manager's instructions to subordinates that they are not to worry about things "beyond their control." This mistake is often made in the following words by a department manager: "Understand this. We'll work hard to improve what goes on here in our department, but let those in the other departments take care of their own problems." Sometimes this view is expressed as "We need to clean our own house before we start talking about the other guy's dirty house."

Any manager who makes such statements is totally ignorant of the basic elements of organizational quality. Such statements are nothing more than a manifestation of the traditional style of management which we are trying to change. Not worrying about what is "beyond our control" is like so many other beliefs in the traditional style of management. It sounds so right, but it is entirely wrong! Pure nonsense! Managers who make such statements assume organizations are equal to the sum of their parts. They assume if every department does its job, usually with MBO, things will go well for the organization as a whole. Nothing could be farther from the truth! What about the interactions between departments? What about the way departments must work horizontally with each other, through processes?

The first step to improving critical interactions between departments is to teach everyone how dependent departments are on each other. Contrary to the thinking of traditional managers, as exemplified in the view that "We won't worry about what's not under our control," every person in a department must be responsible for departments upstream of him- or herself because what goes on there affects quality downstream. In other words, "You can't get your house clean unless the person upstream gets his or her house clean first." Furthermore, every person in a department is responsible for downstream departments, too, because the quality of his or her own department upstream affects quality downstream. In other words, "The person downstream can't get his or her house clean if I leave mine dirty." Talking about processes as being upstream and downstream is good if it helps people understand that what happens upstream always floats downstream.

The improve constantly and forever strategy identifies every barrier and obstacle in the flow diagram of a targeted process, regardless of how small. Some say it gets the "nits and gnats." Its disadvantage, however, is that flow diagraming a large process can take time. And, for organizations on the brink of financial disaster, a lot of time is not available.

Two other strategies operate more quickly to get at the major barriers and obstacles in cross-functional processes. Their main advantage is they take far less time; but, they don't immediately identify every nit and gnat in processes. They go after the biggest problems first, the rogue elephants, and defer the smaller stuff. These strategies are ideal for organizations teetering on the brink of financial disaster. More organizations are in this category than their CEOs often know or are willing to admit. These organizations must get their costs down and eliminate the most serious process barriers to quality as soon as possible. They always can go back later and work off the smaller barriers.

Don't look for these strategies for faster process improvement in the tool boxes of traditional managers. They aren't there. Traditional managers don't think about cross-functional processes. The names of these quicker acting TQM strategies are *the customer defines quality* and *the tyranny of the supplier.*

## Team Improvement Strategy 2: The Customer Defines Quality

Deming teaches us to adopt a new philosophy, including realizing that the customer defines quality. But, the traditional style of management requires everyone to please his or her immediate boss. After all, it's your boss who decides whether you get a salary increase, promotion, or letter of commendation. Therefore, we all feel pressure to please the boss, to stay within our budgets, and not to worry about other departments located somewhere far off in the organization.

Some CEOs formalize this as MBO. In any case, we're all inclined to say, "Other people's problems are their lookout, not mine. I've got my hands full just trying to do what my boss requires of me." The customer defines quality strategy is designed to change this kind of harmful thinking. It is designed to begin the improvement of processes and bring employees around to a new way of thinking.

*How This Strategy Works.* For purposes of explaining how the customer defines quality strategy works, let's focus on a department where improvements are sought. This department is an internal supplier to other internal departments, its customers, all downstream of it. We will call this supplier department the *target department,* and let's assume it has a DIT in operation.

First, the team leader gets DIT members to agree on a definition of the term *customer.* To do this, members discuss the question What is a customer? and come to consensus on a definition. A good definition is suggested by Juran as ". . . anyone who receives or is affected by the product or process. . . ."[3] of a target department.

Second, the team leader uses brainstorming or the ENGT to get DIT members to develop a list of their customers. This can be done with a simple question, Who are the customers of our department? This question will stir up a lively discussion because many members will be reluctant to accept downstream departments as customers. They're used to seeing their department manager as their customer. So, this discussion will take some time. But, time must be allowed because it will begin to change attitudes about the importance of downstream customers. In my earlier book, I explained how to use the NGT to identify customers.[4]

The third step is for DIT members to prioritize their list of customers. All customers are important and deserve to be treated well. But improvement has to start somewhere, and it might as well be on behalf of the target department's most important customers. To prioritize, DITs must agree on the criteria to be used to decide which customers are most important. Many criteria are available for this purpose. Among the best is to rank customers on the basis of percentage of the target department's output, products and services, that goes to them. The highest volume customer is ranked first, the second highest volume customer is ranked second, and so on. DIT members may suggest better criteria. (Incidentally, prioritizing any list, including customers, may be done easily with the voting method explained in Appendix C.)

After customers have been prioritized, the fourth step is to take them one-by-one, in order of their importance, and ask what they want from the target department. Here, the leader poses for DIT members the following question: Exactly what do our downstream customers want us to do for them? You would think supplier departments would know what their customers want; but, remember, they've been looking for years to their bosses for guidance on what to do. And, CEOs may have had them competing with their internal customers' departments, so they don't see these departments' members as people they would want to help in the first place. In fact, according to the sports mentality, they want to try to keep other departments from scoring.

To help identify the needs of downstream departments, personnel from these departments can be invited to DIT meetings and asked to explain what they want. But, first, consider a word of caution about doing this. If the CEO has been pitting these departments against one another, there can be some tense moments when these rivals first sit down across a table from each other. It should be thoroughly explained to them beforehand that these meetings are opportunities to begin to break down barriers. They should be reminded of Deming's point 9, which deals with this subject.

Other ways to get information on the needs of downstream customers include interviews and questionnaires. Also, employees of target departments can take turns working for a period of time, perhaps as long as several months, in customer departments to get a better understanding of their needs.

Once downstream customer departments have been identified and their requirements determined, the fifth step is to find ways to measure how well the target department is meeting its customer's requirements. For an explanation of how to develop such measures or indicators, see Weaver and Harrington. The sixth step is to see what can be done to improve on these measures. This should involve flow diagraming and improving the processes in the target department that produce the output required by downstream customers. Another statistical tool often used to identify opportunities for improvement is the cause-and-effect diagram. In this approach, a measure developed in step 5 of how well the target department is meeting its customer's requirements is used as the effect in a cause-and-effect diagram. This effect's causes are identified, prioritized, and influenced by target department DITs, as needed. For an overview of cause-and-effect diagrams, see Brassard. For a detailed explanation, see Ishikawa.[5]

***An Example of the Customer Defines Quality Strategy.*** Consider an example of how one department used the customer defines quality strategy to improve its effectiveness. In this case, the target department was a sales department. The DIT in this sales department identified its highest priority downstream internal customer as the business office. This choice came as a result of education for the SMEs of the sales department DIT because they used to think of their customers as only the people who walked in off the street to buy something. In any case, the DIT learned that the business office had a requirement to receive information on the addresses of credit customers. The measure of this requirement was the frequency with which the business office was delayed in mailing statements to credit customers because the sales department's billing addresses were incomplete or inaccurate. The exact measure was computed at the end of every month as follows: number of billing addresses complete and correct divided by number of billing addresses provided by the sales department multiplied by 100. The larger this percentage, the better.

The sales department used the percentage of correct billing addresses as a measure [called a *key result area* (KRA) or *key quality characteristic* (KQC)] of its effectiveness in providing correct billing information to the business office. Improvement opportunities in the sales department's processes for collecting and transmitting billing addresses were identified with flow and cause-and-effect diagrams. Many opportunities for improvement were identified. Some part-time sales staff had not been trained to get zip codes. Some did not have access to zip code directories. Carbon paper bought at the lowest price was not making clear copies of orders, and it was these copies that were sent to the business office. And, occasionally, the pouch mail system delivered mail from the sales department to the wrong internal address. In any case, as this process was improved by the sales department DIT, the percentage of correct addresses slowly went up.

Improving the customer address collection and distribution process was, as one impatient sales department DIT SME said, painstakingly slow work. But as fewer statements were delayed in being mailed out by the business office because of incorrect or incomplete addresses, customer bills got paid sooner. And, through time, work by the sales department and a DIT in the business office itself increased the organization's cash flow gradually to higher and higher levels.

*How Do PITs Use This Strategy?* The discussion thus far has explained how the customer defines quality strategy is used by DITs. What if a team is a PIT? How do PITs use this strategy?

PITs use the customer defines quality strategy less often than DITs, but they can use it successfully. Remember, PITs have members who are SMEs from every department in their cross-functional process, from upstream departments to downstream departments. And, remember, too, PIT SMEs are liaisons to their department managers, and DITs gradually develop in each of those departments.

There are several ways PITs can use the customer defines quality strategy. One is when the DITs in the departments in the cross-functional process have matured to the point that they are searching for improvement opportunities. Remember that in addition to bringing about improvement in their assigned processes, an aim of PITs is to help departments undergo transformation away from the traditional style of management. This aim is to get departments to abandon the philosophy of the one best way and become believers in continuous improvement. When this happens, department personnel are no longer defensive and worried that they will be punished because someone found a problem in their area. On the contrary, they will be actively searching for improvement opportunities. They will welcome anyone bringing a problem to their attention because they see problems as opportunities to get better. Thus, when DITs are in place and are searching for improvement opportunities they welcome taskings from PITs about how to improve things.

Now let's be specific about how the customer defines quality strategy works for PITs when DITs are already in place in each department. First, a DIT liaison SME gets a homework assignment from the PIT. The homework is to get with the department manager (the DIT leader) to whom the SME is the liaison. The DIT is tasked to accomplish each of the six strategic steps outlined under "How This Strategy Works" earlier in this chapter. The PIT should communicate to the DIT its willingness to provide technical assistance and help ensure management support with any of the steps. The PIT leader should ask for periodic progress reports through the DIT liaison SME. In rare cases, a PIT leader may need to discuss lack of progress on the steps with a DIT leader.

Another way PITs use the customer defines quality strategy is to carry out the six steps for each department in the cross-functional process during PIT meetings. To accomplish this, the SMEs from each upstream and downstream department work together during PIT meetings to develop the information required in each step for each department. Some department managers (DIT leaders) may wish to attend PIT meetings when steps relevant to their department are discussed. These meetings can be a powerful vehicle for breaking down barriers between departments. The meetings work best when department managers have worked themselves away from the traditional style of management, to the point that they are enthusiastic about continuous improvement.

*Resistance to This Strategy.* There are at least two levels of resistance among departmental personnel to the customer defines quality strategy. The first, as mentioned, is their initial hesitation about recognizing downstream departments as customers. Under the traditional style of management, they ignored these departments or competed with them. They were taught to make their immediate bosses happy and not worry about other departments. They were taught to stay within their budgets despite the fact that doing so denies needed support to other departments and prevents them from doing their best. When this happens, it suboptimizes an entire organization. There may be middle managers, and even senior managers, who are resistant to seeing downstream departments as customers. They represent serious barriers to the success of TQM and need training.

A second level of resistance to the customer defines quality strategy can occur after downstream departments have been accepted by a target department as customers. At this point, it is common for target department personnel to become fearful because they realize they've been ignoring the requirements of their internal customers for years. They realize this has caused unnecessary trouble for these departments and great loss to the organization. Some may experience intense embarrassment or even shame over it. Some may see it as a slap in the face to have to have a PIT teaching them what they should have known all along—that serving their internal customers is vital to the success of the organization. They may wonder what they could have been thinking to have ignored this part of their job for so long. Others will be fearful that management will blame them for this serious oversight and that they will be singled out for punishment. Of course, the fact is they've been doing their jobs as management defined them, but they may feel badly nonetheless. There are occasions when these feelings of guilt and shame require the counseling of psychologists who understand the situation, that these well-meaning employees are psychological casualties in the transition away from the traditional style of management.

It is important that education take place to avoid these kinds of resistance altogether. This education should emphasize that the barriers and obstacles to good work are in processes, not in people. People do the best they can. Thinking otherwise gets us nowhere. Everyone must understand that when an improvement opportunity is identified in a department it's a reason to be pleased, not embarrassed. It's a reason to smile and think how lucky we are to have this chance to improve, not to frown and look for someone to blame and punish. To identify an improvement opportunity really means that, in time, one of the organization's processes will be improved. As these kinds of improvements accumulate, they will, as suggested by the Deming chain reaction, improve quality, lower the cost of operations because rework and waste will be eliminated, increase productivity, expand the market share with lower prices, enable customers to live better, allow the organization to stay in business, and provide jobs and more jobs.[6] People who understand this are less likely to be fearful when they learn of an improvement opportunity. The impact of TQM on organizations is discussed more fully in chapter 12.

There is a third team strategy that does not cause the embarrassment for target departments that can occur in the use of the customer defines quality strategy. But, as you will soon see, it merely *defers* the embarrassment and places it on upstream supplier departments. There is a justification for deferring this possible embarrassment. Every precaution must be taken to ensure the survival of TQM in the early phases of the process improvement stage. This is because it is here that TQM is most vulnerable to cancellation by management or the board. Given some time, TQM efforts pay rich dividends, as managers will see, and then it will be almost impossible to cancel. It may be best, therefore, to use this third strategy in the first few DITs because it avoids the initial resistance and potential embarrassment associated with the customer defines quality approach and, therefore, increases the chances of success for the first teams.

A further justification for the third team strategy is that, later in a process improvement effort, sufficient education will have taught everyone that problems are in processes and not in people. Problems will be seen as improvement opportunities. When this viewpoint is accepted, there will be less reason for anyone to feel embarrassment, shame, or fear about the need to make improvements in his or her area.

## Team Strategy 3: The Tyranny of the Supplier

In point 4, Deming teaches "End the practice of awarding business on the basis of price tag alone." The way this point is worded and Deming's discussion of it places the emphasis on external suppliers, but the concept has a powerful meaning for internal suppliers, too.[7] Target departments should work with their upstream supplier departments to ensure they provide what is needed downstream. With this strategy, target departments look upstream to their suppliers rather than looking downstream to their customers, as they do in the customer defines quality strategy. To use this strategy, any department can be the target department in the sense that every department has internal suppliers. Thus, this strategy can be used by any and all departments.

*The Most Acceptable Improvement Strategy.* The customer defines quality strategy carries the implication for some that the target organization hasn't been doing a good job for its downstream customers. No one says this, but the implication is there nonetheless: "Why didn't you make these improvements before now? How could you have abused your downstream customers for so long?" This, of course, is not an implication department personnel want to think about. Everyone wants to do a good job.

On the other hand, the tyranny of the supplier strategy implies something much more acceptable to target department personnel. "Your efforts to do a good job for your downstream customers have been frustrated all this time because your upstream suppliers haven't done a good job for you! How could you do a good job when you didn't get the support you needed?" These are words that departments new to continual improvement can live with. These words don't imply anything about which to feel embarrassment, shame, or fear. "If those other guys would just do their job, everything would be okay for us." And, the fact is that every target department is subjected to tyranny by its suppliers, so this irritation is real and entirely justified.

*Tyranny by Suppliers Is Widespread.* In all the years I've worked in process improvement, I've never seen a department that wasn't affected in serious and substantial ways by its upstream suppliers. I've seen this kind of tyranny in hundreds of different kinds of organizations in both the public and private sectors—from microbiology sections in hospital laboratories that were oppressed by the main laboratory and nursing units, to flight crews in heavy bombardment wings that were subjugated by their support groups. Regardless of the organization, you can be certain that every department has tyrannical suppliers. I am so convinced of the universality of this concept that I teach my clients to refer to Deming's point 4 as the *tyranny of the supplier* rather than as *don't deal with suppliers on price alone.* To stress the inadequate support departments get from their internal suppliers, I've renamed Deming's point 4.

Before we go on, consider an important question. Are the upstream suppliers that abuse their downstream customers a bunch of bad guys? Do they deliberately set out to abuse their downstream customers? The answer is: Of course not. They are merely doing what they've been taught by managers who practice their trade in the traditional way: "Do what it takes to make your boss happy. Stay within your budget." It is this practice, commonly called MBO, that results in the tyranny of the supplier.

*How the Tyranny of the Supplier Strategy Works.* In the first step of the tyranny of the supplier strategy, personnel of a target department DIT are asked by their team leader (the department manager) to define the term *supplier.* After some discussion, they will come around to a definition such as any person or department that provides inputs, goods, and services, to them. They will probably realize these inputs are of two types: (1) whatever comes to them through horizontal processes from upstream suppliers, and (2) support resources they need to do their job or accomplish their aim, such as janitorial services, heating and air conditioning, plumbing, computer support, maintenance, supplies, and food service.

In the second step, DIT members identify their own suppliers according to their definition. In my earlier book, I explain how to use the ENGT to identify suppliers.[8] Suppliers are identified and their names written on a board for all team members to see. Each supplier is thoroughly discussed with members explaining why each is a supplier.

In the third step, these suppliers are prioritized, by consensus, in response to a question such as "If all these suppliers stopped providing their inputs to us, which would have the most serious negative impact on our ability to accomplish our aim?" (How to reach consensus is explained in Appendix C.)

DITs should be encouraged to prioritize their suppliers separately in the two categories already defined: those who provide inputs through horizontal processes and those who provide support resources. Generally speaking, suppliers who provide inputs through horizontal processes will be considered most in need of improvement and dealt with first. There are a few exceptions, however, when departments that provide support are the sharpest thorn in the foot of operational departments. In my experience, computer support departments, also known as management information systems (MIS) and data processing, are the worst offenders.

Once suppliers have been identified and prioritized, DITs move to the fourth step of taking each supplier, in turn, beginning with the most important and posing the following question for a brainstorming or ENGT session among its members. (For an explanation of how to use brainstorming, see my first book.[9]) "What could this supplier do to help us do a better job?" Because department personnel always know how their suppliers are tyrannizing them, this question will generate a wealth of suggestions about what the selected supplier can do to improve. These ideas are written on a board and discussed until they are made discrete and everyone understands their meaning.

In the fifth step, ways the selected supplier can improve are prioritized, by consensus, in response to a question such as "If this supplier improved in all the ways we have listed, which improvement would do the most to help us do a good job for our customers?" The result of this is always a Pareto outcome, that is a few improvements in the selected supplier's operation will be critical while many improvements will be nice to have, but not critical. The nice to have improvements can be put on the back burner for now and worked on at a later date. The DIT will want to deal with the selected supplier's critical few problems first because these are the biggest barriers to its own work.

In the sixth step, the DIT gathers data on the negative effects on its department of the critical problem in the supplier department identified in the previous step. To do this, DITs need to develop measures of these negative effects. (Again, for a discussion of how to develop measures, or indicators, see my first book.[10]) These data should be gathered for a period of time, say two weeks, and extrapolated to a month or year to show the cost of poor quality produced by the supplier.

Finally, in the seventh step, the DIT puts together a memorandum containing these data to support a request, or tasking, to the supplier department to make improvements in the critical area. (Tasking is discussed in detail in chapter 10.) After the most serious problems in the work of the most important supplier are dealt with in this manner, DITs consider the second most important supplier and repeat the seven steps outlined here. Then, the other suppliers are similarly dealt with in terms of their priority.

## The Role of External Suppliers and Customers

Thus far, only suppliers and customers inside organizations have been discussed. What about the role of suppliers and customers outside organizations? Deming is plain in his answer to this question, and he refers to suppliers and customers in his point 4 (don't deal with suppliers on price tag alone), point 3 (adopt a new philosophy: the customer defines quality), and in his thoughts on appreciation for a system (our suppliers and customers are part of the same system to which we belong). In other words, it makes no difference whether suppliers and customers are internal or external. They should be treated as part of the system that is being optimized.

Perhaps there is a need to be clearer about how to deal with external suppliers and customers in process improvement. Let's begin with external suppliers. Relations with external suppliers are governed by my renaming of Deming's point 4, to the effect that all suppliers tyrannize their customers. You can be sure a significant reason any organization does not do its best for its customers is the failure of its external suppliers. To remedy this, Deming suggests forming long-term relationships with external suppliers—that is, with one supplier of each product or service—and working with them to improve the quality of what they provide.[11] The method for doing this is, of course, the seven-step tyranny of the supplier strategy described in this chapter.

Relations with external customers, on the other hand, should be governed by the viewpoint that the customer defines quality. Many managers benefit from being educated in this concept as their departments go through the customer awareness stage, described in chapter 4. The customer defines quality strategy, described in this chapter, provides a method for reducing the tyranny any organization deals its customers.

# Moving Forward

Throughout this chapter, the term *tasking* is used. In general, a tasking occurs when one organizational unit, PIT, or DIT requests improvements from another organizational unit, usually a department. When done correctly, tasking can be a powerful force for implementing the Deming style of management. Tasking is so important that the entire next chapter is devoted to it.

# Notes

1. Peter R. Scholtes, *The Team Handbook: How to Use Teams to Improve Quality* (Madison, Wis.: Joiner Associates, 1988).

2. W. Edwards Deming, *Out of the Crisis* (Cambridge, Mass.: MIT Press, 1986), p. 86; Scholtes, *The Team Handbook*; Michael Brassard, ed., *The Memory Jogger: A Pocket Guide of Tools for Continuous Improvement* (Methuen, Mass.: GOAL/QPC, 1988); and H. James Harrington, "Flowcharting: Drawing a Process Picture," in *Business Process Improvement: The Breakthrough Strategy for Total Quality, Productivity, and Competitiveness* (Milwaukee, Wis.: ASQC Quality Press, 1991).

3. J. M. Juran, *Juran on Leadership for Quality: An Executive Handbook* (New York: Free Press, 1989), p. 17.

4. Charles N. Weaver, *TQM: A Step-by-Step Guide to Implementation* (Milwaukee, Wis.: ASQC Quality Press, 1991), pp. 64–75.

5. Ibid., chapter 6; Harrington, "Measurement, Feedback, and Action (Load, Aim, and Fire)," in *Business Process Improvement*; Brassard, *The Memory Jogger*, pp. 24–29; and Kaoru Ishikawa, "Cause-and-Effect Diagram," in *Guide to Quality Control* (Tokyo: Asian Productivity Organization, 1982).

6. Deming, *Out of the Crisis*, p. 3.

7. Ibid., pp. 31–49.

8. Weaver, *TQM*, pp. 76–80.

9. Ibid., p. 181.

10. Ibid., chapter 6.

11. Deming, *Out of the Crisis*, pp. 35–49.

# Chapter 10

# The Process Improvement Stage: Tasking, a Tool for System Optimization and Empowerment

Many CEOs know it's important to optimize their organizations as a system, but there has never been a practical, manageable tool for bringing system optimization about. Many CEOs also agree with the advice in the management literature about the need to empower employees. But, like system optimization, empowerment sounds great in theory, but no one has ever said in print what empowerment really means or explained how to provide it. A tool is now available for both of these purposes. It's called *tasking*.

## Deming's View of System Optimization

A key part of Deming's famous profound knowledge is appreciation for a system, according to which he suggests that organizations are systems in the sense that they are ". . . network[s] of functionally related components that work together to try to accomplish the aim of the system." He explains that organizations are like orchestras in which the players must work together to produce beautiful music. In organizations, departments must work together to produce their own beautiful music, the accomplishment of the organization's mission. Each player in an orchestra must contribute his or her best to the orchestra and not draw attention to him- or herself by playing too loudly. Similarly, departments in organizations should be judged by their contribution to the organization, ". . . not to maximize [their] own production, profit, or sales, or any other competitive measure." But, Deming cautions, a system must be managed; it will not manage itself. If left alone, departments become ". . . selfish, competitive, independent profit centers."[1] But, we know managers of traditional organizations do not leave departments alone. They

153

deliberately pit departments against each other, making optimization virtually impossible.

It is critical to understand the need to optimize organizations as systems, but few traditional managers achieve this understanding. However, once this understanding is achieved, an enormous obstacle stands in the way of its realization. That obstacle is "How do you do it?" By what means do CEOs bring about optimization in their organizations? It does little good to know of the need to optimize and to exhort subordinates to do it. This leads to frustration. Eliminating MBO and profit-centered accounting is a step in the right direction, but it's a passive, wait-and-see approach. Most CEOs are interested in a more active and manageable approach. The tool they seek is tasking.

## The Real Meaning of Empowerment

Another flaw in the traditional style of management is what it teaches about empowerment. Empowerment is not about delegation. It is not about achieving a certain state of mind, positive politics, or getting in touch with one's feelings. Nor is it about giving employees the right to check the personnel records to see how much money someone else makes. Empowerment occurs when employees have the resources they need to meet the needs and expectations of their customers. As I have explained, practitioners of the traditional style of management seldom provide this empowerment for their employees. They don't know about the tyranny of upstream suppliers.

Consider an example of some employees who are not empowered. Doctors take their patients (their customers) to a certain hospital for treatment. They order laboratory tests to be done on their patients. They want the results of tests ordered the previous day to be in patients' charts when they make hospital rounds at 7 the following morning. Nurses at this hospital know of the doctor's (their customers) wishes and realize, moreover, that many bad things can happen when test results are not on charts at 7 A.M. For instance, doctors can't release patients whose test results show they are recovered. They have to keep patients until they get their test results, a half to a full day later. This is a waste because it can cost $1,000 or more a day to keep a patient in the hospital. Furthermore, doctors can't be timely about changing medications for improving or deteriorating patients because they won't know of test results until later. A test might show a patient needs 500 milligrams instead of 250 milligrams of a certain drug. But, because the lab results aren't there when the doctor needs them, the needed increased dosage is delayed. The nurses want to meet the needs of their customers, the doctors and patients, and get the results on the charts by 7 A.M., but they can't. When asked why, they say "We can't post what we don't have, and the lab doesn't usually get results to us until 8:45 A.M." This is another case of the tyranny of the supplier. The same would be true if patients complained about the tasteless hospital meals, unclean bathrooms, or noise outside the window. Nurses want desperately to take care of patient concerns, but they can't without the support of such upstream suppliers as the dietary department, housekeeping, and physical plant. When upstream suppliers don't do their jobs for their downstream customers, people who work downstream are unempowered. Providing the support employees need to do their jobs is what empowerment is really all about.

## What Is Tasking All About?

Imagine an orchestra is playing along, and suddenly the second bassoon begins playing too loudly. The loud bassoonist is suboptimizing the orchestra. The delicate sounds of the violins and piccolos are drowned out. What will happen? A violinist may use his or her bow to poke the errant bassoonist gently in the ribs, or the conductor may get the bassoonist's attention and signal "Softly, softly." And, eventually, things return to optimal. The music is beautiful. Everyone involved enjoys the experience.

Now consider suboptimization in an organization. When any department can't take care of its customers because it's not getting what it needs from one of its upstream suppliers, this supplier is suboptimizing the organization. What will happen? In traditional organizations nothing happens. Everyone accepts suboptimization as a way of life in traditional organizations. But suppose the downstream department is trained to practice the tyranny of the supplier improvement strategy and identifies what the errant supplier needs to improve on its behalf. This needed improvement is written up in a memorandum called a *tasking* and sent to the supplier. The supplier makes the necessary improvements, and the organization moves one step closer to optimization and the employees in the downstream department feel empowered. Or, suppose a certain PIT has used the improve constantly and forever strategy. It flow diagramed a cross-functional process and prioritized the improvement opportunities it discovered. These improvement opportunities represent areas of suboptimization. These needed improvements are written up as taskings for the departments where they exist. As these taskings and others are worked through, the organization moves closer to optimization, and employees feel more empowered.

Both these teams needed to get improvements underway, but, remember, they wanted to do it in a way that would help move the organization's culture away from the traditional style of management and toward Deming's teachings.

## The Aims of Tasking

A tasking is a written request made of an organizational component, usually a department, by a team (a PIT or DIT) for an improvement or series of improvements that will bring the organization closer to optimization. Said another way, an opportunity for tasking occurs when a team identifies something beyond its control that is suboptimizing the organization. Taskings are like opportunity statements, but taskings are sent from teams to departments while opportunity statements are sent from quality councils to teams.

Tasking is at the heart of TQM improvement activities; yet, to my knowledge, there is nothing in print on this important subject. When tasking is done well, it contributes to the optimization of an organization and increases employees' sense of empowerment. But, be careful, when tasking is done poorly, it reinforces the traditional style of management.

The first aim of tasking is to generate improvements. Improvements of any kind can be the subject of tasking. Examples include getting something right or on time a greater percentage of the time, reducing costs, standardizing, improving equipment, reducing duplication and unnecessary storage, rearranging the skill mix of personnel in a department, reducing cycle time, reducing bureaucracy, and automating.

But, if teams are to change an organization's culture, their taskings must do more than improve something. Thus, tasking has a second aim, to provide opportunities in which employees can learn, practice, and model Deming's teachings.

Tasking has a third aim which is the most powerful part of this team approach to implementing the Deming philosophy. Tasking is the only direct, deliberate, and manageable method of optimization of a system. I know of no other direct way to do it. Tasking clearly targets areas within organizations where MBO is practiced and where profit centers are in place. Educated CEOs take action on these horrid vestiges of the traditional style of management so that system optimization can occur. Some CEOs can understand the role of tasking in optimizing a system by reading about it; others learn about it through practice.

The fourth aim of tasking is to provide empowerment. Employees feel genuine empowerment when they can call upon their upstream suppliers to provide the resources they need.

# How Tasking Occurs

To achieve these aims, how do teams go about tasking? The answer depends on the state of the PIT–DIT infrastructure. For instance, if PITs are in place but no DITs exist, tasking occurs one way. But if both PITs and DITs are in place, tasking occurs differently. Consider several illustrations of different tasking situations.

## *Tasking Situation 1*

Let's begin with the most common form of tasking, called *orthodox tasking*. As explained in chapter 7, an infrastructure of PITs and DITs develops for most organizations in a particular way. First, a quality council charters a small number of PITs—I recommend three—to improve cross-functional processes. I recommend also that the first processes selected for improvement be in high-cost areas. In any case, each of these PITs has a leader, a facilitator, and liaison SMEs from the departments into which the chartered processes flow. PITs almost always follow the improve constantly and forever strategy, described in chapter 9, and flow diagram their processes to identify improvement opportunities. When opportunities are identified, PITs pass them off through liaison SMEs to the managers of the departments where they exist. Team leaders, department managers, and SMEs should be taught to appreciate the importance of the SMEs' liaison role.

As an orthodox tasking begins to take shape, a department manager who is about to be tasked learns about it as it's being developed from regular briefings from his or her liaison SME. Recall that in their liaison role SMEs brief their department heads after each team meeting on events that occurred. It is also important that there be conversations about a planned tasking, as it is being developed, between the PIT leader and the department manager whose DIT is about to be tasked. As explained in chapter 7, PIT leaders and the managers of the departments in the cross-functional process being worked on get to know each other in earlier conversations when PITs are first started. For purposes of documentation, taskings are eventually written up as memoranda from PIT leaders to the department managers.

In the initial conversations between PIT leaders and department managers about forthcoming taskings, PIT leaders should explain that taskings are intended to get improvement started, but their second aim is to help departments learn and practice Deming's teachings. In addition, PIT leaders should discuss the need to establish DITs to help carry out improvements. It is essential that this conversation be non-threatening to department managers and be focused on system optimization rather than implying that anyone is to blame for problems. It is not uncommon for a department manager to attend a number of PIT meetings as a tasking for his or her department is being developed. The first taskings carried out by PITs must be handled well, or they can reinforce the traditional style of management and set the wrong norms for future taskings.

Orthodox tasking satisfies the first aim of tasking: It kicks off improvement activities in departments. It also satisfies the second aim of tasking: It impacts culture because it causes department managers and their subordinates to begin to think about barriers between themselves and other departments and continual improvement as they get exposed to PITs operating according to Deming's teachings. As explained in chapter 7, as departments take tasking after tasking from various PITs, two important things happen: Departments gradually develop DITs to carry out improvements, and department personnel begin to realize things are going to be done differently. Orthodox tasking also satisfies the third and fourth aims of tasking because it works to eliminate whatever was being done or wasn't being done upstream that caused suboptimization downstream, and employees in downstream departments feel more empowered because their concerns about inadequate or missing support from upstream get remedied.

Memoranda that go from PITs to department managers to document taskings should contain at least four parts.

1. A complete explanation of the improvement opportunity
2. Data showing the frequency with which the opportunity occurs and the cost to the organization of not making the improvement
3. When known, a recommendation on how to make the improvement
4. An offer to assist with the improvement

*The Need for Data.* To write the second part of a tasking memorandum, PITs gather data to prove there is an improvement opportunity. Why is it necessary to prove this? The reason is that in the beginning of a process improvement effort some department managers and their subordinates won't believe anything in their department needs improvement. They will believe they already do things the one best way. They won't believe they contribute to the suboptimization of the organization. They are victims of the traditional style of management. Thus, a memorandum suggesting they need to improve something won't make sense to them. The extent to which they will be reluctant or enthusiastic about improvement opportunities depends on the strength of their belief in Deming's teachings, especially in point 5 about the need to constantly and forever improve the system of production and service.

In any case, until the culture has changed so that department managers and their subordinates are enthusiastically searching for improvements and glad when they find them, it is best to back up recommendations for improvement with proof in the form of cost data. As taskings get more numerous and difficult to keep up with, tasking memoranda are useful as documentation trails on the status of what departments have been asked to improve.

Because proof must be provided in tasking memoranda to back up requests for improvements, PIT SMEs periodically pick up homework assignments to gather data on how often certain problems occur. They must be trained in how to gather data and how to use them to estimate the cost to the organization of these problems. Juran suggests these costs can be estimated by the "quick and dirty" approach or by ". . . enlarging the accounting system."[2]

Data should be gathered for a representative time period. This can be for as little as a few days or a week, but should be extrapolated to a year to show the cost of poor quality in an annual time frame. It is also best to translate the cost of poor quality (rework, waste, delays, duplication, and other bottlenecks) into dollar amounts, rather than in, say, time lost or pounds of scrap, because managers still under the influence of the traditional style of management understand two things: making money and not losing money. It is easier for them to accept PITs if they see them as powerful ways to reduce costs and not lose money.

*A PIT Leader's Program Management Role.* PIT leaders have important, ongoing responsibilities for their taskings after they have been sent to DITs. These responsibilities are discharged through a program management relationship. This relationship has two key parts.

1. Ensuring that DITs receive any technical assistance or management support they need in carrying out taskings

2. Receiving periodic reports on the progress of DITs in carrying out taskings

An important responsibility of quality councils is to ensure that team recommendations get implemented. PIT leaders are tasked by quality councils, and they should be given adequate support to carry out their work. But PIT leaders need to report periodically to quality councils on their progress. There may be instances when someone is in need of special assistance to get team recommendations implemented.

## Tasking Situation 2

Now, consider tasking under a different set of conditions. Suppose a certain PIT has been in operation for a few months and has, through taskings, brought about the creation of several DITs. Some of these DITs have worked off one or two taskings and are passively waiting for more taskings before they improve something else. But other DITs have matured to the point that they are not only improving in reaction to PIT taskings, they are also self-generating taskings for themselves and even for other DITs. This is a highly desirable transition for DITs, from working only taskings from PITs to self-generating taskings for themselves and others. This is really what tasking is all about—getting departments into the spirit and practice of improvement.

Suppose one of these self-generating DITs is using the tyranny of the supplier strategy, described in chapter 9, to improve its operations. Its leader (the department manager) used the ENGT among DIT members to identify its major upstream supplier department and to identify what this supplier doesn't do right that is the greatest source of errors, rework, and frustration in the DIT's department. Speaking in traditional terms, the DIT wants to get this supplier to fix this problem which contributes to the suboptimization of its department. To make this happen, the DIT gathers data to document the errors, rework, and frustration caused by the supplier's nonperformance. These data show the frequency with which the problem occurs and its consequent cost to the organization. These data are written up in a four-part memorandum, as outlined under "Tasking Situation 1." The question is to whom should the DIT send this memorandum? The answer again depends on the extent to which PITs and DITS have developed in the organization.

If the DIT and the upstream supplier department are both members of the same PIT, the answer is easy. The memorandum goes to the PIT leader. The PIT leader looks at the cost-benefit analysis presented in the memorandum. This ensures that from the organization's perspective—not from the perspective of any department—the benefits that will result from implementing the request in the tasking outweigh its costs. Taking the organizational viewpoint in cost-benefit analyses is important to avoid suboptimization. The PIT leader then forwards the memorandum to the manager of the upstream supplier department through that department's liaison SME. It is important that the PIT leader also make personal contact with the department manager to ensure that the tasking is understood in the nonthreatening spirit of system optimization. If the upstream department has a DIT in place, this DIT works the tasking. If the upstream department does not have a DIT in place, the department manager can work the tasking alone or form a DIT to work it.

In terms of the aims of taskings, this tasking memorandum gets improvement activities started or continued in the upstream DIT. In addition, it has some cultural impact to the extent that the department's employees are exposed to a PIT practicing Deming's teachings. Furthermore, it contributes to system optimization and the sense of empowerment.

## *Tasking Situation 3*

Consider a variation of tasking situation 2. Suppose a PIT has initiated a number of DITs. One of these DITs is practicing the tyranny of the supplier strategy and identifies an upstream supplier department in need of improvement. The DIT prepares a tasking memorandum for the upstream department, but it turns out that the department is not a member of this DIT's PIT or any other PIT. Where should the tasking memorandum be sent?

In the first place, an error may have been made in the way the membership of the PIT was constituted. If the upstream department's products and services are important to the downstream DIT, why wasn't that department included in the PIT? Such an occurrence would not come as a surprise to anyone experienced in the workings of PITs and DITs. It is not uncommon for PITs to be in operation for months without the departmental representation they need to streamline their chartered process. The reason is that quality councils and PIT leaders often simply don't know processes well enough in the beginning to see all the departments they include. In any case, the action required is clear.

When a PIT leader realizes a key department was inadvertently left off the team, the leader requests that the quality council add the department. After the council's approval of the new department's membership on the PIT, the PIT leader approaches the manager of the new department (in this case, the upstream supplier), as described in chapter 7, to discuss Deming's teachings and to secure the department's participation in the PIT through a liaison SME. After the department is added, its SME takes the tasking that surfaced this issue in the first place back to his or her manager. The manager can either work the tasking or create a DIT to work it.

The aims of tasking are again satisfied: Required improvements get started, department managers and their subordinates get exposed to PITs modeling Deming's teachings, further system optimization occurs, and the sense of empowerment is heightened. Again, the PIT leader should maintain a program manager relationship with the tasked DIT.

## Tasking Situation 4

Consider another tasking situation. Suppose management discovers a DIT that is not a member of a PIT and never got tasked. This is a common situation, and it raises some interesting questions.

In the first place, how could such a DIT get started? Recall, the usual way DITs get started is by receiving a tasking from a PIT. So, if this DIT is not a member of a PIT and never got tasked, how did it get started?

The answer is that in most process improvement efforts "renegade," "wildcat," or "rogue" DITs start up. Such DITs are not created by taskings, nor are they members of PITs or authorized by a quality council. They are started by managers and their subordinates, and often by subordinates alone, who are sick and tired of the many barriers that prevent them from taking pride in their work. They attended training conducted by senior management on the Deming philosophy. They saw videotapes on Deming's teachings. They heard about continual improvement. They heard about removing barriers that rob people of their right to pride of work. They are among the few employees who actually read the books about quality in the organization's library. All this education was motivational. And, after waiting a while, they became impatient for some action. They felt unempowered. They wanted to see an end to the problems that had plagued them for years. Furthermore, they knew from experience that programs come and go, and they worried that PITs, DITs, and Deming would soon be just another program. They saw a window of opportunity to get some of their departmental problems straightened out so they could take joy in their work for a change. So, they started up a DIT of their own.

Thus, as renegade DITs work through their flow diagrams and cause-and-effect diagrams, usually secretly in the beginning, they come up with taskings for their upstream suppliers. This is because they, like all customers, are tyrannized by their suppliers. The question is what should quality councils do when they hear about a renegade DIT or its taskings?

Thoughtful quality councils find it difficult to restrict process improvement efforts to a few authorized showcase PITs and DITs, and they find it awkward to disestablish renegade DITs. Renegade DIT members are highly motivated. They are so motivated, in fact, that they accept the risks of going around the system to create their own DIT. They don't wait around to be jump-started into improvement by taskings from PITs. Furthermore, they are known for bringing about outstanding improvements. Their disestablishment can be a severe blow to the morale of members of their team and to other employees who hear about it. Because an important aim of a process improvement effort is to get departments involved in improvement, how can quality councils tell the enthusiastic members of a department they cannot participate in its improvement? To onlookers, disestablishing a renegade DIT would be another in a long series of management blunders. Thus, thoughtful quality councils look through their fingers, so to speak, allowing renegade DITs to operate, and eventually they authorize them.

Renegade DITs often force the issue of their own authorization when they route their tasking memoranda to an upstream supplier department by way of the quality council. Here, the council must fish or cut bait. On the one hand, the council can, in effect, authorize the renegade DIT by forwarding its memorandum to the supplier department. The disadvantage of this action is it shows the council is breaking from its publicized plan for evolving DITs from PITs. The council thus runs the risk of employees thinking it plans for one thing and does another. Employees have witnessed irrational behavior by management for years. The advantage, however, is that the organization benefits from the improvements identified in the renegade DIT's memorandum and from other improvements that are almost certain to come from these enthusiastic employees.

On the other hand, the council may refuse to forward a renegade DIT's memorandum, thus denying it authorization. In this case, the integrity of the council's plan for evolving DITs from PITs is maintained, but the organization loses the benefit of the improvements identified in the renegade DIT's memorandum and other memoranda that are almost certain to come from it. Most quality councils opt for recognizing renegade DITs and taking advantage of the improvements they identify.

# How to Know How Well TQM is Going

A question often asked by members of boards of directors, CEOs, and senior managers is "How's our TQM effort going?" There are many ways to try to answer this question: very few right, almost all wrong.

A common, but worst, way to try to find out how a TQM effort is going is to conduct a survey of employee opinion. Those who advocate this approach argue that valuable information can be gained from such surveys. If samples are representative and employees are not too fearful to respond truthfully, there is little doubt about the value of information from employee opinion surveys. But this argument misses the point. The problem with employee surveys is that they show that the CEO is so isolated from TQM activities he or she has to do a survey to find out what's going on. In other words, this approach acknowledges that employees know more about how TQM is going than the CEO. Nothing could be worse for a TQM effort than an isolated CEO!

Successful TQM demands the day-by-day involvement of CEOs. They should be students in the classroom TQM training offered to employees. They should learn Deming's teachings and the statistical tools and team strategies so well that they can comfortably substitute for the regular trainers in any part of the training. They must frequently attend the meetings of PITs and DITs and stay for the full time. They must not drop by for a few exhortations, a few pats on the back, a quick cup of coffee, and depart. While attending team meetings, CEOs must not do much talking, but listen to understand the aims of their teams and how they are progressing toward those aims. When CEOs don't attend meetings, they should receive and read team minutes. Remember, we are talking here about the first three PITs put in place, not 40 or 400. And, after DITs get established, CEOs should maintain a visibility in them also. Except for the largest organizations, this should be feasible. For large organizations, division managers should assume the role described here for CEOs.

Most teams never see their CEOs at their meetings. What message does this send? Some CEOs think it means empowerment; most team members think it means the CEO doesn't consider their work important. Some team members hope to never see the CEO. Employees have thoughts about their CEOs as shadowy figures in plush offices hidden away from where the real work takes place, working political issues behind closed doors, romancing the board of directors to cement his or her job, or hanging out at the country club. Sending a staffer to team meetings is no substitute for the CEO.

The point is, CEOs who are genuinely involved in TQM don't need employee surveys. They know how the TQM effort is going. And, based on real knowledge, they know what actions are needed to keep things going. There are many legitimate aims for employee surveys, but using them to learn how well TQM is going is not one of them.

## Two Sure Signs of TQM Progress

How do CEOs who are directly involved in TQM assess its progress? The best answer is simply that they will know. These are the CEOs who duck out of lunch at the country club to eat with their nonsupervisory personnel in the employee cafeteria or at the snack truck. CEOs who are in the trenches—where they ought to be—know how TQM is going.

CEOs who are genuinely involved in TQM will tell you there are two key things to know about how TQM is going. This knowledge goes to the deepest issues of TQM. But, this knowledge sounds like a foreign language to those who are ignorant of TQM because they don't speak the lingo. Terms like *cross-functional processes, PITs, DITs, SMEs,* and *tasking* throw them.

The first of the key knowledge about how TQM is going comes from this question. Are PITs working major cross-functional, or core, processes, and are DITs established and working in every department? This will show if the infrastructure is in place and operating. On the other hand, if major cross-functional processes have no PITs and many key departments have no DITs, the TQM infrastructure has not yet fully developed. How are improvements going to be made and the culture changed without PITs and DITs? By showing TQM videos and exhorting employees? Very doubtful. Of course, developing PITs and DITs takes time, so it's unfair to make serious judgments about how things are going in this way too early in a TQM implementation effort.

Here's the second part of this key knowledge. The most powerful way to assess the health of a TQM effort is to know how well tasking is going. CEOs who are running their TQM programs in name only won't know what the word *tasking* means. The question to be asked is whether taskings from downstream departments are received with open arms or with resistance by their upstream suppliers. Resistance is a reflection of the barriers referred to by Deming in his point 9 and in his discussion of system suboptimization. Do department managers delay or reject taskings because they don't meet the budget-neutral standard of acceptability required by senior managers? The requirement of budget neutrality is a horrid manifestation of MBO imposed by CEOs who are ignorant of the neéd to optimize their organizations. Do upstream suppliers balk at carrying out the requests made of them in taskings because *they* know what's best for their downstream customers? When department managers think that way, their CEOs haven't taught them that the customer defines quality. They haven't been taught by their CEOs that they should adopt a new philosophy. They haven't been taught an appreciation for a system.

# CEO Responsibilities in Tasking

It should be clear that CEOs have significant responsibilities in tasking. When discharging these responsibilities, they should remember that tasking has four aims: (1) to increase organizational effectiveness by improving processes; (2) to bring about changes in the organization's culture, specifically to give employees a stream of opportunities as they serve on teams to learn, practice, and model Deming's teachings; (3) to optimize the organization; and (4) to provide empowerment.

CEOs who are seeking to accomplish these aims should bear in mind the second law of organizational development.

*Any attempt to increase organizational effectiveness will eventually get washed out unless it has adequate cultural support.*

In other words, tasking won't work well unless CEOs provide training in Deming's teachings so everyone understands how things are going to be done differently. Everyone must see that the organization is moving away from the traditional style of management. In particular, this means practicing the 14 points, observing the obstacles and diseases, and understanding profound knowledge. Recall that the 14 points are the road map to cultural change away from the traditional style of management.

## How CEOs Can Stumble in Tasking

CEOs can stumble in tasking in three main ways, as described in the following sections.

**Failure to Continually Educate Management.** CEOs can stumble in tasking by believing they and their senior staff have mastered Deming's teachings after a cursory exposure to it, such as reading one book or attending one seminar on the subject. Personal transformation away from the traditional style of management takes much time and continuing education. Deming's philosophy is not merely common sense.

It's the exceptional CEO who doesn't backslide into the traditional style of management a number of times in the journey of transformation. Even for CEOs who are diligent in their studies of Deming's teachings, backsliding is normal and should be expected. The frequency and severity of backsliding can be reduced with continuing education in Deming's philosophy.

*Failure to Implement the Customer Defines Quality Strategy.* A key part of the Deming philosophy is that the customer defines quality. CEOs can stumble in tasking by failing to ensure, with training and personal example, that department managers and the managers' subordinates understand that the customer defines quality philosophy applies when they receive taskings from their internal customers. Department managers and their subordinates must be taught the importance of discovering what their internal customers need and working hard to provide it.

*Failure to "Walk the Talk."* CEOs can stumble in tasking by failing to "walk the talk." The "talk" is setting up an infrastructure of PITs and DITs and encouraging continual improvement, system optimization, and empowerment. The "walk" has two parts: (1) adequately staffing and (2) ensuring that taskings that meet organization-wide, cost-benefit criteria are fully implemented in a timely manner.

CEOs often understaff departments but still expect them to meet the needs of their downstream customers. Overworking employees is a shortsighted management abuse in an effort to keep costs down. CEOs also often fail to provide temporary employees to fill in for SMEs when they attend team meetings and do homework. SMEs should not be expected to carry out all of their regular duties plus the additional work as team members. SMEs selected to serve on teams are the best persons from their departments for the job, and it's abusive to ask them to do double work. When SMEs are at team meetings or doing homework, CEOs must ensure there is adequate funding for additional staff.

Failing to walk the talk by not ensuring that taskings meet organization-wide, cost-benefit criteria comes from continuing to manage departments with MBO or as profit centers. This is the traditional style of management at its worst and the lowest use of the honorable profession of accounting. It assumes an organization will prosper if departments are managed as separate businesses unto themselves. "If each department does its best, the organization they make up will prosper." The fact is that the whole is not equal to the sum of its parts. This approach ignores the interactions between departments.

Using MBO and profit centers is a confession by CEOs of their ignorance of the need to manage their organizations as systems. In practice, the profit center approach encourages departments to become selfish and competitive. It makes cooperation among them virtually impossible. This ruinous practice is revealed in CEO dictums to department managers that choke off their efforts to respond to taskings: "Stay within your budgets!" or "All improvements must be budget neutral!"

## An Example of How Management Can Stumble in Tasking

Consider an example in which a tasking fell through the cracks. We will search for the causes of this failure. A product division of a certain manufacturing plant needed to upgrade part of its computer software. Using the tyranny of the supplier improvement strategy, a carefully researched tasking memorandum was prepared by the department's DIT and sent to the computer support division. It showed that an estimated one-time investment of $9,000 in programmer time would save $216,000 annually by reducing rework in the product division. But, instead of welcoming the tasking as an opportunity to support a customer, the manager of the computer support division gathered data to support her own argument that the product division didn't really need what its memorandum said it needed. She concluded that it should simply fully utilize the computer software already available to it. The manager of the product division (the DIT leader) responded to this argument saying the available software was difficult to learn and not user-friendly. He further said that the available software was so user-unfriendly that it contributed to fatigue, and fatigue contributed to costly errors and rework. The computer division manager retorted that the personnel in the requesting division were simply not adequately trained to use the software. To say it plainly, she believed she knew more about her customer's needs than the customer did.

The irony of this situation is that the computer support manager was not trained in computer science but was trained in the traditional style of management. Her subordinates were computer programmers who privately anguished over her lack of customer orientation. They were helpless to do anything about it, other than support customers when they could behind her back. They were not empowered. They occasionally did help their customers in this way, and, when she caught them at it, she punished them. She was uniformly decried by plant personnel below the senior level who had no choice but to deal with her. She had a monopoly; her in-house customers had to go to her for computer support. She maintained sole approval authority on requests for computer support. Her subordinates claimed she okayed requests on the basis of friendship or power. (The CEO's requests got immediately pushed to the top of the priority list.) She seldom answered her telephone, and had a reputation for responding to requests for support by shaking her head and saying, "I can do it, but it'll take 200 work hours and six months." Below the senior level, she was regarded as the number one barrier to quality improvement in the plant.

This is not to say that computer support units aren't tyrannized by their own customers. They can be tyrannized when their customers fail to plan ahead for their needs and expect instant service as if adding computer support is like plugging in a toaster. Computer technology is advancing at a bewildering pace, and in-house customers must plan ahead if their suppliers are to do a good job on their behalf.

But let's examine this situation more closely. Are you convinced that the manager of the computer support division is the barrier she's believed to be? If so, think again. Remember, our problems (opportunities) are not in our people but in our processes. Suppose the CEO has not adequately staffed this computer support division. What would that mean? It could mean the manager is doing the best she can with what she has to work with. She may struggle anxiously every day to meet customer needs by shifting workers here and there to solve crises, meet unplanned requirements, and keep the ship afloat. To herself, she's a hero. Or, let's suppose she lives in a world of MBO where her work is managed by annual objectives and budgets. She would like to provide the one-time $9,000 in programmer support to save the product division $216,000 a year, but if she does she'll overrun her budget. This would put her in the doghouse with the vice president, who stands between her and the CEO. And she doesn't dare ask for overhire authority because she's been told repeatedly how tough times are and to stay within her budget. She's a good soldier doing the best she can in the environment the CEO allowed to be built for her. So maybe she's not to blame after all.

Ask yourself what kind of CEO would allow these kinds of things to happen in a computer support division. What kind of CEO would understaff any department in the organization so it cannot fully support its customers? What kind of CEO would manage with profit centers so there's insufficient budget to support downstream customers? After thinking about these question, maybe you are beginning to blame the CEO for letting this happen. If so, think again. Remember, our problems (opportunities) are not in our people but in our processes. The CEO is a person, too, so you can be pretty sure the problem is not there. Maybe the CEO doesn't have a work force model for balancing staffing in the computer support division against its customer requirements. The CEO and her staff simply haven't been trained for this part of their job. And maybe the CEO hasn't been trained to appreciate the need to optimize the system. Maybe the CEO hasn't studied Deming enough. Maybe the CEO skimmed through only one book on the subject and considers herself a fast study. So, maybe down deep at the roots of this situation the blame does not lie with the CEO.

Who, then, is to blame? The answer is don't think about blaming someone. Think about the process. The process is to blame. Here the flawed process is the traditional style of management. After all, management is a process, too. And, here, the management process needs to be transformed from the traditional style to the style advocated by Deming.

## How to Handle Resistance to Taskings

As an organization is in this stage of the transformation from the traditional style of management, resistance to tasking memoranda requires special attention by PIT leaders and CEOs.

To carry out their responsibilities as program managers, PIT leaders should keep careful records of their taskings and ask tasked DIT leaders to provide periodic updates on progress. This updating may be as simple as the PIT leader receiving a copy of the minutes of DIT meetings. Having these minutes shows whether a DIT is, in fact, meeting to work on taskings, the frequency of its meetings, and the goings-on at its meetings. However, PIT leaders should go further than that. They should know or get to know DIT leaders well enough to discuss their progress on taskings. This is part of breaking down barriers. Getting DIT leaders into the spirit of Deming's teachings, especially to believe in continual improvement, system optimization, empowerment, and that the customer defines quality, is a major part of any PIT leader's job.

When DITs have more than one tasking to work, they should be taught to prioritize the taskings in terms of their impact on the organization as a system. The aim is to optimize the system, not one or a few departments. This may require a meeting between the department manager with the multiple taskings and the PIT leaders who sent them. The CEO should be asked to attend this meeting. In the meeting, attendees should use consensus to prioritize the taskings. The optimization criterion for prioritization is "Which tasking is more important to our organization as a whole?"

Early in the process improvement stage, CEOs must keep an eye on taskings to ensure they don't fall through the cracks. This can be accomplished through monthly meetings of CEOs and PIT leaders to discuss the status of taskings. CEOs can learn much in these meetings. These meetings can be half-day sessions with attendees including the CEO, the master facilitator (if one is being used as a technical adviser), and team leaders. The CEO should already know every team leader by name since he or she periodically attends PIT and DIT meetings.

Perhaps the first meeting could begin with an ice breaker to drive out some fear, but CEOs should continuously work to drive out fear because it is the most serious barrier to the success of these meetings. The next step could be to identify the perceived barriers to team success with an ENGT session on a question such as "What are the major barriers to the implementation of taskings in our organization?" Subsequent meetings could develop more detail about the issues unearthed by this ENGT question. The CEO's attitude in these meetings should be "What can I do from my end to help you team leaders do a better job from your end? How can I help your teams better accomplish their opportunity statements?" This attitude from CEOs will be much appreciated by team leaders, but the key to the success of these meetings is action, if needed, by CEOs to remove barriers to team success, in particular to ensure that taskings don't fall through the cracks.

Taskings almost always show that a relatively modest investment in improvements upstream will result in huge savings downstream. Taskings must be evaluated with simple cost-benefit analysis from the perspective of the entire organization, not from the profit center perspective of individual departments. But, remember Deming's teaching in deadly disease number 5, that "he that would run his company on visible figures alone will in time have neither company nor figures." In other words, the cost-benefit analysis of taskings, even from the perspective of the organization as a system, must be tempered with judgment because the most important figures for running any business are unknown and unknowable.[3]

As has been stressed, one aim of team activities is to increase organizational effectiveness. This may require some departments, such as a computer support unit, to operate period after period at a loss.[4] Why? Because that's in the best interests of the organization. Overrunning one department's budget by $9,000 is wise if it means a $216,000 saving in another department. It's as simple as investing $9,000 to get back $216,000. Ask yourself if you would make a one-time investment of $9,000 if you could get back $216,000 every year from now on? The answer is obvious. Yet, there are traditional managers everywhere who don't spend money regardless of its great benefit on other parts of their organizations because it'll overrun their budgets. Why do they think this way? The answer is that in the past when they overran their budgets it got them in trouble with their MBO-trained bosses. It went on their records, and they didn't get good performance evaluations that year. It kept them from getting raises and promotions. Is it any wonder some department managers resist taskings? CEOs who hold their departments to budgets based on last year's figures plus 6 percent and who use performance evaluations need long-term education in Deming's teachings on optimization of a system. In any case, as everyone comes to appreciate and practice Deming's teachings, the need for oversight of taskings by CEOs will gradually lessen.

CEOs have an additional responsibility when they meet periodically with their team leaders. Not only should they use these meetings to keep an eye on taskings, but they should use them as a way to learn whether the culture in the part of the organization that PITs are touching is changing. How would CEOs know this? Recall that the road map to getting away from the traditional style of management is Deming's 14 points. Thus, CEOs should look for evidence of changes from the old way to the new way of doing things in the attitudes and behavior of their subordinates. They must realize, however, that the most important determinant of whether subordinates will change is whether the CEO him- or herself is changing. There is no escaping this fact. There is no substitute for the practice and modeling of Deming's teachings by CEOs.

## How Tasking Can Break Down Barriers

Another question should be considered in tasking. Because an aim of tasking is to break down barriers between departments, it is helpful to consider the question "What would tasking be like if there were no barriers between departments?" This question should be asked at a meeting of all department managers who sooner or later will be tasked. The meeting could be introduced by the CEO with a brief review of the relevant Deming philosophy, including emphasis on point 9 on break down barriers between departments and appreciation for a system in profound knowledge, and the role of PITs and DITs in cultural transformation. Department managers could also be reminded of the four aims of tasking explained earlier in this chapter.

After these preliminaries are completed, a question about how to task could be posed for discussion. Alternative questions to the one stated in the preceding paragraph include "If there were no barriers between our departments, how would we get each other to change things in our departments that would benefit others?" and, as Deming might suggest, "How would tasking take place if our departments were a network of interdependent components that work together to accomplish the aim of our organization?"[5]

I've talked to many department managers about tasking. They consistently say they would like to have the kind of relationship with other department managers where problems, or improvement opportunities, could be handled smoothly in a friendly conversation in the hall, over diet sodas beside the snack truck, or simply on the telephone. They want to be cooperative. If department managers decide this is what tasking should eventually look like, the way they do tasking now should be a step in that direction. How big a step in that direction they take now is up to them and how much they are imbued with the traditional style of management.

A meeting of department managers to discuss how to do tasking is beneficial in a number of ways. They see again that the CEO supports the TQM effort because the CEO makes the introductory remarks and stays for the entire session, listening carefully to what is said. Managers get more exposure to Deming's teachings on a system. They see again that all the brains are not at the top of the organization because their input on tasking is being solicited and very probably followed. They see that no one at the top is directing them in how to task. And, they get more experience in cooperation because in this meeting they will come to a consensus about how to task.

If barriers between departments are to be broken down, many things must happen that are beyond the control of department managers and their subordinates. First, and most important, CEOs must eliminate the poisonous effects of human resources policies based on the traditional style of management. Although traditional CEOs and human resources directors don't like to hear me say it, I am convinced of the following:

*Personnel policies and procedures are the foundation of most barriers between employees and between departments.*

These policies put pressures on managers and other employees to compete against one another for salary increases, promotions, and bonuses. They do far more harm than good and must be ripped out.

Recall chapter 3 where CEOs' misunderstanding of the ruinous effects of such policies is discussed. Personnel policies must be brought into line with Deming's teachings.

The behavior of department managers will change for the better when they are not forced by the CEO to compete against one another and when it is understood that problems are in processes and not in the people. When managers pass in a hallway, they see a friend, not a competitor. They are glad to see each another. They smile. They kid around. They laugh. Some go fishing together. Some entertain at one another's homes. They get to know each other on a personal level. As a matter of fact, when CEOs have created an environment of cooperation and friendship, no one will have to tell department managers how to work together. They are friends, and they can handle problems, or improvement opportunities, routinely without fanfare. They can take pride in their work, and they will see that continual improvement is part of their jobs.

Tasking is another part of the transitional administrative structure, along with the quality council and PITs and DITs. Like the other parts, when an organization has moved away from the traditional style of management, this part, too, can drop off. Barriers come down, empowered people handle improvement opportunities routinely, and systems move toward optimization.

## Moving Forward

Many CEOs are in marketplace wars where products and services are not perceptibly different and competition is based on low prices. Unfortunately, many CEOs achieve low prices through the economic exploitation of their faithful, hardworking employees, by such practices as not paying enough to provide a life of dignity, hiring as many part-timers as possible to avoid paying retirement and health care costs, and filling many important jobs with low-skill minimum-wagers. Not only are these practices morally reprehensible, but it is also unwise to put people in jobs where they lack the experience and education to handle them properly.

Furthermore, from a purely economic viewpoint, labor is not the largest cost of doing business. The largest cost of doing business is inefficient processes. Consider the evidence that much of the work done in organizations is rework. Add to that the additional cost of unnecessary delays, bureaucracy, storage, duplication, and management, and you've put your finger on the highest cost of doing business. This cost doesn't show up on the profit and loss statement, so accountants don't know about it. And, it's invisible to traditional CEOs. It's these costs that must be reduced. How to reduce these costs by improving processes was explained in this and the preceding five chapters. This concludes the six chapters on the process improvement stage of TQM.

Almost all CEOs believe process improvement is as far as TQM goes. They believe having smoothly working, improving processes that delight internal and external customers is the ultimate in TQM. These CEOs are surprised when they learn there is more to TQM. The innovation stage is discussed in the next chapter.

# Notes

1. W. Edwards Deming, *The New Economics for Industry, Government, and Education* (Cambridge, Mass.: MIT Press, 1993), pp. 50, 51, 99–100.

2. J. M. Juran, *Juran on Leadership for Quality: An Executive Handbook* (New York: Free Press, 1989), pp. 53–54.

3. W. Edwards Deming, *Out of the Crisis* (Cambridge, Mass.: MIT Press, 1986), p. 121.

4. Deming, *The New Economics*, p. 100.

5. Ibid., p. 50.

# Chapter 11

# The Innovation Stage

When CEOs learn there's more to TQM than customer awareness and process improvement, many are surprised and ask, "How can there be anything more to TQM than splendid, cost-efficient processes that provide the highest in customer satisfaction? What else can there be?" Before drawing on Deming's teachings to answer this question, let's set the stage by briefly reviewing the changes organizations make as they journey through the customer awareness and process improvement stages. This journey builds knowledge that makes it possible to move into the next stage of TQM, the innovation stage.

Of course, calling the next stage of TQM the innovation stage is not meant to imply that no innovation occurs in the earlier stages. Certainly, organizations in the customer awareness and process improvement stages innovate. But almost all this innovation occurs randomly, usually coming from brainstorms or bursts of creativity. Innovations of this type can be useful to customers and rewarding for those developing them, but they can't be predicted. This is because brainstorms and bursts of creativity do not result from well-defined steps that can be repeated. This is not the kind of innovation to be explained here.

A second activity that some call innovation also occurs in the early stages of TQM, and it, too, can be highly successful. It involves refining innovations others created but were unable or unwilling to develop fully and bring successfully to market. But this, also, is not the kind of innovation to be explained here. What will be explained here is how to make original innovations in a systematic and predictable manner.

## *Learning in the Customer Awareness Stage*

Let's begin with a brief review of what is learned in the customer awareness stage of TQM, as presented in chapter 4. In this stage it is learned that everyone, from one-person mail rooms to the largest corporations, has customers. Customers are external to organizations, say walking around on the street; but they are also internal, in the form of downstream departments in extended processes. In the TQM transformation, knowledge of the importance of external customers almost always comes first. Regardless, organizational members come to know who their customers are, what their customers want, and that satisfying customers is a survival issue. Said another way, in the customer awareness stage it is learned that satisfying customers determines, in the long run, whether an organization will survive. In a nutshell, the organization has learned that customers define quality.

The origin of the customer-oriented view of quality is attributed to a number of different people, including Juran and Deming, but it has been known for many decades in business textbooks as the *marketing concept*. For instance, the authors of a popular marketing research text, now in its sixth edition, make the following observation.

> *The marketing concept suggests that the resources and activities of the organization be focused in an integrated way on the* needs and wants of the consumer *as opposed to the needs and wants of the organization.*[1]

When organizational members realize they must formally and systematically learn who their customers are and what their customers want, marketing research flowers and is recognized as a tool for organizational learning.

## Learning in the Process Improvement Stage

Consider next what is learned in the process improvement stage, as presented in chapters 5 through 10. Perhaps the most valuable lesson in this stage is that it is of little benefit to have information about what customers want unless organizations can produce products and services that satisfy those wants. And, managing organizations to produce what customers want means recognizing, developing, managing, and continually improving horizontal processes.

Learning in the process improvement stage ordinarily builds on what was learned in the customer awareness stage. Consider an illustration of how one organization, a large industrial wholesaler, learned the lessons of customer awareness but had little effectiveness because too little was known about process improvement. This organization had a sophisticated marketing research operation. The marketing research employees conducted monthly surveys of customer attitudes toward specific dimensions of their products and services. They used control charts to know when the processes that produced these dimensions were in and out of control. They, thus, had an early warning system to signal when and where things weren't going right. They understood that the customer defines quality, and they vigorously sought to understand customers' wants. Unfortunately, after they got this information, they didn't know what to do with it. At best, they distributed survey results to department managers where problems were identified, but the managers were not trained in what to do with this valuable information. Too frequently, senior managers used heavy-handed methods to blame department heads and individual employees for problems. The real limitation of the organization was that senior management had not institutionalized a systematic means of making improvements in the support areas upstream of where their surveys indicated something was wrong. The organization was sophisticated about discovering what their customers wanted, but they were ignorant of how to improve upstream operations so they could provide it. In short, they had not learned the lessons of the process improvement stage.

Organizations learn from their journey through customer awareness and process improvement that they must have customer feedback systems that provide information with which to fine-tune their processes. In addition, they must have a culture that endorses continual improvement. (An infrastructure of PITs and DITs is a vehicle by which both process improvement and cultural transformation can be brought about.) When the culture is right, departments are happy to receive customer feedback because they recognize it as an opportunity to improve. They see making improvements as an important part of their job. When the culture is right, recipients of customer feedback pounce on it and are delighted to make the indicated improvements.

Exceeding customer expectations with the best, most efficient processes is important. In fact, it's a matter of survival. But something more is needed if organizations expect to expand their markets and prosper. This something else is the ability to see into the future. To use the phrase *see into the future* may seem strange. It may sound like gazing into a crystal ball or reading tea leaves. But, there's nothing magical about seeing into the future as it's about to be explained here. Seeing into the future is the job of every CEO, and it revolves around innovation.

## Deming's View of Innovation

Deming makes an interesting and challenging comment about innovation. He says customers are able to ask for improvements in existing products and services, but they are unable to ask for new products and services. In other words, customers can complain that your product costs too much, was delivered too late, or wore out too soon. These are requests for improvements, and you can do something about them. You can improve the processes that produce these outputs. On the other hand, Deming says you cannot expect customers to identify new products and services that you could provide. To illustrate his point, he names a number of products which customers did not ask for, including electric lights, photography, telegraphs, telephones, automobiles, pneumatic tires, integrated circuits, pocket radios, and facsimile equipment. For instance, no customer asked for the invention of the telephone. What customer would have even dreamed the telephone was possible?[2]

Deming further suggests that while customers are unable to ask for new products, they are always willing to buy new products that will make their lives easier and better.[3] For instance, customers were willing to switch from gas lights to electric lights. They were willing to send messages by telegraph instead of Pony Express and, later, by telephone instead of telegraph. Deming concludes that it is not enough to have happy, loyal customers because they will desert you as soon as something better comes along. Even if your products and services delight them and exceed their expectations, they'll still switch when something better comes along. To illustrate this point, he recalls the carburetor. Regardless of how flawless the processes that produced carburetors and how satisfied and loyal their customers, carburetors were out virtually the minute fuel injection came along. The same was true when the vacuum tube lost its market to the transistor. Countless examples could be added to those given by Deming.

Let's recap the two lessons Deming is teaching here. First, it's important to get customer feedback about improvements needed in the processes that produce your existing products and services. Second, customers will leave you when a better product or service comes along, no matter how good your existing products and services are.

Now comes the important question. What should we do in response to these two teachings? Our response to the first teaching is more obvious. We should constantly gather information on customer attitudes toward our products and services so we can improve the processes that produce them. How to improve processes is explained in chapters 5 through 10. But what about Deming's second teaching? What are we to do in response to the fact that our customers will leave us if better products and services come along? The answer is that we should think about new products and services we can offer our customers next season, in five years, and even 10 or more years from now. If we want to secure our own presence in the marketplace, we must begin today to find new products and services that will help our customers live better than they do with what's available to them now. In short, we must innovate.

# Deming's Advice on Innovation

Deming has some advice about how to innovate. To innovate, he says organizations must ask themselves two questions: (1) What business are we in? and (2) What new product or service will help customers more than what is currently available to them?[4] To illustrate the value of these two questions, he suggests the makers of carburetors would have been better off if they'd thought of themselves in the business of putting a stoichiometric mixture of fuel and air into the combustion chamber, and invented something that would do it better than a carburetor. Instead, they were preoccupied with making better carburetors. They were preoccupied with improving their processes so they could make better and better carburetors. They were stuck in the process improvement paradigm and not open to seeing into the future through innovation.

Now, keep Deming's advice in mind while we consider the specific actions required to get organizations into innovation. I refer to these actions as the *principles of innovation.*

# The Principles of Innovation

After organizations accept the importance of satisfying customers and understand the need to improve processes, innovation can be the natural next step. Innovation is, indeed, the next stage of TQM.

Organizations in the innovation stage practice at least one of the principles of innovation, and some organizations are mature enough in their innovation style to practice all three. These principles are universal. They apply to all organizations whether large or small, public or private, and regardless of whether their customers are external, internal, or a combination of both.

## Innovation Principle 1: Know Your Customers' Processes

The following is the first principle of innovation.

> *To discover the products or services that will help customers live better, understand their processes.*

To understand this principle, consider that innovation is similar to process improvement. Recall from chapters 5 through 10 that the first step in process improvement is to build knowledge of how a process works. This is accomplished using a simple tool, the flow diagram. Building knowledge of how a process works uncovers opportunities for improvement in areas such as rework, delays, unnecessary costs, and bureaucracy. Once processes are understood, their improvement is easy. It is important not to get overly concerned about the action step in process improvement, however. Instead, you should concentrate first on building knowledge about how processes work. When you know enough about how processes work, how to improve them will become apparent. Recall, in chapter 9, the iron law of process improvement.

> *When a team sees no way to improve a process, it's always because the team lacks sufficient knowledge of how the process works.*

Identical reasoning underlies the first principle of innovation. In fact, the first principle of innovation could be reworded to be similar to the iron law of process improvement.

> *When organizations don't know how to innovate products or services, it's always because they lack sufficient knowledge of how their customers' processes work.*

Thus, don't worry about inventing something. Don't stick a bunch of scientists out in a research center somewhere hoping they'll have a brainstorm. That works, but its results can't be predicted. Instead, create a department in which employees continually build knowledge of how customers' processes work. This knowledge will reveal the problems, difficulties, inconveniences, and frustrations that your customers face. Ways to do away with these problems, difficulties, inconveniences, and frustrations are the innovation opportunities for you to make your customers' lives easier and better.

Remember, Deming says customers are anxious to buy products and services that make their lives easier and better. All you have to do is walk around in any shopping mall to see this kind of anxious searching going on, people searching for products and services that will make their lives easier and better. When you innovate a way to make their lives easier and better, you'll expand your market and prosper.

***The Example of the Nail Manufacturer.***  Let's consider an example of how innovation takes place by broadening the definition of the business you're in and by understanding customers' processes.

Suppose you manufacture and sell general-purpose and woodworking nails. Customers come into your outlet every day. Some buy common nails, some buy finishing nails, some buy casing nails, some buy annular ring nails, and so on. Suppose you have continuously improved your manufacturing processes so you produce the highest quality nails, and trade association data show you have the highest customer satisfaction in the industry. But, you want to do even better. You want to innovate to expand your market and prosper even more.

To innovate new products, you take Deming's advice and think of yourself in a broader line of business than merely nails. You do this by asking yourself "What is the larger category of which nails is a part? What's the generic category into which nails fall?" One answer is that nails are a type of fastener. That sounds good, so you may want to think of yourself as being in the fastener business. But, on second thought, you think fasteners is too narrow, and you prefer fasteners, hardware, and adhesives.

Beyond expanding the definition of the business you're in, you also need to understand your customers' processes. Because you make many kinds of nails, you have many different kinds of customers. So you select one type of customer to start with, maybe the one that accounts for most of your sales revenue. What are these customers doing when they use your products? What are their processes? How do fasteners, hardware, and adhesives fit into their processes? In particular, what problems, difficulties, inconveniences, and frustrations in their processes are related to fasteners, hardware, and adhesives?

To build knowledge about customer processes, you get your engineers out in the field with customers. They discover customers use sledge hammers to drive your nails into masonry and concrete, but the nails often buckle, bend, and break when used this way. You ask your engineers to think about what they learned. You ask them how fasteners could be innovated to make the lives of these customers easier. They experiment. In time, they come up with a new special heat-treated nail and holding tool for fastening to masonry and concrete surfaces. After some field tests and refinements, this product works. This product makes customers' lives easier and better. It expands your share of the market. You and your employees prosper.

On another occasion, you get your engineers out in the field with another important class of customers. Here they observe these customers using old-style nails that require drilling when used with concrete. Again, your engineers think about what they've learned, and they ask themselves what innovation they could come up with to make the lives of these customers easier. They experiment. As a consequence, they think up round, square, and fluted concrete nails that drive straight and set firmly. Again, this product enables your customers to live better. Your share of the market expands. You and your employees prosper.

Another discussion with your engineers gets focused on the work processes of roofers and carpenters. It is observed that these customers use hammers to drive nails. Someone remarks how nice it would be if you could somehow innovate away from the use of hammers. Hammers are heavy, tire those who use them, and are occasionally a safety hazard. After some thinking along this line your engineers come up with an air gun for use when a large number of nails must be driven in a short time period, such as when applying shingles or siding or when roughing in a room. You innovate and market such products. They save time and money in the building trades. They make your customers' lives easier and better. Your market share expands, and you and your employees prosper.

Could your customers have asked for these innovations? In their frustration with the old products for working with concrete, could they have come to you and asked for heat-treated nails and a holding tool or for round, square, and fluted nails? It is true that they could have complained about the existing products, but few of them could have identified these innovative fasteners. To do that would require knowledge of both your processes and theirs, and few of them have that knowledge. But you did.

*The Grocer Example.* Consider another illustration of innovating by expanding the definition of the business and understanding customers' processes. This time, you are a grocer who owns stores all over town. You've spent big bucks on marketing research to discover what grocery customers really want, and after you found out you did everything you could to continually streamline your processes to give it to them. Research showed that what most grocery customers want is low prices, so you've become a master at cost control. It is true that some customers don't mind higher prices. They want other things, such as no waiting to check out, carryout service, and gourmet and specialty items. But, you let those smaller market segments go to your competitors. You concentrate on the massive segment of customers where low prices is the key.

To innovate, you take Deming's advice about broadening the business you're in. You ask yourself, "What's the larger category of which grocery store is a part? What is the generic category?" One answer is that you can begin to think of yourself as a retailer rather than as a grocer. Retailing is a larger category into which grocery store falls.

Next, you go to the second step. You seek to understand how your customers' processes work. Through marketing research you get an important insight about customer processes. This insight was as plain as the nose on your face, but you overlooked it. When customers go out to buy groceries, they also run their other errands. On the way to the grocery store, they do other things, like drop off laundry, leave film to be developed, swing by the garden center, pick up a prescription, drop off a pair of shoes to be half-soled, or get fast food. Your research into their processes shows they don't like to leave the house to do one errand; they save up errands and do them all when they go for groceries. Small retailers know how customers do errands on their way to the grocery store, so they like to locate their shops near grocery stores like yours. They know they'll pick up lots of customers who are doing errands en route to your stores.

When you finally understood the customers' running errands process, you decided to experiment with selling the products and services offered by the small retailers located around your grocery stores. For instance, you added pharmacies inside your stores. Then you added garden supplies centers. Then shoe repair counters. Then floral sections. Then dry cleaning counters. Your customers can still do their errands on their way to the grocery store, but now they don't have to go to as many stores to do it. They can get more of what they need in your store. And, with your big volume and experience in cost containment, you're able to offer lower prices on these products and services than customers pay at small retailers. As a consequence, rather than your stores attracting customers for the little retailers, you began to compete with them. Eventually you drove many of them out of business with more one-stop shopping and lower prices. As a consequence, what used to be strip centers or shopping malls with clusters of small retailers around your grocery stores has changed. It is now your grocery stores with a lot of empty shops around them. The empty stores are the "dead bodies" of the small retailers.

Other small retailers have moved into many of these vacant stores offering products and services that you don't sell. These retailers hope you don't become interested in selling what they sell. These small retailers are like birds living near an alligator. The birds survive by eating insects stirred up by the alligator's thrashing around after fish. As long as the alligator is satisfied eating fish, the birds are safe.

In any case, you got into innovation by expanding how you thought of yourself from grocer to retailer, and by understanding an important dimension of your customers' shopping processes. Now your customers live better with one-stop shopping and lower prices on more of the products and services they require. You expanded your share of the market, and you and your employees prospered.

Before you made these changes, would any of your grocery customers ever have come up to you and said, "Hey, why don't you carry the products and services offered by the small retailers located around here? I know you could beat their prices, and I wouldn't have to shop at so many different stores. My time is valuable. I need to get back home to see the football game." Could they have identified ways for you to innovate? It's doubtful. To do so would require knowledge of both your processes and theirs. Few of them have this knowledge, but you did.

To test Deming's assertion that the customer is not a source of innovation, see if you can answer this question about innovation for a grocery store. Imagine some particular grocery store located near where you live. What could that grocer do now to innovate? What could that grocer do to make your life easier and better? This is a difficult question for any grocer unless customer processes are understood. And this question is impossible for customers, like you, who know neither the grocer's processes nor customers' processes. Oh, sure, you know your own grocery shopping processes, but without research it's impossible to know if your processes are representative of the shopping processes of any segment of grocery customers.

*A Hospital Example.* Innovation can come from simply understanding customers' processes; it doesn't always require expanding the definition of the business you're in. For instance, consider an example of a department that innovated its service to make life easier for another department in the same organization, a hospital. The first department is admitting; the second department is patient accounts. Admitting is responsible for gathering a wealth of information from persons as they are admitted as patients. A partial list of this information includes patient name, address, social security number, insurance carriers, insurance carrier account numbers, addresses of insurance carriers, third party guarantors, address of guarantors, discounts applicable, next of kin, address of next of kin, and various signed release documents.

Patient accounts accumulates information from all over the hospital so statements can be prepared and mailed to insurance companies and others for payment. Accumulating this information is complicated, and the correctness of statements is based on the accuracy and completeness of information received from admitting and other departments. Any omission or error in any one of hundreds of pieces of information input to patient accounts causes rework, delays, and frustration. For instance, if certain pieces of information required to complete patient statements are missing, patient accounts must recover them. Sometimes this means disturbing patients in their hospital rooms or at home after they have been discharged. Sometimes it requires contacting a physician's office. Another example is if insurance company addresses are incorrect, statements mailed to those addresses will be returned. The list of problems goes on almost endlessly when incorrect or incomplete information is provided to patient accounts.

Suppose you accept a job as the director of the admitting department. After you get to know your way around, you form a DIT and start practicing the customer defines quality strategy explained in chapter 9. After 11 months of hard work and much patience, your DIT improves your processes so you produce most of what patient accounts wants when it wants it. You asked the patient accounts employees what they need, and you improved your processes so that you provide it. Now, you're well into process improvement, but beyond providing timely, accurate information—you want to innovate. How do you do that?

To innovate, you might look at the new products displayed by vendors at hospital supplier conventions and wonder if buying them would help patient accounts. Or, you could get ideas from other admitting department managers. You might reason, "If it works for other hospitals, it might work for us." With rare exceptions, results from these approaches are marginal and usually dead ends. See Deming's remarks on the search for examples as an obstacle to the improvement of quality and productivity.[5]

To innovate in the admitting department, you must build knowledge of the processes of patient accounts. You need to find out how patient accounts uses the information you and others provide to it. You need to get admitting people involved with patient accounts people. You should flow diagram its processes. You must build knowledge of the problems, difficulties, inconveniences, and frustrations patient accounts employees have with their processes. This knowledge will reveal ways to innovate in your department that will make their lives easier.

What are some examples of how you could innovate in admitting to make life easier in patient accounts? You may learn from your flow diagram that at a certain step in its processes patient accounts employees collate information on three pieces of paper to construct a final statement. Two of these pieces of paper are sent by your department. You realize you can print the information contained on these two sheets of paper on one sheet. Further study tells you that information you send on another sheet of paper is not used. You stop sending it.

Thus, after this simple consolidation and elimination, life in patient accounts gets easier. There are two fewer pieces of paper to handle. In addition, you rearrange the order of the information on your one sheet of paper so it's easier to compare with the other sheet of paper that comes from another department. And, you plan to coordinate with the other department to see if the two of you can eventually send only one sheet of paper. You hope that eventually you can use electronic mail to eliminate paper information transfers altogether. None of these or dozens of other innovations like them are possible without knowledge of the processes in patient accounts.

*Are Changes Improvements or Innovations?* Consider the changes you made in admitting. Someone might argue that these changes were merely process improvements, not innovations. Actually, they were innovations. There is an important distinction between improvement and innovation.

> *Process improvements can be made without any knowledge of customers' processes, but innovations can seldom be made without that knowledge.*

The word *seldom* is used here instead of *never* because innovations occasionally result randomly from someone's brainstorm or burst of creativity.

Consider this distinction in the hospital illustration. You first improved your processes by ensuring that the information you provide to patient accounts is accurate and timely. You did that without any knowledge of the processes in patient accounts. But, to innovate you had to have knowledge of how that department's processes work. For instance, how could you know to combine the information on the two sheets of paper if you didn't know about the collation step in patient accounts' process?

Next, consider whether your rearrangement of the information on the sheet was an improvement or innovation. Improvement of this sheet would be to ensure the correctness and timeliness of the information it contained, but it was an innovation to rearrange the order of the information. The point is you would not have known to rearrange the information if you hadn't known patient accounts had difficulty comparing your sheet with a sheet that came from another department. You had to be familiar with your customer's processes to know that.

*Can Customers Ask for Innovations?* Another question is could patient accounts have asked for these innovations in your processes? It is true that patient accounts employees could have asked you for

If you plan for the future by monitoring financial results from the past, all you can do is react after revenues trend downward. In our example, revenue would trend downward because older customers begin to trade at stores where they can get carry-out service and the groceries they prefer, such as low-fat foods, more fish, and more fiber. Until you can react to these unforeseen changes, all you can do is try to maintain profits by cutting costs. All you can do is lay off loyal, hard-working employees who may have been with you for years. Then, if you're human, you'll lie awake nights worrying about how these people will feed their families and pay their bills. You need to quit relying on history, your accounting records, as a way of planning for the future. You've got to get out of the reactive mode. You need to learn to anticipate the effects of changes in the environment on your customers' processes.

Environmental factors that affect customers' processes come in all sizes and shapes. They can be psychological, sociological, cultural, emotional, technical, political, legal, military, religious, governmental, and regulatory. Consequently, an organization that wants to innovate not only establishes a way to continually build knowledge about customers' processes, but also establishes a means of continuously monitoring the environments that can affect its customers' processes. Detecting these changes is not easy, but it can give suppliers an early warning that an opportunity for innovation is coming up. Consider more examples.

Suppose a certain customer's processes are affected by government regulations, say on environmental concerns. The wise supplier to such organizations monitors the *Congressional Record* to read the debate in Congress about possible legislation in this area. Or, for a different example, if customers' processes are sensitive to fashion changes, the wise supplier monitors fashion ahead of local customers, say in London, Paris, or Rome. Or, if customer processes are affected by sociological concerns, the wise supplier may accumulate data on demographics in his or her trade area based on census documents and subscribe to relevant sociology journals.

## Innovation Principle 3: Know Your Customers' Customers' Processes

One environmental influence on your customers' processes is so important it deserves to be a separate principle. This is the influence on your customers' processes of their customers' processes. Think of it this way: You're a supplier to customers who are, in turn, suppliers to other customers. The idea is that what happens to your customers'

customers gets passed through your customers to you. Explaining this gets wordy with all the *customers' customers,* but the principle involved is powerful.

To illustrate the effects on your organization of your customers' customers, consider this question. What would happen to you if all your customers' customers went broke? The answer shows that anything that happens to your customers' customers will eventually get passed through to you. CEOs who wish to see into the future develop ways to build knowledge of the processes of their customers' customers. This knowledge is a powerful basis of innovation.

*The Cooking Oil Example.* To illustrate this principle, let's make you a supplier of cooking supplies to fast-food restaurants who specialize in fried chicken and fried fish. For the sake of better taste, these restaurants fry in animal fat. To meet their needs, you provide them with lard, a cooking product made from animal fat. But, let's suppose you are smart enough to monitor your customers' customers' eating habits (processes), and you realize they are changing. They are beginning to demand healthier food. As a result, you need to spend some serious time thinking about how this trend will affect your customers and, eventually, affect you, their supplier. You see into the future that unless customers of fast-food restaurants can buy something healthy at your customers' fast-food restaurants, they may eat elsewhere.

If many fast-food customers go elsewhere for healthier meals, the sales of your customers are going to suffer, and this will mean that you, in turn, will sell less. You don't want this to happen. Seeing this in the future, you decide to find a healthier oil for frying chicken and fish. You see the writing on the wall, and you want to have a solution to the problem before your customers are even aware of it. You find vegetable oil. As a consequence, your sales staff starts pushing vegetable oil and provides free literature to be handed out at your customers' restaurants to inform customers how "This restaurant now cooks with healthier oil with the same great taste!" You deal with the objection that vegetable oil has less taste with the argument that today's customers want healthier food. And, you offer menu recommendations on how to use seasonings and spices to heighten taste. You also have menu recommendations on baking and broiling instead of frying.

If you understood only your immediate customers' processes, you could have only reacted to this change as their sales slumped. But, because you understood the processes of your customers' customers, you were able to be proactive. You got out in front of other restaurant suppliers long before they saw the need for healthier cooking oil. You not only maintained your own customers and delighted them by keeping them in the market, but you increased your share of the market by offering healthier cooking products to your competitors' customers before your competitors could do so. You accomplished this simple innovation by building knowledge of your customers' customers' processes.

*The Child Care Provider.* Consider another example of this innovation principle in a story of the owner of a day-care facility. She had a background in sociology and studied people patterns carefully. Over the years, she benefited from the increasing employment of women and the increasing percentage of both parents working. These factors translated into a greater demand for child care by working parents. But, a new pattern recently caught her attention. Statistics suggest that single parents are entering the work force in increasing numbers, and some of them don't earn enough to afford professional child care. They rely on relatives and friends for child care. And, other data suggest that low-wage single parents are more often late and absent from work because of the unreliable child care provided by relatives and friends.

It occurred to her that if companies would pay for child care the savings to them from reduced tardiness and absenteeism among lower-wage single parents might more than offset its cost. In addition, providing child care on-site would give companies more control and would be more convenient to parents. She approached a number of companies with an offer to operate day care of this type on their premises on a trial basis. Several accepted her offer, and the results were positive.

In this illustration, an entrepreneur detected a trend and foresaw how it could affect the processes of an important class of employees and, in turn, their employers. The result was an innovation that benefited everyone. The businesses benefited because they had less tardiness and absenteeism among a growing segment of their work force. Employees benefited because they were late and absent less often from work. Furthermore, they had reliable, safe, and professional care for their children, and the location of the care was convenient. The entrepreneur benefited because she expanded the market for child care. Her employees benefited because their jobs became more secure, and she hired more employees.

# Moving Forward

It is important to know what customers want and to continually improve the processes that produce what they want. But, it is also important to understand customer processes and the environments that influence them. This is how we see into the future. This is how we innovate. The future belongs to those who innovate products and services, and innovation requires the capability to continually build knowledge about customers' processes and their environments.

A final question is how TQM affects organizations. For instance, when TQM is implemented and operations streamlined, does the size of an organization's work force shrink? Are employees laid off? In TQM does the shape of organizations change so they are flatter? Do they delayer and reengineer themselves so they are more horizontal than vertical? These questions are answered in the last chapter.

# Notes

1. Thomas C. Kinnear and James R. Taylor, *Marketing Research: An Applied Approach*, 4th ed. (New York: McGraw-Hill, 1991), p. 5.

2. W. Edwards Deming, *The New Economics for Industry, Government, and Education* (Cambridge, Mass.: MIT Press, 1993), pp. 7–9.

3. Ibid., pp. 8–9.

4. Ibid., p. 10.

5. W. Edwards Deming, *Out of the Crisis* (Cambridge, Mass.: MIT Press, 1986), pp. 128–129.

*Chapter 12*

# The Effects of TQM
# on Organizations


Traditional enterprises are organized on the basis of the division of labor into functional areas, such as sales, manufacturing, and finance, within often gigantic vertical hierarchies or pyramids of authority. These pyramids are managed vertically, with each functional area seeking to maximize itself and ordinarily having little to do with other functional areas. In fact, many CEOs pit functional areas against one another on the grounds that it brings out their best.

As CEOs make the transition into the process improvement stage of TQM, they learn that all the work does not take place vertically within functional areas. They learn that the most important work takes place horizontally in processes that cut across functional boundaries. They learn that these processes are chains in which functional areas are linked together as customers and suppliers. To their chagrin, they learn there are many costly disconnects as products and services are handed off across the boundaries of their functional areas. In addition to these disconnects, these processes are rife with rework, delays, and bureaucracy that cause gray hair and ulcers for CEOs, the screams and curses of customers, and the anguish and frustration of employees.

As CEOs understand more about TQM, they see that something has got to be done about these processes. They realize this is not a job of mere restoration because these processes never worked correctly in the first place. The solution lies in transforming organizations so that the continual improvement of processes becomes a way of life.

Many CEOs realize effectiveness gains, such as the continual improvement of processes, can be permanent only if they have cultural support. And, many believe that following Deming's teachings is the way to provide this support. Many CEOs achieve both effectiveness gains and cultural support through widespread and continual education in Deming's teachings and through an infrastructure of PITs that initiate the necessary transformation through DITs. As this transformation takes place, it has a number of dramatic effects on organizations and their structures. It is the aim of this chapter to describe these effects.

## Reduction of Full-Time Equivalents

As PITs and DITs improve processes, a clear sign of their success is that departments begin giving back full-time equivalents (FTEs). CEOs say they've heard this happens in TQM, but they never thought it would happen in their organizations. But, sure enough, it does happen. Let's take a moment to explain why.

It all has to do with reducing quality-related costs. It is difficult to precisely measure quality-related costs, but Frank M. Gryna suggests they include internal failure costs, external failure costs, appraisal costs, and prevention costs.[1] Familiar examples of these costs include rework, unnecessary bureaucracy, unnecessary work, unnecessary storage, duplication, errors, delays, unnecessary management, untimely deliveries, and so on. These costs are almost never anybody's fault; they're caused by processes that don't work correctly. Gryna refers to studies that show that quality-related costs are ". . . much larger than . . . shown in accounting reports," and "for most companies are in the range of 20 to 60% of sales." Kaydos refers to studies that estimate ". . . that as much as 30% of a company's resources can be spent correcting quality problems that shouldn't happen in the first place." In my experience, many of these costs should be added to Deming's list of "the most important figures that one needs for management [that] are unknown and unknowable."[2] The bulk of these costs—the ones that don't show up on accounting reports and are invisible to management—are caused by the tyranny of upstream supplier departments. For instance, I've encountered many departments that had personnel doing nothing but correcting errors made by upstream departments. Between correcting what was done incorrectly upstream and what departments themselves do wrong, I have no doubt quality-related costs are as high as the many studies of the subject suggest. In fact, my experience suggests that rework alone may be as high as 30 percent to 60 percent for some departments. Anyway, consider an illustration of what happens to FTEs in a department when rework is stripped out.

Consider a department that's in pretty good shape. Only 25 percent of what it does is rework. Strange as it may seem, 25 percent rework may reflect that a department is doing well. Rework is often far worse. In any case, in this department a quarter of the time things are done twice to get them right. The CEO begins education and process improvement with PITs and DITs, and after months of work, the effort begins to pay off. The percentage of rework begins to fall. Let's say it goes down to zero. (It would be rare that all rework could be eliminated, but you can get close.) The 60 people in this department now have a quarter less work to do. So, if the work load stays the same and it takes a quarter less effort to do it, doesn't it make sense to say a quarter fewer people are needed? A quarter of 60 is 15. The question is, what happens to these 15 extra FTEs?

In the first place, during a typical TQM effort department managers often use temporary employees and overtime to keep up the work of employees serving as SMEs on PITs and DITs. This backfill is needed because it's unfair to ask employees to keep up fully with their regular jobs while devoting time to team meetings and homework. In any case, as rework is eliminated and FTEs are freed up, the first reaction of department managers is to cease using temporaries and overtime. Newly freed up FTEs are put on backfill.

In the second place, an almost universal reaction of department managers to a reduction in work load (because of the elimination of rework) is to pad the books, so to speak, on FTEs because they suspect the reduction is only temporary. And, they've learned from years of dealing with personnel managers that it's easier to keep FTEs than get them back after they've been given up. But, as time goes by and the elimination of rework continues to reduce the need for FTEs, only the most fearful department managers will continue to hoard FTEs.

When department managers give back FTEs, CEOs rejoice. They rejoice because they see labor costs going down and output staying the same. In anybody's language, this means more profit. This is something to take to the board of directors.

Now, consider a key question. When fewer FTEs are needed because of reduced rework, isn't it smart to reduce the size of the work force? In many cases, it is. Yet, if CEOs have learned anything about TQM, they know laying off employees as a result of process improvement will seriously undermine their TQM effort. This is because team members will not be enthusiastic about improving processes if it can cost them their jobs. Therefore, from the start, it should be a visible policy that no one will lose his or her employment as a result of TQM.

But, if a policy is in place that no one will lose their employment over TQM, how can the work force be downsized when process improvement lessens the need for FTEs? The answer is this. Process improvement doesn't happen overnight. It happens slowly and unevenly throughout an organization. As process improvement happens slowly, there is natural employee attrition. People retire or take jobs elsewhere. These FTEs are not replaced. As process improvement happens unevenly, FTEs no longer needed in departments where improvement is happening faster are retrained and transferred (at the same salaries) to departments where improvement is happening more slowly. The answer, therefore, to downsizing that results from streamlining processes is natural attrition. And, this answer allows CEOs to sleep better at night because they don't have to worry about how laid off employees will provide for their families.

But, for CEOs who really understand TQM, other results of process improvement make questions about how to downsize meaningless. Those familiar with Deming's teachings on the chain reaction know he says quality improvement leads to jobs and more jobs.[3] In other words, TQM results in staff increases, not decreases! How does this happen?

## Capture the Market with Better Quality and Lower Price

When processes are improved, three things happen. The first is that the cost of operations goes down. For instance, fewer materials are wasted, time is saved, and less labor is required.

The second thing that happens when processes are improved is that customers get higher quality. Because processes are working, products and services get to customers when they're needed. And, products work like they should. The wheels don't fall off. Fewer warranty calls are required. Customers don't have to yell at service representatives. As a consequence, customers are satisfied and come back again, and they may bring their friends. As word gets around about their quality products and services, organizations capture more of the market, just as Deming predicts in his chain reaction.[4] Therefore, not only does process improvement reduce costs, it increases market share by attracting customers with higher quality.

A third thing happens when processes are improved. Lower costs for the same volume of output allow organizations to either put more money in the bank or lower their selling price. Lowering selling price is a way of sharing the gain from reducing rework with customers.

But, lower prices on high-quality products and services has an additional competitive benefit. Consider the impact on customers when quality is high and prices are lower. Customers will be shocked because higher quality usually means higher prices, not lower prices. But, you can be sure they'll like it, and they wouldn't dream of shopping anywhere else. And, again, they may bring their friends.

There are many examples of how lower prices captured a greater share of the market. Consider retailing, especially discounters and supermarkets. There also are many examples of how higher quality captured a greater share of the market. Many Japanese products illustrate this. With higher quality, sellers can keep prices the same, lower them, or raise them. In the case of most Japanese automobiles, prices are raised as quality improves. The Japanese discovered customers are willing to pay premium prices for automobiles that work reliably. An illustration of higher quality and lower prices is electronics goods, such as stereo receivers and color television sets.

## *The Most Powerful Competitive Strategy*

If it isn't enough to go at your competition with lower prices for high-quality products and services, consider the most powerful strategy available to CEOs who have improved their organizations' processes. These CEOs do not draw the easy conclusion that process improvement leads to the reduction of FTEs. They see things more clearly and more competitively. They know that process improvement with the same number of employees leads to excess capacity. And, they know this excess capacity can be sold, even to competitors, to capture an even greater share of the market. So, when they improve their processes, they don't anticipate reducing FTEs. Instead, they aggressively go after more market share by selling the excess capacity that process improvement provides.

Consider an illustration of how this works. Recall the department with the 60 employees and rework of 25 percent. When it got its rework down to zero, it could have concluded that there were 15 employees too many and eliminated the excess FTEs through attrition and transfers. This would have resulted in the same capacity, but fewer employees. This would make some CEOs happy because of the lower costs and something to take to the board of directors. But, there is a much more aggressive way to manage this situation. In this illustration, the organization retained all 60 employees. This meant excess capacity. The organization sold this excess capacity to existing and new customers.

The organization in this illustration was the laboratory in a hospital. To fill its excess capacity, the laboratory solicited lab work from other hospitals on the grounds that it could do better work at a lower cost. This was true because the laboratory had improved its processes. Other hospitals quickly saw this as a way to get better lab work at a lower cost than they could provide for themselves. So, they folded up their labs and contracted their lab work to the higher quality, lower price laboratory with the other hospital. In time, this laboratory did the lab work of practically every hospital in the area.

Notice that, as this laboratory captured the market, everyone benefited. The laboratory and its employees prospered. More employees were hired. The laboratory was able to spend money to provide more training and get the best equipment. The other hospitals got higher quality lab work at lower prices. Everyone's patients got better lab work at lower prices. Physicians got better care for their patients through more accurate and timely lab results. Society benefited because health care costs were reduced.

CEOs should foresee that they will not be required to lay off, attrite, or retrain and transfer anyone out of departments where processes are improved. The fact is that, with new business from higher quality and lower prices, they will need to hire more people! This is what Deming means when he talks about how improving quality reduces rework, lowers prices, captures the market, and provides jobs and more jobs.[5]

CEOs who don't follow Deming's advice about improving quality are forced to control costs by laying off loyal, hardworking employees in the usual way traditional organizations operate. You see employee layoffs reported every day in the newspaper. These CEOs simply do not know their jobs. All the while, CEOs who follow Deming's advice are adding new employees and giving existing employees big gain-sharing bonuses! It's amazing. For organizations in the same industry, same town, or even directly across the street from one another, these activities will be happening at exactly the same time. Good things happen to organizations that follow Deming's way, and bad things happen to those that don't.

# The Effects of TQM on Organizational Structure: Reengineering

As CEOs journey through the four stages of TQM, they build knowledge. They come to understand the power in the statement "The customer defines quality." And, because they believe the customer defines quality, they work hard to understand their customers' processes and the environments that affect them so they can innovate products and services. They work hard to focus organizational resources through horizontal processes on customer requirements.

CEOs realize survival depends on horizontal processes that work well on behalf of customers. As they work with PITs and DITs to improve their processes, they build knowledge that some processes are highly important and are core processes, while others are feeder or support processes to core processes, and still other processes can be eliminated altogether.

Core processes fall into one of three categories. The first two have to do with customers. Recall that a process is defined as a series of repeatable steps that produce products or services that go to or affect customers. In other words, the last step in any process is a customer receiving or being affected by the output of the process. Core processes that have to do with customers have either one large customer or a collection of customer types at their ends. These processes provide something that makes customers' lives easier and better. So, these are two categories of core processes: those that have either a large customer or a collection of customer types at their ends. The third category of core processes is those that have to do with important internal operations that, in one way or another, support customer-related core processes.

## *An Example of Reengineering*

Consider an example of reengineering a core process. Most hospitals are organized on the hierarchical model. One of their departments, admitting, admits patients and another department, patient accounts, accumulates charges and prepares and mails statements to payers. Much of the information patient accounts needs to get correct statements to correct addresses comes from admitting, and from other departments that provide services to patients, such as nursing, pharmacy, and the laboratories.

Although few hospital administrators appreciate the magnitude of this problem, countless times every day the ball is dropped in hospitals organized functionally when information is handed off from various departments to patient accounts. Vital information is not collected, collected incorrectly, not charged, charged incorrectly, mishandled, stored needlessly or incorrectly, lost, and miscommunicated so that patient statements all too often contain errors and are delayed in getting delivered. The larger these departments, the more times the ball is dropped. The negative effects of these disconnects are too many to list. The more dramatic ones include services rendered to patients but not charged to their accounts, services charged to the wrong patient accounts, patient complaints, employee frustration, and accounts receivable (money hospitals have earned but not collected) far larger than it has to be. For large hospitals, a cash flow delayed by accounts receivable can translate into millions of dollars of lost interest every month.

Flow diagraming builds knowledge of the opportunities to improve cross-functional processes, and understanding more about customer processes can lead to innovation of products and services. Both of these activities were used to improve the situation for the hospital illustrated here. But, the knowledge built also led to a substantial modification, or reengineering, of the way the admitting and patient accounts departments were organized. Rather than leaving them as separate departments, they were consolidated with the medical records department and managed horizontally as a core process under one director. This ensured that complete and accurate paperwork flowed from the time patients were admitted, or when services were rendered on their behalf, to the preparation of their statements. There were fewer departmental boundaries where the ball could be dropped.

This departmental consolidation was brought about smoothly because a cross-functional team, a PIT, had been in place for more than a year. The participation of employees from the admitting, patient accounts, and medical records departments on this team brought them closer together. In addition, DITs were begun in these departments, and they worked with each other on taskings. Barriers between the three departments were broken down by these team activities. These three departments were then reorganized horizontally with these teams as the building blocks. Existing teams, both PITs and DITs, were in place to coordinate the smooth feed of information from ancillary departments, such as nursing, pharmacy, and the laboratories, into the core process. The performance objectives of the core process were horizontally based on missing data reports at the end of the process, accounts receivable days (average number of days statements were in accounts receivable), and customer satisfaction, rather than on separate departmental MBO-type goals, profitability, or shareholder value. Budgeting was based on the aims of the core process, not on departmental goals.

In time, knowledge was further built that this core process could be stratified by customer type, such as Medicare, Medicaid, Champus, private pay, and standard insurance, with separate cross-functional teams coordinating each. Beyond the virtual elimination of ball dropping between departments, many benefits came from the greater sense of cooperation among employees as they saw their work as part of a seamless core process, or system, rather than as separate departments. They came to see their part of the hospital's organizational chart as a block diagram that comprised one horizontal process with the director's office ensuring coordination and support.

CEOs of other health care organizations see the value of placing key ancillary support units, such as radiology, pharmacy, and laboratories, together with their main customer, nursing service, as core processes under one director rather than leaving them as separate vertical empires.

Progressive manufacturers often organize product development, sales generation, and production scheduling cross-functionally as core processes around large customers or many smaller customers that comprise a market or customer type. With functional representation on such multidisciplinary teams, new product development is faster, sales are more appropriate to customer needs, and production scheduling is more flexible.

## Snags in Reengineering Around Processes

Many CEOs understand that it takes more than a pyramid of power to stay flexible and vigorous in today's competitive global marketplace. But there can be a number of snags in reengineering organizations horizontally around core processes.

A dangerous snag can be reengineering without first building knowledge of how processes work by improving them with PITs and DITs and without changing the culture with Deming's teachings. In their rush to instant results, traditional CEOs often hire consulting firms in the hope of an overnight transformation of their top-heavy hierarchical organizations into sleek, efficient horizontal organizations. But this does not permit the necessary up-front understanding of customer processes and their environments or the time to understand the linkages between the requirements of major customers or classes of customers and the aims (vision and mission statements) of organizations. The selection of core processes is, therefore, uncertain at best.

Another snag is the resistance among personnel being moved from functional areas, where narrow specialties and task management are important, to cross-functional teams where multiple competencies, such as systems thinking, problem solving, statistical thinking, and cooperation, are required. There is also resistance among managers to flattening, or delayering, organizations because of fear and uncertainty about their new jobs and roles. And, senior managers can be resistant to the requirement of cross-functional teams for information that was once a basis of power for those at the top. Other technical problems often not foreseen include the need to modify training programs, career paths, and compensation systems based on the new horizontal emphasis in organizations.

Another snag can be CEOs' need to see organizational charts that show how things work. Once they accept that the old pyramid of power is not the one best way to organize, they can be anxious to see the new one best way to organize. This need is reminiscent of the traditional style of management and Taylor's one best way. The answer is there is no one best way to organize. Like everything else, organizational design must be in a constant state of improvement. Why should organizational design be exempted from the TQM requirement for continual improvement? Organizational design must be continually reconfigured as customer processes, customer environments, and technology change.

Few organizations are ever completely horizontal. Most will be hybrids, moving in the beginning to only one horizontal core process and, with time, organizing a few more. And, for most, there always will be a senior management group, also multidisciplinary in nature, that oversees the coordination of processes and ensures support.

## Notes

1. Frank M. Gryna, "Quality Costs," in *Juran's Quality Control Handbook*, 4th ed., edited by J. M. Juran and Frank M. Gryna (New York: McGraw-Hill, 1988), pp. 4.5–4.12.

2. Ibid., p. 4.1; Will Kaydos, *Measuring, Managing, and Maximizing Performance* (Cambridge, Mass.: Productivity Press, 1991), p. 27; and W. Edwards Deming, *Out of the Crisis* (Cambridge, Mass.: MIT Press, 1986), pp. 121–122.

3. Ibid., p. 3.

4. Ibid.

5. Ibid.

# How Teams Can Practice and Model the Deming Philosophy

To reach their full potential, teams must have two aims. The first is well-known and widely attempted: to increase organizational effectiveness through the continual improvement of processes. The second is not well-known or understood, even by the authors of most books on the subject of teams. The second aim of teams is to be a force for changing organizational culture.

There is a road map to follow in changing an organization's culture. It is Deming's 14 points: a list of dos and don'ts that can be followed to transform any organization from the traditional style of management. Many people believe the 14 points are only for management, and even Deming refers to them as "the 14 points for management." But, he also says, "The 14 points apply anywhere, to small organizations as well as large ones, to service industries as well as to manufacturing. They apply to a division within a company."[1] It should be added that the 14 points apply to teams, too.

Teams are more likely to achieve both of their aims when they practice and model Deming's 14 points. They are more likely to achieve effectiveness gains, and they are more likely to influence their organization's culture. Another way to think about this is to understand that teams can influence culture by acting as a training ground in Deming's teachings for team members and as a model of how things should be done in Deming's way for all who come in contact with them. Yet another way to see this point is to think of teams as small organizations that follow Deming's teachings in literally everything they do. Like large organizations, teams should have aims (their opportunity statements), managers (team leaders), employees (team members), customers (downstream departments and others), suppliers (upstream departments and others), and, just like any organization, they can follow Deming's teachings as a guide to what they think is important and how they do things.

At first, running a team strictly according to Deming's teachings may seem awkward. This feeling is only natural because, for most people, it's a new way of doing things. But the more Deming's way is practiced, the more sense it will make. After people serve on teams that work Deming's way, they often wonder how any team ever accomplishes anything when it doesn't do things this way.

Those who have studied Deming's teachings are usually quick to see how his teachings apply to teams. But for others, the connection may not be so plain. This appendix provides a few thoughts on how Deming's teachings can be followed by teams.

Once team leaders and facilitators realize how using Deming's teachings enhances team capabilities, their team skills will improve rapidly. But, here's a word of caution. In the few cases where basing team activities on Deming's teachings failed, it was almost always for one of two reasons: (1) a team leader or facilitator believed he or she had mastered Deming's teachings by reading one book on the subject or by some other limited exposure, or (2) management did not adequately support the undertaking.

For the average person, developing a thorough understand of the Deming philosophy, beyond a nodding acquaintance with the 14 points, takes time. This knowledge cannot be learned by reading one book on Deming's teachings. Learning Deming's philosophy requires continuing study of his books.[2] One should also read the books written by others about Deming's work. One part of Deming's teaching may not be clear in one book but easily learned from another. Every book about Deming's teachings with which I am familiar is listed in the suggested readings sections at the end of this book.

To my knowledge, there is nothing in print or otherwise available that addresses the question of how teams practice and model Deming's philosophy. To take a small step in remedying this deficiency, I provide the following remarks on how teams can practice the 14 points. These remarks assume the reader is familiar with these points as they are discussed in other contexts.

### Point 1—Create Constancy of Purpose

No one can have constancy of purpose unless he or she has first decided on a purpose. To this end, everyone who wishes to practice constancy of purpose must begin by stating his or her purpose or aim. In the case of a PIT, it seeks constancy of purpose to accomplish its opportunity statement, or aim, as chartered by a quality council.

A PIT's opportunity statement should appear at the top of its meeting agendas, and a different SME should be asked to read it aloud to begin each meeting. This starts every meeting by focusing on what the team is trying to achieve. Then, team members can work constantly to achieve this aim.

Opportunity statements identify processes targeted for continuous improvement. Team members are chosen for their belief that their assigned process can be improved. Team members must agree on their team's aim.

Meeting agendas outline what teams intend to accomplish during their meetings and provide time frames, including stop and start points during meeting times, for each agenda item. It should be clear to team members how each agenda item contributes to the accomplishment of team aims.

During meetings, team members should be trained always to consider the team's aim before getting involved in any activity. If what the team is about to do does not contribute to its aim, members should resist doing it. For instance, ask, "Why are we gathering these data? What will these data be used for, and how will having them help us achieve our aim?" "Why are we using this cause-and-effect diagram?" "Why are we using voting with the ENGT? How will these activities help us achieve our aim?" When team members report homework results, they should always begin by reminding the team of the aim of their assignment. They also should show in their report how the product of their homework assignment helped move the team toward its aim.

The question, "What is our aim?" should be asked so often by leaders and facilitators that it gets branded into team members' brains. Hopefully, they will come to see the value of knowing the aims of everything they do, and they will take this practice back to their regular jobs and even to their personal lives.

Knowing one's aim so one can work constantly to achieve it is a concept with universal application. It applies to teams, but it also applies to everyone's professional and personal lives. Team members should be reminded of how the aim of their team ties in with the aim (vision or mission statement) of the organization.

In addition, members should be asked how their personal aim fits in with the aim of the team and organization. If team members don't have a personal aim, they should be encouraged to develop one. Most people have a vague idea of what their personal aim is, but they should be encouraged to think it through and write it down on paper. Individuals can begin to develop a personal aim by asking themselves to identify the main things they're trying to accomplish with their lives. They should review their aims from time to time and rethink the important issues involved.

Beyond having a personal aim, team members should be trained to see the value of having their spouses and families come to consensus on their common aims. Like teams, families with aims do better than families without aims. How can a family accomplish something unless every family member knows what it is they're trying to accomplish? In developing a family aim, team members should ensure that all family members have a voice. They should ensure that family aims are in harmony with Deming's teachings on the aim of a system.[3]

Discussing the value of personal and family aims will deepen team members' appreciation of the value of constancy of purpose in their work on teams. Using the ENGT and voting (see Appendix C) to develop an aim with their families also is a valuable learning experience for team members.

## Point 2—Adopt a New Philosophy

There are two new philosophies to emphasize in point 2: Understand that the customer defines quality, and replace competition with cooperation. With respect to the first philosophy, facilitators should help team members work away from the viewpoint that they know what's best for their internal and external customers. As a matter of fact, a team strategy, described in chapter 9, is based on the philosophy that the customer defines quality. It involves simple steps that a team can work through: (1) define the term *customer*; (2) identify your customers; (3) prioritize your customers; (4) select a customer from the prioritized list, and learn what this customer wants; (5) develop measures of how well you're providing what the selected customer wants; and (6) work continuously to improve the processes that affect the measures of how well you're providing what this customer wants. For different customers, cycle through steps 4 through 6.

Teams must avoid the trap of believing they are already doing the best they can for their customers considering their staffing level and thin resources. This belief leads to the conclusion that customers have to accept organizations as they are. "Our customers are already getting the best we have to give" is a viewpoint that ignores the fact that your processes are choked with unnecessary rework, duplication, bureaucracy, and delays. When these barriers are stripped away, your ability to meet customer needs will increase dramatically.

The second new philosophy is to replace adversarial competition with cooperation. It has been said many times in this book that, with rare exceptions (such as in professional sports), the effects of competition are ruinous to individuals and teams.

If team members are encouraged to compete either among themselves or with other teams, their results will come much more slowly, if at all, and will not approach their potential. For instance, think of the devastating consequences when a team leader and facilitator do not agree on their team's aim. One interprets the aim one way; the other interprets it differently. Pity the unfortunate team members whose leader and facilitator don't agree on the aim. That's almost as bad as a husband and wife who don't agree on the aim of their marriage. It leads to trouble without end. To reduce the possibility of this problem occurring, leaders should ensure that their team aim is discussed to consensus at the first team meeting and is occasionally reviewed.

To remind everyone of the importance of cooperation, some leaders place a large poster in the team meeting room with the word, *cooperate* lettered boldly on it. This, of course, is an exhortation, and exhorting team members to cooperate will not work unless they are taught how to do it. Consensus building, negotiating, and mediation techniques are available to help get team members into the spirit and practice of cooperation, and they should be taught to appreciate the damage competition does to a system. (See Deming's thoughts on a system.[4])

In addition to team members learning to cooperate with each other, they must also cooperate with other teams to whom they spin off taskings for process improvements. Team leaders and facilitators must be alert always for signs of adversarial competition and act quickly to point them and their negative consequences out. Cooperation must become normal behavior on teams. In addition, cooperation must be modeled for others who come in contact with teams so it will eventually become commonplace throughout organizations.

Teams and other personnel, including managers, must be taught cooperation through the practice of consensus. Consensus and how it is achieved is discussed in Appendix C.

Management must endorse cooperation with appropriate administrative policies, especially to cease the use of performance appraisals and pay-for-performance programs. These programs create competition.

## Point 3—Cease Dependence on Inspection to Achieve Quality

Sometimes, inspection is necessary. If a nurse is about to give you an injection, for example, don't you want him or her to double-check that the medication you're about to receive is correct? And wouldn't it be a good idea to see if there's enough antifreeze in your radiator before a blizzard blows in? The idea is not to do away with necessary inspection, but to understand that inspection alone will not achieve quality. Separating the good from the bad and reworking the bad will eventually produce a defect-free batch. But it's inefficient, costly, too slow, and unpredictable.

The better way to achieve quality is to improve processes so the products and services they produce don't need rework. These are the very processes that teams are chartered to improve. Processes that cross departments are improved by PITs; those that cross sections within departments are improved by DITs.

Team members should be taught that processes are composed of components—including materials, methods, environment, machines, and personnel—and each of these components can be the subject of improvement.

The flow diagram is a tool for building knowledge of how the components of processes fit together in a series of repeatable steps. It uses symbols—such as ovals for start/end points, rectangles for actions or steps, diamonds for decision points, and bullets for delays—to describe these steps. Processes should always be flow diagramed to build knowledge of how they work, and this knowledge will point to improvement opportunities. Before flow diagraming a process, a team must work to a consensus on the aim or aims of the process.

When considering Deming's point 3, teams should take special note of diamonds on their flow diagrams. Diamonds represent yes or no decisions of all kinds. These decisions can be inspections, where yes/no decisions indicate where something either passed (yes) or failed (no) inspection. At inspection diamonds, teams must ensure that inspections are necessary, not redundant, valid, and not being relied on to achieve quality. Teams must ensure that quality is built in upstream of inspection points. When flow diagrams are used to build sufficient knowledge of how processes work, teams will know what to do to improve them.

## Point 4—End the Practice of Awarding Business on the Basis of Price Tag Alone

Point 4 sounds like it has to do with only external suppliers, those suppliers from whom you buy products and services. But, working with internal, upstream suppliers for process improvement is usually of more concern to teams.

In my experience, the quality of the output of any department is dependent, usually as much as 90 percent, on the support of its upstream suppliers. When upstream departments are not managed in the interest of system optimization, it is virtually certain that they will tyrannize their downstream customers. These customers, in turn, can't help but tyrannize their own customers farther downstream. Teams must end this chain of tyranny.

A team improvement strategy for dealing with suppliers is explained in chapter 9. It's called the *tyranny of the supplier*. This strategy involves the following steps carried out by a DIT or, occasionally, by a PIT: (1) define the word *supplier*; (2) identify your suppliers; (3) prioritize your suppliers; (4) take your suppliers in order of their priority, and list the ways the selected supplier tyrannizes you; (5) prioritize the list of ways the selected supplier tyrannizes you; (6) gather data on the effects of the highest priority tyranny; and (7) prepare a tasking memorandum to initiate continuous improvement in the supplier's processes. Cycle repeatedly through the highest priority suppliers and their highest priority tyrannies, initiating improvement in each cycle. Seek to develop long-term relationships of trust and loyalty with suppliers to build quality into their products and services. This involves breaking down barriers and practicing all of Deming's 14 points.

## *Point 5—Improve Constantly and Forever*

This point is the companion to point 3. Deming's 14 points work together as a unified theory of management, and points 3 and 5 emphasize the need for continual process improvement. You must not rely on inspection to build in quality, as explained in point 3; you must, instead, practice point 5 to build in quality by constantly and forever improving the system (or processes) of production and service.

Teams should take the lead in changing the belief that there is a one best way to do things. They must not see their aim as merely restoring broken-down processes. Few processes worked right in the first place, so what's the sense of restoring them to their former state? Before teams can improve processes, they must first build knowledge of how processes work. When sufficient knowledge is built about how processes work, teams will know what to do to improve them. The best tool for building knowledge about how processes work is the flow diagram.

Teams practice and model for the rest of the organization the concept of constant and forever improvement of the system of production and service. Teams, themselves, must practice what they preach. They must constantly and forever improve the way they do their team business. For instance, they must improve the way they conduct their meetings. To make this happen, the last item on each team's agenda is meeting evaluation. The last few minutes of each meeting is devoted to the leader going around the room soliciting thoughts from members about what the team did well and what the team didn't do so well during the meeting. This activity builds team knowledge about how to make meetings better. Other ways teams can continually improve is in how they assign homework, how homework is conducted and reported, how statistical tools are selected and used, how improvement strategies are selected and used, and how teams learn about and practice Deming's teachings. Team members must understand there is no one best way; everything must be continually under review for improvement—even the way teams conduct their meetings.

## Point 6—Institute Training on the Job

Like anyone else, team members must be trained for their jobs. Team leaders and facilitators should have the benefit of formal classroom training in Deming's teachings, team meeting skills, improvement strategies, consensus building, and statistics tools under the direction of a master. They should also have the opportunity to practice applying this knowledge during actual team meetings under the watchful eye of a master. When handled in this way, there is no better training than experiencing Deming's way as it is practiced by teams.

Members come to teams as SMEs on their part of the process, but they need training in Deming's teachings and on the quality improvement tools. This training can be done on a just-in-time basis by leaders or facilitators during team meetings. As teams conduct their meetings, members have the best opportunity to learn about Deming's way of doing things because they see it being practiced.

## Point 7—Institute Leadership

Remember, we are talking about how Deming's 14 points apply to teams, so when we say *leadership* we're referring to the leaders of teams. Deming's teachings on leadership are made plain in his recent book, *The New Economics for Industry, Government, and Education*.[5]

Team leaders must understand that teams have two aims. The first is to initiate improvements in chartered processes. To improve processes, team leaders must understand how processes contribute to the aim of the organization. They also must understand how to use the team improvement strategies, explained in chapter 9.

The second aim of teams is to be a force for changing an organization's culture. By the time they are assigned to teams, leaders should be well down the road to understanding Deming's teachings. They should have an appreciation for systems, or processes, and how it takes cooperation among all the suppliers and customers in a process to accomplish an aim. They must be capable of communicating this understanding to others on teams. They must be willing to take the risks involved in teaching and working by cooperation and in adopting Deming's teachings. They should be interested in self-improvement and, therefore, be unceasing learners. They should be interested in learning how to improve their leadership skills and how to make their teams more effective.

Team leaders should be models, coaches, and counselors to team members. They should help team members improve and understand that inspecting, judging, policing, and ranking people doesn't help them. They should understand how these practices harm team members and reduce any team's effectiveness. A team leader's job is to create trust and an open environment that encourages cooperation, freedom of expression, imagination, and creativity.

## *Point 8—Drive Out Fear*

Wise CEOs know that all the brains are not at the top of the hierarchy. They accept that the best persons to improve processes are the employees who work in those processes. These employees are SMEs. They are gathered together as a team and are chartered to improve processes. Nothing can be a bigger roadblock to their success than fear.

Like most people, SMEs want to do a good job and be proud of their employer. But to do a good job, they must feel free to tell the truth about what's wrong with their processes. More often than not, however, there is a code of silence among team members because they are afraid.

Many things can cause fear. In their excellent book, *Driving Fear Out of the Workplace,* Kathleen D. Ryan and Daniel K. Oestreich discuss fear and estimate its high costs to organizations.[6] CEOs, managers, team leaders, and facilitators should read this book.

One source of fear is teams themselves. Remember, teams are a force for change from the traditional style of management. Change of any kind worries anyone who doesn't understand it. Hence, team members may be fearful when they sit down for the first time at a team meeting. They may be fearful that they can't learn all they need to learn. They will wonder, "Am I getting in over my head?" They may be fearful of what their coworkers will think of their new role as a subject matter expert (sounds pretty fancy) or a SME. They may be fearful that they're in for some kidding, or maybe some humiliation. They may be fearful that someone on the team will repeat outside the team something they say. They may be fearful about whether the team leader and the facilitator can be trusted to observe the ground rule about confidentiality.

Managers of departments that contain processes targeted for improvement may be fearful about what's in store for them. They may be fearful about whether they're up to learning all that's required and making continual improvements in their departments. They may be fearful that the CEO will ask how they could have allowed their part of these processes to stay flawed so long.

When team leaders walk down the hallway with a master facilitator to conduct their first team meeting, they may have fears about whether they can correctly lead according to Deming's teachings. They'll privately worry, "Am I up to the task ahead of me? I was never any good at statistics."

Such fears as these and countless others are not unusual, but they must be bravely understood and accepted. Team leaders and facilitators should be alert for signs of fear on their teams and take steps to remove it. They should ensure that no one feels small as a result of anything that happens during team meetings or as a result of a team's work. Team activities should enhance everyone's sense of self-respect. Leaders and facilitators should establish and strictly enforce a team ground rule that "What's said in this room stays in this room," and surface for team discussion any incident when this rule is violated. It must be known that the CEO supports this ground rule on confidentiality and expresses support for it at quality council meetings and at presentations to team leaders.

## Point 9—Break Down Barriers
## Between Departments

Perhaps no part of a team leader's job is more important or difficult than breaking down barriers between departments. Team leaders often remark that they knew there were barriers between departments in their organization, but they never knew how many there were and how tall and wide they were until they led a team. They often express astonishment that every department is doing its best, but that every department's best always tyrannizes its downstream customers. Of course, the traditional style of management, in particular the functional form of organization and competition, causes this. Managing teams to break down barriers between departments is a major part of a team leader's job.

To set the stage for a team's role in breaking down barriers between departments, leaders must teach team members to appreciate the organization as a system. They must understand that all a system's components, or departments, must work together in cooperation to accomplish the organization's aim (as expressed in its vision and mission statements). Members must appreciate that no department can maximize its own interests through competition with other departments without severely suboptimizing the organization.

Team members should be taught to appreciate that some departments must subordinate their own interests, maybe lose money month after month, so other departments can do their jobs. This optimizes the larger organization and benefits everyone. The aim of every department is to contribute its best to the organization, not to maximize itself.

Teams can do much to break down barriers between departments. For instance, when a PIT leader has initial conversations with the department managers into which his or her targeted process extends, the systems perspective should be taught and emphasized. When SMEs from departments serve on teams they should see how teams work to optimize the organization as a system. Any remark that suggests or even hints at competition between departments should be identified and openly discussed. As the PDSA cycle is used, team leaders must emphasize the need for cooperation between departments and staff areas. When guests are invited to team meetings to provide expert information, the entire experience must demonstrate cooperation with them and the departments they represent. Guests must see a multidisciplinary team of SMEs working cooperatively toward a common aim.

A team activity that can be of great help in breaking down barriers is tasking, discussed in chapter 10. A tasking is a request of a department by a team for an improvement or series of improvements. One aim of tasking is to initiate improvements, but another aim is to bring the departments involved closer together. Care must be taken by team leaders to do tasking correctly. If tasking is done poorly it reinforces the traditional style of management, which is just what we're trying to get away from.

## *Point 10—Eliminate Slogans and Exhortations*

It is wrong to use slogans and exhortations with individuals, and it is also wrong to use them with teams. To urge team members to higher levels of effort with slogans and exhortations can be insulting and discouraging when they are already trying their best. Slogans and exhortations carry the objectionable implication that members won't do a good job unless they are exhorted. This is so rarely the case that it's a waste of time to think about it. Remember, SMEs are selected because they are the best persons from their departments to work on the process. As such, they have distinguished themselves time and again. They are well thought of by their coworkers and supervisors. They take pride in their work, and all they ask of leaders is an opportunity to do a good job and be proud of the team. This is not to say that SMEs don't like a word of encouragement or a pat on the back for a job well done. But, slogans and exhortation are far different from a pat on the back.

Another problem with the use of slogans and exhortations is what it reveals about team leaders who use them. It points to their misunderstanding of what it takes to achieve team success. Team leaders who use slogans and exhortations reveal their belief that "If my SMEs would just do their jobs, this team would be successful." This attitude suggests that the leader who holds it has not been adequately trained. SMEs work hard to do their jobs, and when they don't it's almost always for lack of training or opportunity. To think otherwise gets us nowhere.

Leaders should be concerned about their SMEs only to ensure their continuing training in Deming's teachings. SMEs will do their jobs if the leader does his or hers. The real problem is that many team leaders backslide into the traditional style of management and don't do their own jobs as described in point 7. Instead, they cop out with slogans and exhortations. When slogans and exhortations don't work, they blame any lack of team success on their SMEs. Team leaders should think about doing their own jobs, which is always a handful. They should lead teams strictly according to Deming's teachings, and they should patiently follow a team strategy suggested in chapter 9.

*How to Motivate Teams.* Traditional managers make the assumption that employees really don't want to work. Because of this, managers believe an important part of their job is to motivate employees. This motivation takes the form of rewards and punishment.

Similarly, traditional managers believe employees don't want to work on improvement teams. So, they think it's their job to motivate employees to do so. They offer incentives for the team members who contribute the most. This, they think, will provide the motivation to do a good job. Giving team members incentives is wrong. In the first place, it's impossible to know which team member contributed the most because the members' work is so interdependent. But, even if the best team member could be identified, dangling incentives in front of team members creates competition—the very thing we're trying to eliminate. Members may go through the motions and appear to cooperate, but they don't give it their best shot. They're trying to maximize their own performance and reduce the performance of everyone else. They want to win the incentive provided by management to the best team member. Contradictory as it is, many CEOs spend tens of thousands of dollars on team building to increase cooperation and then cancel the result by creating competition with rewards to the best team members.

Experience has taught many CEOs that offering incentives to team members doesn't work. They've learned this creates competition that ruins teams. They've learned that for teams to be successful, team members must cooperate. But this is often where their knowledge ends. Many who know it's wrong to give incentives to team members still think it's smart to give them to teams, as groups. This approach, they believe, creates the competition between teams that is needed to bring out their best.

Providing incentives to teams is as bad as providing them to team members. Both approaches create competition which leads to suboptimization. When teams compete with one another, cooperation across an organization is reduced, barriers between departments are further built up, and an entire organization is suboptimized. All this goes against what we're trying to accomplish with TQM.

It is incentive enough for team members to be part of an effort to eliminate the barriers that have prevented them, in some cases for years, from taking pride in their work. Remember, all employees ask is an opportunity to do a good job and be proud of the organization where they work. They see improvement teams as a way to make these things possible. They are honored by an invitation to serve as a SME on such a team. That feeling is all the motivation they need. They don't need a 50¢ certificate in a cheap plastic frame or a $2 wooden plaque taken from a closet where they know dozens of such plaques are stored and routinely handed out every month. Team members will reluctantly accept such rewards at ceremonies they are obliged to attend, and they will dutifully display them in their offices. But they know such rewards are a sham, and CEOs are only fooling themselves if they believe team members think otherwise.

Rewards cheapen and lessen the good feeling SMEs get from being part of something important. It's like your spouse giving you $15 for being a good husband or wife. Your spouse could say, "I know this $15 doesn't compensate you for all your work and interest in our marriage over the years, but please accept it as a token of my appreciation." These words still don't make it right. You did what you did because you wanted to, not in the hope of a reward. If the reward is anything more than a simple acknowledgment, such as a single rose in the case of a marriage, the reward cheapens and lessens the feeling. Plainly said, rewards change the nature of relationships. They commercialize something tender and emotional. Deming calls this over-justification.[7]

This is not to say that management has no responsibilities with respect to the success of teams. Rather than taking the easy way out with incentives that never work for the long haul, management has the much harder job of providing the environment in which teams can do a good job. Management must provide training; backfill of jobs while employees are at team meetings; logistical support, such as adequate meeting rooms, flip charts, overhead projectors, and plenty of coffee and soda pop; and action to implement team recommendations.

## Point 11—Eliminate Work Standards and MBO

Facilitators are often asked when a team will be done with its work. "When do you think we'll be finished here? You know, the work on my desk is really piling up." Why do team members ask this kind of question? Like all employees, they have lived in the culture of traditional management with MBO where there are work standards and objectives. So, when they get on a team, they expect to see work standards, suspense dates, deadlines, and objectives for the accomplishment of the work. They want to hear an answer to their question like "Well, I'd say we'll be 50 percent done by August and out of here before New Year's Day."

Saying a process will be improved by New Year's Day indicates something about the speaker. It shows the speaker believes the team is merely restoring a broken-down process to the one best way, and is not thinking about continual improvement. Improvement is continuous, as explained in point 5.

On the other hand, it is true that PITs do cease to exist. They cease to exist when they have accomplished their aims. One of their aims is to initiate a spirit of continual improvement in the departments their chartered process touches. Their other aim is to help get culture change underway with Deming's teachings. Thus, when departments are well underway on continuous process improvement and practicing Deming's teachings, a PIT may cease to exist. It has done its job as part of the transitional administrative structure.

MBO makes it difficult, usually impossible, for departments to respond to taskings. Under the yoke of MBO, departments seek to accomplish their own objectives and stay within their budgets. Despite the fact that all departments tyrannize their downstream customers, those managed with MBO have no interest in taskings that would set things right. To them, responding to taskings is to guarantee that their budgets will be overrun. In MBO, departments think of themselves as separate entities seeking to accomplish their own aims rather than those of the larger system.

## Point 12—Remove Barriers that Rob People of Pride of Work

If given the right training and the opportunity, all team members will do a good job. You can count on that. Unfortunately, there are barriers that keep team leaders, facilitators, and SMEs from doing their best. These barriers are countless and almost all under the control of CEOs. Team leaders must identify such barriers and seek to remove them. This takes courage because it means identifying barriers to the CEO and requesting, sometimes insisting, they be removed. CEOs should be given some slack, however, because they usually don't know that barriers exist or they misunderstand their importance. They are blinded by the biggest barrier of all, the traditional style of management. But, they, too, are trying to learn. Team leaders must deal with CEOs, as Deming's teachings suggest, in ways that break down barriers.

There are many barriers to the pride of work of teams. Barriers include inadequate meeting rooms; no flip charts; no chart paper; markers that are out of ink; a building that is too cold; a dirty environment; an inadequate training budget; not enough copies of training materials to go around; no copiers; no money to hire a master facilitator; no money for statistics training; an inadequate budget to backfill work left by employees attending team meetings and doing homework; senior managers stalling out in their long-term efforts to provide training to everyone in Deming's teachings; inadequate training by senior managers to middle managers in their role and responsibilities in the transformation to TQM; the failure of CEOs to monitor taskings; the failure of CEOs to have eye-to-eye sessions with senior and middle managers who don't get the message that their organizations are going to do things Deming's way; the failure of CEOs to strip out personnel policies and practices based on the traditional style of management, especially performance appraisals and pay-for-performance plans; and CEOs unable to model for everyone the attitudes of cooperation, patience, continual improvement, and security.

## *Point 13—Institute a Vigorous Program of Education*

How does point 13 apply to teams? Deming would say there is no shortage of good people to serve as leaders, facilitators, and SMEs.[8] However, what we need is not just good people, but people who are improving with education. What does this mean?

How many people do you know who have a good mind and were once vibrant and enthusiastic, but somehow they've gone stale? Somehow they've slipped into a reactive, complacent frame of mind. They may be the most knowledgeable persons from their departments serving as SMEs, but when they begin their work, they seem half asleep, they explain all the ways something can't be done, or they agree to do something and then allow it to slip off their to-do list and never mention it again. When they're on a team, they do homework and put in their 2¢ worth on ENGTs, but they don't seem to have their hearts in it. There are many reasons for this kind of behavior, but could it be these people aren't growing any more? Some of them may not have read a book in years. Outside of watching television and reading the sports page, they may not have been exposed to a new idea in years. What they need is something to get their minds in gear again.

Teams can't really be successful unless their members have their minds in gear. It takes SMEs who are thinking about better ways to do things. Deming suggests everyone needs education to keep his or her mind engaged and active.

Training in the skills needed to work on teams often provides the necessary stimulation. Training in Deming's teachings, the statistical tools, and consensus-building techniques are, for many people, a fresh and stimulating way to see things.

Often this works best when a team leader challenges members to apply TQM in their personal lives. For instance, leaders might say, "Does your family have a mission statement? If not, your homework assignment for the weekend is to facilitate an ENGT session with your family, seated around the dining room table, to develop one." The leader ensures that members have the necessary skills to make this homework easy and fun. This assignment should not be shoved down anyone's throat, but most people are interested in it because they see it as a way to help their families.

Another example of TQM in one's personal life is to ask members to use one of the statistical tools. A homework assignment in this area can produce impressive results if members feel comfortable accepting it. In this assignment, the leader teaches the tally sheet and Pareto principle and suggests that these tools can be used to reduce the number of quarrels team members have with their spouses or children. Most team members will find this suggestion fascinating and will be interested in trying it. Those who don't should not be forced to participate, other than listening to the results at the next team meeting.

To bring this assignment about, these steps should be recommended. First, family participants must agree on the aim of working toward reducing their number of quarrels. They will need to agree on an operational definition of the word *quarrel*. Second, they should agree to keep a tally of the reasons for their quarrels for two weeks or a month. Third, when the time is up, this tally will form a Pareto outcome; that is, a few reasons will account for most of the quarrels and many reasons will account for only a few quarrels. Developing the tally sheet ends the homework assignment.

Members should not be forced to report their results to the team. Some results may be too sensitive, but some members will be enthusiastic about reporting their results. Members will understand or perhaps can be told that the vital few reasons for quarrels could be addressed by family participants in the exercise. (Occasionally, the assistance of a counselor is required.) In recommending that the participants address the most common reasons for quarrels, the Ishikawa diagram can be explained and used as a tool to further analyze the reasons for quarrels. One of the vital few reasons is placed in the effect box on the right of the diagram, and participants brainstorm causes for this effect. The causes are grouped on the main branches on the left of the diagram. In any case, with a little imagination from the team leader, this kind of personal learning about TQM fascinates many team members. It can help get their minds back in gear. Education for this purpose need not be job-related, but can be translated easily for benefit to the job.

## Point 14—Put Everybody in the Company to Work to Accomplish the Transformation

To many, point 14 is the most difficult of the 14 points. They ask, "Just how do you put everyone to work to accomplish the transformation away from the traditional style of management?"

The transformation can't be done by senior managers merely training and exhorting employees to practice Deming's teachings. This certainly puts senior management to work (in the training mode), and it shows management's commitment and generates enthusiasm. But how does it put anyone besides management to work to accomplish the transformation?

The transformation can't be accomplished with TQM books and expensive videotapes either. A few employees will read these books, and most will be willing to sit through the videotapes, if for no other reason than to satisfy their curiosity. These training aids can help in building knowledge of what Deming's teachings are all about, but they don't put everyone to work to accomplish the transformation required to escape the prison of the traditional style of management.

Many people can learn Deming's teachings by practicing them on the job. Practicing and modeling Deming's teachings is one of the aims of teams. The other aim is to initiate continual improvement in processes. Thus, as teams practice Deming's teachings, team members get a stream of chances to learn them. As teams model Deming's teachings, all who come into contact with them also get exposed to training by seeing this new approach in action. In these ways, the practice of Deming's teachings moves from a few teams in the beginning—I recommend three PITs—to every department (by means of DITs) and to every employee in an organization. This is how everyone in an organization is put to work to accomplish the transformation away from the traditional style of management.

## Notes

1. W. Edwards Deming, *Out of the Crisis* (Cambridge, Mass.: MIT Press, 1986), pp. 23. The 14 points are covered in pp. 23–96.

2. Deming, *Out of the Crisis;* and ———, *The New Economics for Industry, Government, and Education* (Cambridge, Mass.: MIT Press, 1993).

3. Deming, "Introduction to a System," in *The New Economics.*

4. Ibid.

5. Ibid., chapters 5 and 6.

6. Kathleen D. Ryan and Daniel K. Oestreich, *Driving Fear Out of the Workplace* (San Francisco: Jossey-Bass, 1991).

7. Deming, *Out of the Crisis.*

8. Ibid., p. 86.

# The Transformation
# of Decision Making

As personnel make the transition away from the traditional style of management, many changes in their behavior occur. Few changes are more important to the success of the transformation than how they make decisions. Broadly speaking, there are three ways to make decisions. As personnel learn more about Deming's teachings, they move from the worst way to the best way. The three ways to make decisions, from worst to best, are judgmental, data-based, and scientific.

## Judgmental Decision Making

The owners of organizations delegate authority to CEOs who, in turn, delegate it to managers at various levels in the hierarchy. With the authority they are delegated, managers incur responsibilities to carry out the owners' wishes. To discharge these responsibilities, managers are presumed to have knowledge of what goes on beneath them in their part of the hierarchy. With their heads presumably full of this knowledge, they walk the halls and shops making decisions.

For many reasons, managers don't always have complete knowledge of the work they manage. Organizations are complex and difficult to understand, and most organizations are changing constantly. In addition, managers themselves change, moving from job to job in the same organizations and to jobs in different organizations. To the extent that these and other factors occur, managers have less than complete knowledge of the details of the work for which they are responsible. And, what they pass off as judgment is sometimes, in part at least, guesswork.

In other words, judgment is composed of two parts: knowledge and guesswork. When judgment is based on knowledge, decisions tend to be correct and work well. But, when judgment is based on guesswork, the result can be another management blunder. Blundering managers may be asked to resign, but their bad decisions are usually chalked up as valuable learning experiences for them. More often than not, unwitting subordinates pay the price for managers' blunders in extra work, and these blunders reduce the value of the organization for stockholders and customers who never hear about them.

Many managers strive to get away from judgmental decision making. You hear them give advice like, "Get the facts before you decide." This kind of advice suggests that getting the facts will reduce the guesswork part of the equation (judgment equals knowledge plus guesswork) so that judgment is based more on knowledge and less on guesswork. This kind of advice is best when it suggests that facts are data. Before making decisions, these managers ask to see the data. Some place signs on their office walls, "In God we trust; all others bring data." When decisions are based on data, the style of decision making has improved from judgmental to the data-based approach.

# Data-Based Decision Making

Managers consider themselves progressive when they use the data-based approach to decision making. In this approach, they don't simply use judgment to solve problems. They get whatever data they can to supplement their judgment, to fill in the guesswork gap between judgment and knowledge. They listen more to subordinates. They read background reports. They look at accounting, financial, production, and market research data. They apply statistical techniques to gather, analyze, and present data. They take a little extra time to be more certain of their decisions. It was explained in the previous section that the judgmental approach to decision making is *action based on judgment*. The data-based approach is *action based on data*. Data-based decision making is usually slower than the judgmental approach. It takes time to get data. But, while it takes more time, the results are better.

Those who practice the data-based approach kid those who use the judgmental approach. Data users accuse the judgment users of using "the genius approach." Data users poke fun at the judgment users, claiming they all get around a conference table, and the first one says, "I've got an idea!" Then the second one says, "I've got an idea!" Then the third one says, "I've got an idea!" and so forth. After all the ideas are out, they fight to see whose idea is selected for action. The winner is usually the one with the highest rank or most aggressive personality. Having facts and data always leads to better decisions than pure judgment.

There is another approach to decision making that goes beyond the data-based approach. This third approach doesn't disregard the value of the data any more than the data-based approach disregards the value of judgment. Managers need judgment to the extent that it represents knowledge gained from years of experience. It is important to be able to make good guesses, to have intuition, and to have a sense or feel for the right decision. Furthermore, complete knowledge is seldom available. Usually, data are incomplete.

Something is needed to tie judgment and data together. This something is the third and most powerful form of decision making.

## Scientific Decision Making

In scientific decision making, there is an important role for judgment and data, but neither of them, by itself or together, is a sufficient basis for decision making. The better approach is the widely familiar scientific method, which has been explained as a decision-making technique by a number of different people, including Shewhart, George E. P. Box, and Deming.[1]

In scientific decision making, *judgment* is a source of hypotheses about problems. A hypothesis is a tentative explanation for a problem made so its truth can be tested. Then *data* are used to test hypotheses to determine whether they are true. Thus, scientific decision making relies heavily on both judgment and data. Consider the following story to clarify how scientific decision making works.

### The Escaped Dog

Suppose you get a new dog. One Sunday afternoon, you drive to the grocery store to pick up some milk, and you leave the dog in your fenced backyard. When you get back from the grocery store, you are surprised to see your dog running around in the front yard! You ask yourself "How could this happen? How could my dog have gotten out?" You have a problem. The dog might have run out into the street and been run over by a car.

To figure out how your dog escaped from the backyard, you decide to try the scientific decision-making approach. First, you form a hypothesis. You say to yourself, "I must have left the gate open." Then what do you do? You gather some data to see if this hypothesis is true or false. In this situation, you gather data by simply checking the gate. Suppose you find that the gate is closed and locked. You conclude the dog could not have worked the lock, opened the gate to get out, and then closed and relocked the gate. You are satisfied that your tentative explanation (hypothesis) is incorrect. What do you do next? If you're still interested, you form a second hypothesis. "There must be a loose slat in the fence," you speculate. To test this hypothesis, you walk around the fence looking for loose slats. You find none. Second hypothesis exploded. You hypothesize further, "Maybe she dug a hole." Checking reveals no holes. Third hypothesis exploded. As you put the milk in the refrigerator, your child walks into the kitchen. "Did you let the dog out of the backyard?" you ask. "Yes, we were playing ball in the front yard, and I came in to answer the phone." Explanation found. Now you are ready to take action to prevent the problem from occurring again. You say to your child, "Honey, please don't leave the dog in the front yard. I'm afraid she'll run out into the street and get hit by a car."

*Lessons of the Escaped Dog Story.* What can we learn about scientific decision making from our escaped dog story? One lesson is that getting to the point where action can be taken may require testing a number of hypotheses. In our example, one hypothesis was the gate was left open. Another was a loose slat in the fence. Another was a hole in the ground. Another was that your child let the dog out to play ball with her.

A second lesson from our story is very important: As you test hypotheses you build knowledge. In the story, you built knowledge that the gate was not left open. You built knowledge that there were no loose slats in the fence. You built knowledge that there were no holes under the fence. You built knowledge that your child took the dog out of the backyard to play with her.

There are two more lessons in our story of the escaped dog. First, when you test a hypothesis, both positive and negative results build knowledge. In our story, when you disproved the hypothesis that the dog escaped through a loose slat in the fence, you built knowledge. Negative results like this build knowledge just as surely as do positive results. After a negative result, you know more than you did before. After finding no loose slats, a negative result, you didn't have to worry about loose slats anymore. Another lesson is that knowledge is the best basis for action. In our story, the more hypotheses you tested, the more knowledge you built. And, when you finally built enough knowledge, you knew what action to take. You knew to say to your child "Honey, please don't leave the dog in the front yard. I'm afraid she'll run out into the street and get hit by a car."

The key to scientific decision making is this: When you face a problem, you need to ask yourself, "How can I build knowledge about this problem?" It is important to understand that action is best when it is based on knowledge, not on judgment or even data.

This is not to say that judgment and data are unimportant. They are key parts of the scientific decision-making approach. Judgment is an excellent source of hypotheses. Suppose in our example you've had the dog for two years, and you know from experience how she gets out of the backyard. She paws at a slat in the fence until it gets loose. Then she squeezes through. So, for a few weeks she won't get out; she's behind bushes busily pawing at a slat. But, when she eventually gets out, your judgment (based on past knowledge of her behavior) gives you a good hypothesis to test, and you look behind the bushes. And, sure enough, you find a slat she's loosened to get out. Notice, judgment from experience was the source of this hypothesis.

Notice, also, you didn't go straight from judgment to action. When you saw the dog running loose, you thought, "Boy, she got out through a slat again," but you did not immediately hire somebody to drive bigger nails into the slats. You tested your hypothesis first. You went around to the backyard and looked for a loose slat. What if your hypothesis had been wrong, and you took action instead of testing it? Suppose the truth was she really got out through a hole she dug. You'd have wasted your money by putting nails in the slats when that was unnecessary. That's a danger of basing action purely on judgment.

Data are also important in the scientific approach to decision making. *Data* is a loose term for all the things you do to test hypotheses. Data can be real data, numbers that measure something; but, data also can be looking for a loose slat in the fence. It's anything you do to test hypotheses. In organizations, it can be looking up something in the financial records, or it can be the results of an experiment or survey.

In summary, the basic idea in the scientific approach to decision making is to go back and forth between a series of hypotheses and data to test each hypothesis and, thus, build knowledge. When you have enough knowledge, you'll know what action to take.

Let's consider one last lesson from our escaped dog story. Many things can go wrong in the process of going back and forth between hypotheses and data. So, to make this part of the scientific approach to decision making easier, Shewhart and Deming suggest that this back and forth activity should be thought of as a cycle composed of four steps, the PDSA cycle.[2] Figure B.1 shows how these four steps fit in between hypotheses and data to build knowledge. This sounds easy, but most people misunderstand how to use the PDSA cycle. So, let's consider an example of how this cycle works.

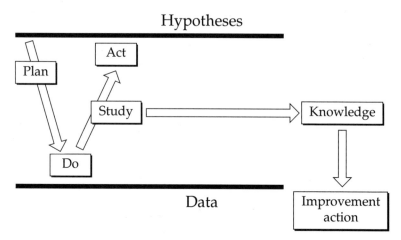

**Figure B.1.** Scientific decision-making model.

## *The Role of the PDSA Cycle in Decision Making*

Consider how the PDSA cycle works in our example of the escaped dog. Suppose your first hypothesis for how the dog got out of the backyard was that she has grown large enough to jump up on top of the iron gate, which is lower than the fence, and crawl over. How would you test this hypothesis? Let's suppose you decide to use the PDSA cycle to go back and forth between hypothesis and data.

First, you do the plan step of PDSA. You plan how you're going to test the hypothesis. You really think about it. First, you think about getting a bone and holding it up high to see how high the dog can jump. If she could jump high enough, it still wouldn't show whether she's motivated to jump the fence or whether she knows how. You finally decide to test this hypothesis with an experiment. You lay out a plan to put the dog in the backyard and simply watch her to see if she jumps the fence. The plan includes a place to hide where she won't see you, but from which you can see the gate. And, you plan to have a soda pop and some cookies in case the wait is a long one. That's the plan step of PDSA.

Next comes the do step. Here, you carry out your plan. You do exactly what your plan specifies. You put the dog out and hide in the selected place. After a period of time, sure enough, the dog comes up to the gate, looks around to see if anyone is watching, and jumps up on the gate and crawls over.

Next, you do the study step. What did you learn from your observation? You study the outcome of your experiment. Here the result is pretty clear. Sometimes results require considerable study to determine exactly what they mean.

Finally, you do the act step. In this step, you either take action or don't take action, based on the outcome of your experiment. Suppose, after watching for hours on two different days, the dog does not jump up on the gate and crawl over. Negative result. Good or bad? Good, because you built knowledge. Now you have pretty good evidence that the dog doesn't get out of the fenced yard by jumping over the gate. The act step adds to your knowledge regardless of whether results are positive or negative. Suppose, however, the dog did jump over the gate while you were watching. Positive result. Again, good. Now you have enough knowledge to act to do something about the problem. Maybe you have the iron gate built higher.

In the case of either negative or positive results, you need to use the PDSA cycle again. Why is this? In the case of negative results, you need the PDSA to test another hypothesis. In the case of positive results, you need it to test the hypothesis that the *new* gate is so tall that the dog can't jump over it.

## How Teams Use the Scientific Approach to Make Decisions

Transformed managers know that all the brains are not at the top. Managers know workers have valuable knowledge of what goes on in their part of the organization. In fact, as explained in chapter 1, workers commonly have greater knowledge of customer needs and how to fulfill them than any manager. Consequently, in transformed organizations everyone is encouraged to increase his or her knowledge (Deming point 13), and the knowledge of everyone is used in making decisions that affect him or her.

An important part of the role of team leaders is to ensure that teams practice and model Deming's teachings. And, a key part of Deming's teachings is that teams make decisions according to the scientific approach. For instance, a team should be discouraged from basing decisions on judgment, from using the "genius approach," and from sitting around a table and playing "I've got an idea" for a solution to a process problem. SMEs should be taught that their judgment and experience are important, but only as sources of hypotheses, not as a basis for action. Furthermore, they should be taught to test hypotheses with data. They should be taught the value of the PDSA cycle in going back and forth between hypotheses and data. They should be taught that this builds knowledge. They must understand that knowledge is the only safe basis for action.

## The Continuing Story of the Innovating Grocer

To further demonstrate scientific decision making, consider again the grocer, discussed in chapter 11, who is trying to innovate in response to understanding his customers' processes. Suppose the grocer had the wisdom to create a DIT to work innovation issues. To begin with, remember from chapter 11 that the grocer and his DIT had knowledge that customers run errands while on their way to the grocery store. To capitalize on the customer need to do one-stop shopping, the team decided to brainstorm some new nongrocery product lines that could be offered in the grocery store. It hypothesized that customers would buy these items in the grocery store rather than make an additional stop at small retailers on the way home. DIT members asked themselves what new departments could be added in the grocery store? Suppose the result was a list which included a garden center, a pharmacy, a shoe repair counter, a film developing center, a laundry, a flower shop, a barber shop, and a United Parcel Service (UPS) station.

The DIT members were taught to consider each of these potential new product lines they developed from judgment as a hypothesis. They were taught that each hypothesis must be tested. Consider how this might work with the first innovation they considered, a garden center. The DIT hypothesized that the addition to the grocery store of a small department to sell garden supplies would be successful. The team knew of a large, successful nursery located two blocks from the grocery. The DIT reasoned that on trips to the grocery store customers would buy garden supplies rather than make a second stop at the nursery, especially if the supplies didn't require an expert to explain their use.

Should the DIT take action based on its judgment and recommend that management begin handling garden supplies? Not at all. The DIT needs to gather data to test its garden center hypothesis. The DIT was trained to do this with the PDSA cycle. First, the team needs to plan some kind of data-gathering activity to test its hypothesis. The team decided to conduct an experiment. It planned to add a small number of garden supplies and see if they sold. The DIT planned every detail of this experiment. It planned to offer supplies, such as fertilizers and insecticides, that required no advice from a gardening expert; to conduct the experiment in the spring, when the demand for fertilizer and insecticides was high; to advertise to support the effort; and to find a good location for the supplies. The team planned to place commonly used garden supplies, such as big sacks of organic compost peat and lawn food, on pallets on the sidewalk in front of the store. It also planned measures so members would know if their experiment was a success. The team planned what it would do if the garden center was a success and what it would do if it wasn't a success.

Second, the DIT did the do part of the PDSA cycle. It executed the experiment. Everything was done according to the plan. Next, the DIT carefully studied the result, the study part of the PDSA cycle. Did the result of the experiment show that the hypothesis was true or false? In this case, suppose the hypothesis was true. The garden supplies experiment was a great success. The store sold out its initial inventory and ordered more. What next? The DIT followed the part of its plan that had to do with acting on the results. It acted to add other garden supplies. And, it again tested its additional supplies with the PDSA cycle. Eventually, the DIT had enough knowledge to support a recommendation to management that garden supplies be a seasonal, but regular, part of the store's offerings.

With the scientific approach to decision making, the grocery store added a garden section, a pharmacy, a film developing center, and a flower shop. Eventually, it put the nearby shops selling these products and services out of business. On the other hand, the evidence from the DIT's experiments went against the hypotheses for a barber shop, a shoe repair counter, a laundry, and a UPS station.

There is a busy barber shop in the shopping center right alongside the grocery store, and the grocer gets his hair cut there. As he sits in the barber's chair, the grocer wonders if his innovation DIT will ever reconsider getting into the barber shop business. Little does the barber know of the dangerous thoughts in the head whose hair he is carefully trimming.

## Notes

1. Henry R. Neave, *The Deming Dimension* (Knoxville, Tenn.: SPC Press, 1990), pp. 139–149.

2. W. Edwards Deming, *Out of the Crisis* (Cambridge, Mass.: MIT Press, 1986), p. 88.

# How to Reach Consensus

In organizations that practice TQM, it's understood that all the brains are not at the top. Leadership is based on consensus. Consensus is a way of making choices and decisions that marshals the emotional and intellectual resources of everyone toward common aims. There's no room for adversarial competition; everyone works cooperatively.

This appendix offers a definition of consensus and explains how to achieve it. The discussion focuses on teams, but it applies to all groups that make choices and decisions.

## What Is Consensus?

If the Deming management philosophy is to be practiced on teams, there must be a method of making choices and decisions that captures the contributions of all team members. The method must not make any member feel defeated. Every member must feel good about the experience. And, the method must not kindle feelings of competition, but make cooperation easy.

These features call for a way to make choices and decisions that all team members can support. Each member need not be totally satisfied with choices and decisions, but each must favor them enough to support them.

The first problem was to find a name for a decision-making method defined this way. One possibility is *unanimity*, which means *having the agreement or consent of all* or *being of one mind*. But what we're talking about here is not the 100 percent agreement, but enough agreement so that everyone can support the choices and decisions that result. Another possibility is *consensus*, and the definition of this word revolves around *general agreement*. That definition seems to capture what we're after here.

### Two Concerns About Consensus

One of the two main concerns some people have with consensus is it feels like compromise. They think consensus and compromise mean giving up something, or making concessions, to reach agreement.

And, they assert that making concessions is losing something, and losing is contrary to the win–win requirement of the Deming management philosophy.

As on many other occasions, I was asked to explain the difference between consensus and compromise in a PIT/DIT leader seminar I was teaching with Dr. Karl J. Krumm, a consulting organizational psychologist in Austin and San Antonio, Texas. As I was trying to answer this question, he quickly made some notes on pairs of terms that show the contrast between compromise and consensus, and he handed them to me to help with my answer. I think his pairs of terms address the fundamental and wide differences between consensus and compromise. In Figure C.1 are the words, with one addition, that Krumm handed to me.[1]

A second concern about consensus is that it takes more time than the old way, which is management by fiat. It is true that there are situations where consensus does take too much time, and, in these cases, it should not be used. Examples include deciding how to leave a building in case of fire or how to modify a product to beat the competition to market. In such cases, time isn't available. It's best to let someone who knows make the decision. "These stairs lead to safety! Hurry!"

Consensus on teams takes time for several reasons. It takes time to get people from different departments to trust one another, and hearing everyone out takes time. Because of this up-front time commitment, some people think teams can lose momentum. But arguing that consensus takes too much time is really a misperception of what making choices and decisions is all about. Making choices and decisions is a two-part activity: making them and implementing them.

| *Compromise* | *Consensus* |
| --- | --- |
| Positions | Underlying needs |
| Competition | Cooperation |
| Limited solutions | Third option |
| Subtractive | Additive |
| Differences | Similarities |
| Individual | Common ground |
| Individual power | Group power |
| Give up something | Gain something |
| Negative feeling | Positive feeling |
| Win–Lose | Win–Win |

**Figure C.1.** The differences between compromise and consensus.

The advantages of consensus are more than enough to offset its up-front time commitment. In the first place, a group choice or decision is usually better because of synergism, or, said more plainly, because people working together produce far more than the sum of each working separately. In the second place, implementing a choice or decision is always faster if the people who are charged with making the implementation had a say in the choice or decision in the first place. This second advantage is really the key. Consensus doesn't take longer if you count the time it takes to implement a choice or decision. If you compare the time it takes to both make a choice or decision and implement it between consensus and fiat, the shorter time always goes to consensus in situations where it applies. The answer seems to narrow down to two alternatives: shoot from the hip with a fast, uncertain decision by fiat that is almost certain to run up against time-consuming resistance throughout its implementation; or take some extra time up front to get consensus and have smooth sailing in implementation.

## How to Bring a Team to Consensus

Before consensus will work, members must be trained to appreciate Deming's teachings that teams must eliminate adversarial competition in favor of cooperation and that the aim of teams is to optimize the overall system. Teams need to do what's best for the organization, not individual departments. In fact, teams need to be agents for breaking down barriers between departments. For PITs or DITs, breaking down barriers between departments narrows down to the idea that employees are a team, not a bunch of lone wolves, each struggling to do what's best for his or her department. Employees better achieve their aim by working together.

The NGT is the general framework to bring teams to consensus. The NGT was originally described by Andre L. Delbecq, Andrew H. Van de Ven, and David H. Gustafson, and I explained it in my first book.[2] However, I recently enhanced the original version (I refer to this version as the *enhanced NGT*, or ENGT), so the eight steps I now recommend are the following:

1. Consider the aim.
2. Pose the nominal question.
3. Gain group acceptance of the question.
4. Conduct silent generation of answers.
5. Round robin list answers.
6. Discuss and clarify answers.

7. Vote to work toward consensus.

8. Document the result.

In his point 1, Deming teaches us to consider our aim so we can have constancy of purpose in accomplishing it. Thus, before team members begin an ENGT exercise they should consider their aim. "What is our aim in doing this ENGT exercise?" The aim should be discussed, at length if necessary, and made clear how accomplishing the aim of doing the ENGT will help move the team toward the accomplishment of its opportunity statement.

There are four possible aims in using the ENGT.

1. Generate a list, such as of customers, suppliers, or perceived barriers to good work.

2. Generate a list and prioritize it; that is, put a list of items in rank order, from highest to lowest. For instance, "Let's rank this list of barriers in terms of which cause the most delays in our response time to customer requests."

3. Generate a list and prioritize it so the result shows a Pareto outcome; that is, the vital few and trivial many items.

4. Generate a list and choose one item from the list, such as to select the upstream department that a team wants to task first to make improvements.

Notice all the aims of ENGT include generating a list. Once a list is generated, different things can be done with it. Sometimes nothing is done. Generating a list was the aim. So, that's the end of the ENGT exercise. But, besides that, there are three other things that can be done with a list. All three include prioritizing. One is to prioritize a list from high to low. Another is to prioritize to look for a Pareto outcome, to identify the vital few and trivial many. Another is to prioritize to select one item.

Prioritizing anything requires a criterion or criteria by which to evaluate the alternatives. For instance, to prioritize 10 different flowers there could be one criterion, say beauty, or there could be more criteria, say beauty, fragrance of blossoms, and resistance to disease. To prioritize six different soda pops, the criteria could be sweetness, caloric content, flavor, appearance, and shelf life. Teams must come to consensus on the criteria they plan to use for prioritizing. And, each criterion must be carefully defined to everyone's satisfaction.

## The Steps in ENGT

Knowing the aim is the key to the successful use of the ENGT. That's the first step in conducting an ENGT exercise.

The second step is stating a nominal question for a team to work with. For instance, the team leader might ask, "Who are the customers of our department?" "What are the barriers to our pride of work caused by our supplier, the MIS department?" "What are the reasons the accounts don't balance the first time?" "Why would data be lost in the transfer from Department A to us?"

In the third step, the leader ensures that team members understand and accept the nominal question. Here, team members may ask a question of clarification or request an operational definition, such as "What do we mean by *customer?*" or "When you say 'our department' do you mean to include the technicians out at the Onion Creek station? And what about our line workers out on the rural roads?"

After the nominal question is accepted, the fourth step begins. Here members take three minutes or so to silently generate and write down all the answers they can think of to the nominal question. Working silently to develop this list taps individual creativity.

In the fifth step, round-robin listing, the leader asks each member, in turn, to call out one answer from his or her list and quickly writes it on chart paper or a board. The leader goes around and around the room getting answers until everyone's list is exhausted. Members are asked to say "pass" when all their items have been listed; but, after they pass, they can add to their lists if what another member says makes them think of another item. No questions are allowed during this step; the time for discussion comes next.

Note that after this step, the first aim of using the ENGT has been accomplished: A list has been generated. Thus, a team may decide to stop the ENGT exercise at this point. It may decide, however, that it wants to continue on to the next step, discussion and clarification, to remove duplications from its list, and then stop the exercise.

In the sixth step, discussion and clarification, the leader takes each item written on the board, in turn, and asks its owners to explain the thinking behind it. For instance, "Donna, why do you think XYZ department is our downstream customer?" or "Tom, why do you want to offer our services to the Hotel California? What's your reasoning there?" After each owner has had all the time needed for his or her explanation, other members may remark about the item or ask a question to clarify it. Members may add new items during this step, and this is another way creativity is stimulated in the ENGT, this time under the influence of what others have said. The discussion and clarification step always reduces the original list because duplicates are removed, members voluntarily drop their items after the discussion shows their relative unimportance, and items are combined. Some facilitators prefer to combine items as they are discussed and clarified;

others prefer to wait to combine items until after they all have been discussed and clarified.

Because the discussion and clarification step reduces the original list, it is a powerful force for consensus. The next step is to vote. Voting is needed only if the aim of an ENGT exercise is to prioritize a list.

## Two Earlier Voting Methods

In my first book, I described two methods of voting, one by show of hands and one with 3 × 5 cards, to help teams reach consensus.[3] The well-known show of hands method is easy to understand and fast, but it has the disadvantage of denying team members the opportunity to weight their votes. They can vote for or against every item on a list; but, there is no mechanism by which members can express their degree of support for items. Another disadvantage of the show of hands method is that it creates winners and losers. Those voting with the majority win, and those voting with the minority lose. This can polarize a team, build barriers, and suboptimize a team's efforts.

The second voting method described in my first book uses 3 × 5 cards. This method has the distinct advantages of allowing team members to weight their votes and providing more information about the outcome of voting than any other method with which I am familiar. It displays in detail and in summary, without attribution, the number of votes cast for each item as well as the sum of the weights cast for each item. But, this use of 3 × 5 cards is not especially easy to understand, and its use can lead to errors when voting. Furthermore, it takes a lot of time.

*The Need for a Better Means of Voting.* Facilitating teams almost every day, I felt a need for a voting method that is somewhere between the show of hands and the 3 × 5 card methods. It must not take much time, must be easy to understand, must allow members to weight their votes, must not create winners and losers, must help teams reach consensus, and must be fun to use.

There's a lot of good information about voting in the various team handbooks, but I wasn't fully satisfied with the methods suggested there. So I gradually developed a voting method that satisfies all my requirements. I call it the *fingers method.*

*The Fingers Voting Method.* Suppose a team has finished the discussion and clarification step of the ENGT with 19 final items on a list written on a board. Before they vote, the team members should be reminded of the aim of the vote. It can be to prioritize the list by ranking items from highest to lowest, to identify the vital few and trivial many items on the list, or to select one item from the list.

Before voting, leaders should number the items on the board, if they weren't numbered when originally written there. Also the number of votes each team member is allowed to cast must be determined. If the number of items to be voted on is large, members should get votes equal to about 20 percent of that number. For instance, if there are 50 items for voting, members should get 10 votes (20 percent of 50). But if the number of items is small, say 10 to 25, the number of votes members get should be a greater percentage, as much as 50 percent. There is no need to worry about the precise number of votes members may cast. Within a broad range, the number of votes allowed will produce essentially the same result.

It is important to be clear about how team members cast their votes. If members get 10 votes, they may cast their votes in any manner they choose. All ten votes could be cast for one item, or five votes could be cast for one item and five votes cast for another item. Or, four votes could be cast for one item, three votes for a second item, two votes for a third item, and the remaining vote for a fourth item. This option of allocating votes among items as members see fit is how they weight their vote to show their degree of support for items. The opportunity to weight votes is satisfying to team members.

Sometimes, members get mixed up as they are casting their votes. They forget how many votes they have cast already. To make it easy to remember, it is best to ask members to use a T-table. When I start the discussion of a T-table, I make two fists but allow my index fingers to stick out straight. I hold my index fingers up in front of me so they make a *T*, one finger for the horizontal top of the *T* and one finger for the vertical bottom of the *T*. In any case, each member is asked to draw a *T* on a sheet of paper. They are then asked to use their *T* to write the numbers which identify the items for which they plan to vote in the left column, or left side of the *T*, and write the votes they want to cast for those items in the right column.

Consider an example of a T-table. Suppose a list on a board has 19 items numbered 1 through 19, and you get to cast 5 votes. You decide to cast 3 votes for item 2 and one vote each for items 6 and 10. Here's what your T-table would look like:

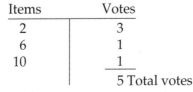

| Items | Votes |
|:---:|:---:|
| 2 | 3 |
| 6 | 1 |
| 10 | 1 |
|  | 5 Total votes |

Members are given a few minutes to complete their T-tables, recording how they will allocate their votes to the 19 items. The leader calls for the votes for item 1 in these words: "How many votes for item 1?" Members hold up fingers to correspond to the number of votes they want to cast for item 1, as shown in their T-tables. In your case, you would not hold up any fingers for item 1. The leader goes around the team counting the fingers held up and writes the sum of the fingers beside item 1 on the board. The vote for item 2 is then called for, and members hold up fingers to correspond to the votes they want to cast for item 2, as shown on their T-tables. Here, you hold up three fingers. Voting in this manner continues until all items have been voted on. The method is called the fingers method for the obvious reason that fingers are used to vote.

To begin to work toward consensus, the team is invited to view the results of the voting on the board, and it is reminded of the aim of the voting. If the aim was to prioritize the items in rank order, one round of voting may be sufficient. The item with the greatest number of votes gets the rank of 1, the item with the second greatest number of votes gets the rank of 2, and so on. Ties are permitted or not permitted according to the wishes of the team. If ties are not permitted, the team should be asked to discuss how to decide which of the tied items is more important. Sometimes this requires another round of discussion, clarification, and voting to reach consensus on how to rank the tied items.

If the aim of voting was to identify the vital few and trivial many, the team needs to come to consensus on an operational definition of the terms *vital few* and *trivial many* with respect to the results of its voting. (An operational definition is a definition upon which a team of SMEs can agree.) There will probably be consensus to declare the items with the highest number of votes in the vital few and the items with the lowest number of votes in the trivial many. But a second round of voting may be required for items that the team regards as neither in the highest ("vital few") or lowest ("trivial many") groups. This second round of voting should be preceded by clarification and discussion of the items to be voted on. Someone who voted for an item could be asked to speak in its behalf, and someone who voted against the same item could be asked to speak against it. Discussion is encouraged, and members are asked to consider that how they vote on the remaining items should take into consideration what other members have said.

If the aim of voting was to identify the one item from a list, the team may reach consensus simply based on seeing the results of the first vote. The result may be that one item got all the votes. Or if one item got most of the votes, the owners of the votes for other items may feel that

# Suggested Reading

## Books About the Deming Management Philosophy

Aguayo, Rafael. *Dr. Deming: The American Who Taught the Japanese about Quality.* New York: A Lyle Stuart Book, 1990.

Deming, W. Edwards. *Out of the Crisis.* Cambridge, Mass.: MIT Press, 1986.

———. *The New Economics for Industry, Government, and Education.* Cambridge, Mass.: MIT Press, 1993.

Gabor, Andrea. *The Man Who Discovered Quality.* New York: Random House, 1990.

Gitlow, Howard S., and Shelly J. Gitlow. *The Deming Guide to Quality and Competitive Position.* Englewood Cliffs, N.J.: Prentice Hall, 1987.

Kilian, Cecelia S. *The World of W. Edwards Deming.* Washington, D.C.: CEEPress Books, 1988.

Mann, Nancy R. *The Keys to Excellence.* Los Angeles: Prestwick Books, 1985.

Neave, Henry R. *The Deming Dimension.* Knoxville, Tenn.: SPC Press, 1990.

Price, Frank. *Right Every Time: Using the Deming Approach.* Milwaukee, Wis.: ASQC Quality Press, 1990.

Scherkenbach, William W. *The Deming Route to Quality and Productivity.* Milwaukee, Wis.: ASQC Quality Press, 1986.

———. *Deming's Road to Continual Improvement.* Knoxville, Tenn.: SPC Press, 1990.

Walton, Mary. *The Deming Management Method.* New York: Putnam Publishing Group, 1986.

———. *Deming Management at Work.* New York: Putnam Publishing Group, 1990.

## Books About Performance Appraisal and Merit Pay

Aguayo, Rafael. *Dr. Deming: The American Who Taught the Japanese about Quality.* New York: A Lyle Stuart Book, 1990.

Celnicker, Mary, Lonnie Weiss, and Peter Scholtes. *Performance Appraisal and Total Quality Management.* Madison, Wis.: Joiner and Associates, 1992.

Gitlow, Howard S., and Shelly J. Gitlow. *The Deming Guide to Quality and Competitive Position.* Englewood Cliffs, N.J.: Prentice Hall, 1987.

Kohn, Alfie. *Punished by Rewards: The Trouble with Gold Stars, Incentive Plans, A's, Praise, and Other Bribes.* Boston, Mass.: Houghton-Mifflin, 1993.

McLean, Gary N., Susan R. Damme, and Richard A. Swanson, eds. *Performance Appraisal: Perspectives on a Quality Management Approach.* Alexandria, Va.: American Society for Training and Development, 1990.

Neave, Henry R. *The Deming Dimension.* Knoxville, Tenn.: SPC Press, 1990.

Scherkenbach, William W. *The Deming Route to Quality and Productivity.* Milwaukee, Wis.: ASQC Quality Press, 1986.

Scholtes, Peter R. *An Elaboration on Deming's Teachings on Performance Appraisal.* Madison, Wis.: Joiner Associates, 1987.

———. "Total Quality or Performance Appraisal: Choose One." *National Productivity Review* (Summer 1993): 349–63.

# Index